SPORT

SPORT
A Critical Sociology

Richard Giulianotti

polity

First published in 2005 by Polity Press

Polity Press
65 Bridge Street
Cambridge CB2 1UR, UK

Polity Press
350 Main Street
Malden, MA 02148, USA

ISBN: 0-7456-2545-2 (Hardback)
ISBN: 0-7456-2546-0 (Paperback)

A catalogue record for this book is available from the British Library

Typeset in 10.5 on 12 pt Sabon
by TechBooks, India
Printed and bound in Great Britain by MPG Book Ltd, Bodmin

For further information on Polity, visit our website: www.polity.co.uk

Contents

Acknowledgements   vii

Abbreviations   ix

Prologue   xi

1   Durkheimian Elements: Religion, Integration and Social Order in Sport   1

2   Weberian Trends: Meaning and Rationalization in Sport   15

3   Marx and Neo-Marxists: Sport, Work, Alienation and Ideology   29

4   Cultural Studies: Hegemony Theory beyond Resistance   43

5   'Race', Ethnicity and Intolerance in Sport   62

6   Gender Identities and Sexuality in Sport   80

7   The Body: Discipline, Conduct and the Pleasures of Sport   102

8   Sporting Spaces: Valuing Topophilia   121

9   Elias on Sport: The Interplay of Figurations   138

10   Bourdieu on Sport: *Distinction*, Symbolic Violence and Struggle   153

11   The Postmodern: Premonitions of Virtual, Post-Industrial Sport   171

Contents

12 Globalization: The Politics of 'Glocal' Sport   190

Epilogue: The Critical Sociology of Sport:
Some Recommendations   210

Notes   218

References   228

Index   254

Acknowledgements

In the process of thinking through and writing this book, I have benefited from the expertise and influence of plenty of people, most notably David Andrews, Eduardo Archetti, Gary Armstrong, John Bale, C. L. Cole, Gerry Finn, Allen Guttmann, Jennifer Hargreaves, Hans Hognestad, John Hughson, Rolf Husmann, William Kelly, Alan Klein, David Rowe, Adrian Walsh and Betül Yarar. There are numerous others whom I have enjoyed meeting and communicating with, especially at conferences and symposia both in the UK and overseas, who have provided me with insights and inspiration. I am particularly indebted to several institutions for providing the finances to travel and meet colleagues overseas over the past five years, notably the British Council, the EC, the ESRC, the Human Rights Council of Australia, and the Swiss Academy for Development. The following universities have also assisted with significant travel funding to enable visits: Aberdeen, Cologne, Glasgow Caledonian, Göttingen, Liège, Liverpool, London, Newcastle (NSW), Norwegian University of Sport and Physical Education, Otago, Toronto, Vienna and Yale.

Many of my colleagues (current and former) at the University of Aberdeen have joined me in direct and general discussions regarding issues and themes that are raised in this book. Particular thanks are due to Roland Robertson for his time and wisdom in developing our collaborative work, as well as to John Bone, David Inglis, Mike Hepworth, Andrew Blaikie and Chris Wright within our department. Across our university, I have also enjoyed cross-disciplinary writing, teaching collaboration and e-mail exchanges with Keith Hart, Ally Macdonald, Peter Sloane and Arthur Stewart, among others. I appreciate too the comments, criticisms and good humour of the many students who have been exposed to arguments in this book, in particular the fourth-year undergraduates who have taken my course on 'Sport and Leisure'.

An earlier version of this manuscript benefited from the comments and constructive criticism of Polity's anonymous referees, the publishing guidance of John Thompson, and the production assistance of Andrea Drugan, Helen Gray, Rachel Kerr and Emma Longstaff. I am also indebted to Jean van Altena for copy-editing the text with great expertise and obligence.

As ever, Donna, Gabriella and Olivia have provided me with plenty of time to work on this project.

Abbreviations

AFL	Australian Football League (elite Australian Rules football league)
CCCS	Centre for Contemporary Cultural Studies
FARE	Football Against Racism in Europe
FDI	Foreign Direct Investment
FIFA	Fédération Internationale de Football Association (world football's governing body)
GAA	Gaelic Athletic Association (Gaelic Games' governing body)
IAAF	International Association of Athletics Federations
ICRC	International Committee of the Red Cross
IMF	International Monetary Fund
IOC	International Olympic Committee (Olympic sport governing body)
IPC	International Paralympic Committee (world governing body of paralympic sport)
LPGA	Ladies' Professional Golf Association (North American)
MLB	Major League Baseball (elite North American baseball league)
MVP	Most Valuable Player (North American sports award)
NBA	National Basketball Association (elite North American basketball league)
NCAA	National Collegiate Athletic Association (US college sport association)
NFL	National Football League (elite US American football league)
NGO	non-governmental organization

NHL   National Hockey League (elite North American hockey league)
NRL   National Rugby League (elite Australasian rugby league)
OECD   Organization for Economic Co-operation and Development
SAP   Structural Adjustment Programme
TCC   transnational capitalist class
TNC   transnational corporation
WADA World Anti-Doping Agency
YMCA Young Men's Christian Association
YWCA Young Women's Christian Association

Prologue

This book seeks to provide a critical sociological interpretation of modern sport. To that end, I employ a critical development of core theories and substantive research themes within the sociology of sport. Other disciplines – notably anthropology, history, human geography, political science and political philosophy – contribute substantially, to broaden the interpretative horizons.

Its global popularity alone ensures that sociologists cannot ignore sport. The 2002 World Cup finals of football (or 'soccer') drew a cumulative 28.8 billion television viewers in 213 countries. The 2000 Olympics involved 199 participating nations in 300 events, assisted by 47,000 volunteer staff, reported on by 16,000 accredited media workers, and watched by 6.7 million spectators. In the United States, the NFL's Super Bowl is watched by over 120 million viewers, and peaked in 1996 at 138.5 million people, the highest-ever national audience. At grass roots level, tens of millions participate in sporting pastimes, notably the football codes,[1] skiing, basketball, gymnastics, track and field athletics, and volleyball.

There is no single reason for sport's huge cross-cultural appeal. Like love, truth and art, sport is a kind of human medium that conjoins people. Modern sport promises playful pleasures to players and spectators; new skills are tutored and learnt. Different sports facilitate controlled, pleasurable interaction with particular landscapes. In our increasingly 'performative' consumer culture, the physical endeavour of sport compensates for sedentary working practices. All sports are rule-governed, enabling easy transmission across cultures; yet the rules and techniques of sports may be transformed to suit local needs. Sport allows different cultures to explore old and new identities and conflicts, in particular concerning community, gender, social class and ethnicity. Sport's political ethics – with reference to 'sportsmanship' and 'fair play' – reflect dominant, liberal-democratic ideologies in the West. Institutionally, sport has been a normative training ground for young elites, notably the English aristocracy and international business leaders. The economics of sport are now dominated by a power matrix that features top sports governing bodies, transnational corporations and global media networks.

The global economic, political, cultural and social growth of sport is indexed by the sudden, rather belated expansion of 'sport studies'. The volume of material published in recent years is staggering, an industry hastened by the founding of new journals. While all academics must now 'publish or perish', sport studies has mushroomed since the late 1980s; new departments or faculties have evolved under a challenging diversity of appellations, such as kinesiology, human movement, sport management, leisure and recreation, or the more prosaic moniker of physical education. While this expansion reflects intensified public and commercial emphasis on leisure practices and body cultures, even the most conservative of teaching institutions cannot deny that sport studies is highly popular within the student 'market'.

Towards a sociological definition of sport

When seeking definition, the word 'sport' is somewhat slippery, and carries significant pre-industrial associations with aristocratic 'hunting and shooting' field activities. For *Chambers Twentieth Century Dictionary*, to 'sport' (as a verb) is to 'frolic', 'make merry', or 'amuse'; and to 'wear' and 'exhibit'. 'Sport' (as a noun) denotes 'recreation', 'games' and 'play'; or 'amorous behaviour', 'mirth', 'jest' and 'dalliance'. The social actor, the 'sportsman', is plainly a 'good fellow'.

Sociological definition of sport requires more modern, systematic classification. Adapting McPherson, Curtis and Loy (1989: 15–17), I suggest that sport is:

1 *Structured* by rules and codes of conduct, spatial and temporal frameworks (playing fields and time limits on games), and institutions of government.
2 *Goal-oriented*: aimed at particular objectives, e.g. scoring goals, winning contests, increasing averages; thus winners and losers are identifiable.
3 *Competitive*: rivals are defeated, records are broken.

4 *Ludic*, enabling playful experiences, germinating excitement.
5 *Culturally situated*, in that 1–4 correspond closely to the value systems and power relations within the relevant sport's host society.

Criteria 1–4 distinguish sport from other practices like walking or exercising that lack, for example, competition. Criterion 5 implies that any transformation of the culture in which sport is played may well lead to the categorical reinvention of sport *per se*. Hence, the sociology of sport must also focus on inter-group struggles to control and change the meaning of sport.

The above criteria enable an inclusive approach towards listing 'sports'. Despite their competitors' limited physical activity or fitness levels, our definition does stretch to include games like darts, bowling, snooker, pool and motor-racing. Each requires intensive physical engagement and proficiency in hand–eye co-ordination. Each pastime is structured, goal-oriented, competitive and ludic. Moreover, these pastimes' custodians and practitioners advocate their sport status; their equipment is retailed by 'sports' shops; and their key news is reported by 'sports' media. Despite their antediluvian goals, I include 'blood sports' here, but only in discussion of historical struggles over the 'culturally situated' meaning of sport.

Sparking sport: historical and international dimensions

Sociology is the inquisitive child of modernity, its questions being traditionally directed towards industrialized and industrializing societies. Anthropological and historical standpoints afford crucial comparative perspectives on the categorical range of sporting practices, and the interconnections between these practices and power relations, community identity, codes of social conduct, and metaphysical belief systems. It is useful to outline the historical and cross-cultural influences in the sociogenesis of modern sports. This reveals both the centrality of power relations in sports' social history and important cultural differences in the foundation of modern sporting traditions and institutions. This sociological dichotomy – concerning structured power relations and elements of cultural agency – is a key theme throughout the book.

Many ball games like polo, the various football codes, and tennis originated in ancient pagan rituals or medieval springtime festivals. The modern Olympic games inherited sporting disciplines from the original Greek games, including sprinting, the long-jump, javelin throwing and wrestling. However, the British were key figures in transforming games and pastimes into codified sports, and then transmitting these cultural practices internationally. Until the late nineteenth century, British schoolboys had been adept in 'hard-drinking, horse-racing, gambling, blood sports, prize fighting and sexual indulgence' (Mangan 1998: 179), but through the 'games cult', discipline was enforced and unruly energies dissipated, establishing sports like football, rugby, field hockey, boxing, lawn tennis, squash, and track and field athletics (Mangan 1981: 15–18). British influence overseas opened up distinctive channels of international diffusion, along imperial and trade routes, for the different games. As Perkin (1989: 217) notes, 'where the public-school boys went in large numbers, inside or outside the Empire, there cricket and rugby prevailed, and where the horny-handed sons of toil, or at least of the counting house, predominated, there soccer fever tended to infect the locals and become endemic.' Dominions like Australia and South Africa embraced the games cult. The Australians were the first to codify football, as their sport of Australian Rules, in 1859. Across southern Africa, football and boxing became particularly popular among indigenous peoples. In the Indian subcontinent, cricket was favoured, although local peoples reinvented its intensely colonial value system. After national independence in 1947, *kabaddi* underwent 'sportization' as different local rules were harmonized and playing procedures standardized.

North America's aristocracy and upper middle classes enjoyed tennis, polo and cricket, but up to 1914 new 'national' sporting traditions were forged. Baseball, spread initially by the army in the mid-nineteenth century, gained mass popularity among the lower classes; young males at leading universities took up American football; meanwhile, the Christian movement invented basketball and volleyball as alternatives to existent sports. Canada's national sports were ice hockey and lacrosse, the latter developed from the game played by the indigenous peoples.

In Germany in the early nineteenth century, Friedrich Jahn founded the *Turnverein*, a set of nationalistic disciplines combining gymnastic drill with military training (notably fencing) (Segel 1999: 209–11). The Czech equivalent, *Sokol*, spread across central and eastern Europe. To meet competitive demands among German sportspeople, handball was invented and popularized after the First World War to challenge football's popularity. France's major contribution has been largely political and administrative, promoting a remarkably prescient, cosmopolitan vision of sport's global potential. Baron Pierre de Coubertin founded the modern Olympic games, first contested in Athens in 1896. The

French were catalysts for establishing football's governing body, FIFA, in 1904. France's distinctive sporting event is the Tour de France, the world's most prestigious cycling race. While football's European hegemony remains intense, shooting and the alpine sports are strong across the Alps and Nordic nations. In Ireland, hurling and Gaelic football were established to counteract perceived British cultural imperialism, and maintained strong grass roots support. In Latin America, there are no noteworthy indigenous sports; football dominates, but baseball is hugely popular in Central America. In Japan, traditional martial arts were transformed into sports like judo and karate according to Western criteria. Baseball has long-standing popularity; gymnastics remains important in school curricula, but football is now rooted within Japanese popular culture.

Contents of the book

To provide this sociological analysis of sport, the book is divided into twelve chapters and concludes with an epilogue. This distribution of intellectual labour, in theory at least, should make for diverse, concise discussions; but obviously they cannot be encyclopaedic. Each chapter, of course, could in its own right become a book twice the size of the one you are now reading; the bibliography would be several times longer, despite it presently being close to twice chapter length. I have endeavoured to deploy a reasonable range of sociological texts, taking account of likely readership interests and, of course, my disciplinary research interests and theoretical commitments.

The opening three chapters explore the broad influence of the three founding fathers of sociology: namely, Emile Durkheim, Max Weber and Karl Marx, in relation to sport. Durkheimian sociology emphasizes sport's function in promoting social cohesion and solidarity through quasi-religious rituals. Sport may be seen to promote social order at two levels: at systemic level, as claimed by structural-functionalists, through harmonious connections between sport and other institutions; at everyday level, as indicated by Goffman, through particular interaction rituals that protect the 'face' of social actors.

Weberian sociology facilitates deeper understanding of sport's interpretative and rationalized aspects. Interpretive sociology focuses on the complex, varying meanings and identities of social actors within sport. Weber, Guttmann and Ritzer point us towards considering the impact upon sport of our highly rationalized, bureaucratized modern society. Despite significant respective strengths, both Durkheimian and

Weberian perspectives underplay political economic factors that shape social relations.

By contrast, Marxist theories address conflicts that underlie sports within modern capitalism. For different 'neo-Marxists', sport reproduces the signature iniquities of industrial capitalism, like exploiting workers/athletes and manipulating consumers/spectators. However, such arguments oversimplify Marx's understanding of the complexity of power relations at any historical moment.

These discussions lead into an analysis of 'Cultural Studies' in chapter 4. More plausible Cultural Studies approaches utilize sustained fieldwork and theory (notably from Gramsci and Williams) to examine how culture (including sport) is a site of struggle for subordinated social groups, notably the working classes, young women and ethnic minorities. The concept of 'resistance' needs to be deployed judiciously, alongside notions of 'transgression', as associated with the carnivalesque. I advocate a 'structured polyphonic' approach towards sociological investigation of sports cultures.

The first four, more theoretical chapters provide the crucial conceptual bases for examining four more substantive themes in the next chapters, relating specifically to 'race', gender, the body and space. The first two of these chapters, on 'race' and gender, have become key research domains within Cultural Studies. I examine each issue with substantial reference to their modern sporting history, highlighting the long-term social construction and cross-cultural complexity of these respective research fields. I explore how sport has contributed to racist mythologies, and whether it offers alternative social mobility for non-whites. I assess sport's role in shaping distinctive gender norms, identities and experiences, with consideration given to both women and men.

The next two chapters examine two key sites of sporting practice: namely the body and the sport landscape (or space). Foucault's theories of the corporeal and spatial disciplining of populations feature prominently. While modern sport facilitates some bodily transcendence, risk of injury and permanent harm remain connected to wider patterns of social inequality. Sporting landscapes generate strong emotional attachments at individual and collective levels, but are bedevilled by spatial rationalization and commodification.

The next two chapters examine the sport-centred contributions of two major international sociologists, Norbert Elias and Pierre Bourdieu. Elias's 'process-sociological' standpoint examines society as a game wherein participants, spectators and governing bodies are 'interdependent' and caught in the constant flux of play. His theory of the civilizing process has been employed to trace sport's social history and, more problematically, to explain sports-related violence. Bourdieu proposes a more critical, concerted sociological standpoint that connects sporting 'tastes' to inter-group struggles. Bourdieu's later work became more overtly politicized through trenchant critiques of social inequality and 'neo-liberal' government policies.

The final chapters, on the postmodern and globalization, examine two of the most important debates within social science over the past two decades. Postmodern trends are located in the growing significance of mediated sport, the interpenetration of sporting codes and disciplines, the reorientation of stadiums towards fantasy consumption, shifting or 'neo-tribal' forms of sports identification, and the collapse of sports-defined distinctions between high and low culture. Latterly, globalization has become the key theme within contemporary sociology. Modern sport illustrates *par excellence* the globalization of cultural practices and social relations, while our focus should now turn to political reforms within the governing bodies of most global sports.

The twelve chapters provide a plethora of critical sociological arguments and observations regarding sport. In the epilogue, I integrate these arguments to provide recommendations for future research and critical analysis within the sociology of sport. My sociological emphasis insists on the complex interrelationships between social structures and institutions, systematic power inequalities, community identities and cultural agency. My overall challenge to the controllers, custodians, competitors and constituencies in and around sport is to enact major reforms that will enhance egalitarianism, democracy and participatory justice within their respective disciplines.

1

Durkheimian Elements: Religion, Integration and Social Order in Sport

Functionalist theories, and their variants of structural-functionalism and neo-functionalism, highlight the importance of social consensus and social order and play down the role of social conflict. Since the late 1960s, functionalism has lost much of its disciplinary influence, partly to more attractive, conflict-based theories (notably Marxism). Functionalist sociologies of sport thus appear as scholastic artefacts, marking the sub-discipline's history while providing little of contemporary explanatory value.

While not ignoring their weaknesses, I seek to indicate here that the functionalist sociology of Durkheim, Merton and Parsons assists in our analysis of social solidarity, rituals, religiosity and anomie within sport. Goffman's more micro-sociological work facilitates intriguing insights into the fragile social order that underpins everyday interaction.

Durkheimian sociology: social order, solidarity and religion

Emile Durkheim (1858–1917) lived through tumultuous historical changes in his native France: notably industrialization, urbanization, secularization, specialization and global warfare. In partial consequence, Durkheim's sociological focus was relatively conservative, focusing on the nature and problems of social order.

Methodologically, Durkheim advocated the sociological study of 'social facts': that is, those social forces which are independent of individual control and which shape our destinies (Durkheim 1938/1895: 13). Durkheim (1970/1897) uncovered social facts regarding differences in suicide rate between specific social categories (such as Protestants and Catholics), demonstrating that people in more integrated communities, families and religious orders are less likely to commit suicide than those in more individualistic contexts. These social facts constitute external social forces that increase or decrease the likelihood of particular individuals committing suicide. This scientific method has obvious, positivistic applicability within sport. For example, consider the social fact of sizeable group differences in sports participation, with working-class women the least active; to reshape this social fact, policy-makers must amend the social structures 'causing' low participation.

One research problem concerns the difficulty of isolating accurately the most influential social forces. For example, Lüschen (1967) found that Protestants are more likely than other religious groups to participate in organized sport, especially individual-based sports. This 'social fact' might fit the argument that modern sports emphasize Protestant values like asceticism and individualism. However, statistics that show differences in sports participation across Europe may have non-religious causes. Smaller class inequalities may explain why more Scandinavians than Spaniards join sports clubs. Moreover, joining a sports club is surely a collectivist act, irrespective of whether that club favours individual sports (Bottenburg 2001: 33–4).

Durkheim's conservatism was reflected in his interpretation of the modern division of labour and modern social order. For Durkheim, primitive societies cohere through a 'mechanical' form of social solidarity whereby group members share similar roles, duties, beliefs and outlooks that are underpinned by a common moral order, or 'conscience collective'. Mechanical solidarity requires a simple division of labour, strong socialization forces, minimal individualism, and reproduction of social roles. Conversely, the 'organic solidarity of industrial societies' features greater specialization and 'functional interdependence' across the division of labour. Modern secularism promotes the 'cult of the individual', a moral framework that in excessive form is unable to sustain social cohesion (Durkheim 1964/1893: 170–2). A major pathology of industrial society is the rise of anomie, the sense of normlessness and lower moral regulation among individuals. Class conflict and crime reflect a weakened conscience collective. While Durkheim (1961/1915: 475) viewed French society's modernization as producing 'a stage of transition and moral mediocrity', he envisioned a more integrated organic solidarity, when 'new ideas and new formulae' would furnish a 'guide to humanity', but how this would occur 'surpasses the human faculty of foresight'.

The mechanical/organic binary opposition features in Durkheim's study of religion. For Durkheim (1961/1915), religious ceremonies functionally reproduce the conscience collective. In traditional communities, religious ceremonies assist communal self-worship, bonding the 'clan' socially and morally. The ambit of religiosity is total: all aspects of the natural and social world acquire religious meaning. Clans value and protect 'sacred' objects against the 'profane'. 'Rituals' constitute 'rules of conduct' that prescribe how people should act in relation to sacred objects (Durkheim, quoted in Birrell 1981: 357). Positive rites set out the ceremony's procedures, thereby maintaining clan members' commitment to important norms (Giddens 1971: 108–11). Negative rites serve to prohibit particular behaviour such as 'profane' language, touching sacred objects, or defecation. This fits Durkheim's reading, at the individual level, of the body as profane and the soul as sacred. 'Totems' are objects, usually in the natural world, that become sacred when represented in emblematic form. Although animals live alongside profane things, they become sacred when represented emblematically. For Durkheim, the totem symbolizes the clan; hence, during ceremonies, the clan worships itself *qua* sacred totemic image.

Sport, religion and solidarity

Durkheim's model has applicability within sports, notably regarding their ritual and religious elements. Numerous anthropological studies examine the rituals of sport and physical culture.[1] For example, Bromberger (1995: 306–9) has identified a seven-fold correspondence between religious ceremonies and football match rituals. First, games occur in 'particular spatial configurations' (the stadium); playing fields possess sacred qualities, and stadiums generate intense emotional states. Second, as in religious ceremonies, spectators are spatially organized according to power, with political leaders and other VIPs in full view. Third, football has critical temporal and rhythmic affinities as matches, cup finals and championship seasons follow a regular calendar. Fourth, role distribution is ceremonial; football supporters, while specially robed, engage in intensive ritual acts. Fifth, football has its own organizational framework, from local to global level. Sixth, the football match ritual possesses a sequential order: pre-match preparations, the warm-up period, player entry on to the field, playing the game according to set procedures, and the game's conclusion, followed by supporter exit. Seventh, the football ritual generates *communitas*, a 'communion of minds', as strangers come to share common purposes, identities and causes. Bromberger's observations on football hold for many other sports rituals in different nations.

Durkheim correctly noted that games habitually mutate from religious ceremonies (Giddens 1971: 111n). Across the Americas as far back as 3000 BC, the indigenous peoples played ball games with highly symbolic religious dimensions. These games symbolized the fateful battle of life and death, often quite literally when team leaders on losing sides were sacrificed. Many ball games originated from pre-Christian, pagan rituals that sought to harness nature's forces to secure good harvests or communal well-being. In Spain, for example, the ball rituals of the Moorish invaders, notably during the spring, were transformed and transferred to Christian festivals, particularly during Lent (Henderson 2001: 32–3). In medieval times, games were played on holidays like Shrove Tuesday, when local peoples sustained their mechanical solidarity through communal ritual. Such pastimes, like religious ceremonies, functioned to forge social bonds and to ward off material, military and spiritual dangers (Muchembled 1985).

The foundation and social diffusion of modern sports show strong religious influences. Modern sports have structured, rule-governed and goal-orientated properties that connect to Puritan and Protestant value systems (cf. Guttmann 1991: 67). Overman (1997) examines how the 'Protestant ethic' facilitated modern sport's sociogenesis. Weber (1958/1905) had argued that capitalism's early development and expansion was assisted by the coterminous influence of Protestant religious beliefs. Calvinism in particular espoused ascetic doctrines of individual hard work and self-denial in the quest for eternal salvation, ethics that also promoted early capitalism's expansion.

For Overman, seven elements of Protestantism promoted modern sporting development. 'Worldly asceticism' preaches discipline, self-denial and endurance of pain to gain rewards. 'Rationalization' connects religious revelation to human reason. 'Individualism' connects individuals to the Almighty while rendering them responsible for their personal destinies. 'Goal direction' ensures that human actions can be evaluated according to results, while 'achieved status' associates success with human virtue. The 'work ethic' depicts labour as a calling, and the 'time ethic' promotes time as a resource to be husbanded efficiently. All of these mores within Protestantism are prevalent in modern sport.

Given Durkheim's point that religion struggles to sustain modern social solidarity, where might we find alternative rituals for social cohesion? Sports events, through their integrative and quasi-religious practices, provide one possibility. Sports events occur at established times, allowing the 'clan' to worship its sacred, totemic objects and thus celebrate itself. Sacred objects here include the sports team that 'represents', in name, the clan. Other sacred objects include the playing field, the trophy room and the stadium. The most sacred, totemic objects may derive from the natural world and be emblematic of club identity (for example, the Toronto Maple Leafs in ice hockey, the Indianapolis Colts in gridiron, or the 'vultures' of Flamengo in Brazilian football). Particular status is accorded to clubs possessing a special 'spirit', 'heart' or 'soul', where players 'play for the jersey'. Conversely, 'passionless' clubs lack appeal to surrounding communities or outside observers. Sports 'heroes' may possess totemic qualities: living in the profane world, among ordinary supporters, but gaining sacred status as community representatives. Supporters publicly express love for the club through positive rites of worship: e.g. stadium songs, seeking player autographs. Significant victories are celebrated through feasting, heavy drinking and other forms of carnival behaviour that promote *communitas*. Negative rites serve to prohibit spectators from encroaching on the pitch or verbally violating players. Among players, negative rites include the avoidance of injured athletes or women, for fear of being polluted and losing energy. In sports like baseball, players also practise superstitious rituals ('magic') to boost their chances of successful play (Gmelch 1972).

Immanentist religious beliefs stress the power of spiritual forces. Some immanentist beliefs, notably in non-industrial societies, imagine the transfer of spiritual powers between objects or persons. The charms and amulets carried by athletes or spectators have immanentist qualities. The chanting and choreography of some spectator subcultures may be interpreted as immanentist ceremonies whereby the clan transfers spiritual powers and energies to the team (Robertson 1970: 50–1).

Nationalism, as institutionally embodied by the nation-state, has been the major modern form of territorially defined collectivism. Llobera (1994: 109–10) observes that Durkheimian thinking is underutilized by anthropologists who try to explain modern kinds of cultural cohesion such as nationalism. Both sport and nationalism may be viewed as mutually complementary forces that strengthen organic solidarity. Modern international events like the Olympics and the various World Cups possess numerous rituals that depict the nation as sacred, thereby enhancing collective integration. The mass media play a crucial role in transmitting these sports mega-events across the nation, deploying commentaries that seek to bind audience identification with representative teams, through reference to assumed national characteristics.

Ideas of 'civil religion' or 'secular religion' help to explain how modern cultural practices perform quasi-religious functions, particularly in reproducing the nation (Bellah 1975). Modern ceremonies, such as royal weddings, civic parades, remembrance gatherings or sporting events serve periodically to bind communities and nations. For example, the 'secular religion' of Australian Rules football pervades many aspects of social life (Alomes 1994). The game offers possible transcendence to its followers, and an antidote to anomic assumptions regarding modern 'loss of community'. Baseball's meaning as an American civil religion has been located in its promise of 'national self-transcendence', while inculcating key masculine norms to the exclusion of women and African-Americans (Evans 2002: 27). Strong patriotic values proclaim, through baseball, the superiority of the American way, and the conviction that 'God is on our side' (Evans 2002: 27–31).

Baseball also illustrates how myths of origin, stories of common tradition, function to promote national solidarity. In the 1900s, A. G. Spalding, a sportswear entrepreneur, volubly supported the claim that in 1839 in Cooperstown, New York State, the Civil War general Abner Doubleday had established the rules, diamond field and name of 'baseball'. To settle the dispute about this, the Spalding Baseball Commission was established and ruled in 1907 in Spalding's favour. Historical evidence, however, demystifies the myth. Doubleday had invented neither baseball (it was, instead, a variant of English 'rounders'), nor the game's name (which pre-dates 1830), nor the baseball 'diamond' (which pre-dates 1810), nor the 11-a-side team system. Doubleday was not *in* Cooperstown from 1838 to 1839, nor did he claim to have invented baseball (Henderson 2001: 189–90). But, in Durkheimian terms, the Doubleday myth at least functioned to provide Americans with a deeper sense of collective identity through baseball. Doubleday's military credentials lent greater appeal to the mythology, notably during a century of continuing conflict; as an architect of the nation, it is logically seductive for Doubleday to become architect of the national pastime.

Functionalism's underplaying of conflicts between different social groups, institutions and belief systems is a major problem. This weakness is exposed by struggles to control sport according to distinctive interests, cultural identities and world visions. Puritans argue that play is dangerous since it diverts energies from productive endeavour. In the seventeenth and eighteenth centuries, Puritans and Quakers in

the new American territories fought hard, but unsuccessfully, to prohibit sports and games against the rising urban male culture centred
on amusement, and led by the new wealth of traders and landowners
(Gorn and Goldstein 1993: 34–41). Only in the late nineteenth century
were more sober values inculcated through these pastimes. In modern
times, religion's disruptive influence within sport is commonly identified in the traditional 'sectarian' rivalry between fans of two Scottish
football clubs, Rangers (with a strong Protestant Unionist and anti-
Catholic history) and Celtic (founded by Irish Catholics and with many
Irish nationalist followers), both based in Glasgow. Notwithstanding
other structural influences upon this club rivalry, the relevance of religious antagonism suggests that sport alone cannot guarantee the social order's functional reproduction. Moreover, sport does not require
Protestant predication. Important non-Protestant elements permeate
physical cultures in societies with alternative religio-moral systems.
The origins and culture of aikido are wrapped in Japanese spirituality, not Western rationalism. Followers of Ueshiba Morihei, aikido's
founder, abhor its sportization through the weighing, ranking and
competing of practitioners; traditionalists instead favour the pursuit
of harmonious relationships between individual and universal *ki* energies (Guttmann and Thompson 2001: 148–9).

To conclude here, Durkheimian approaches help explain sport's
ritual functions and religiosity. The earliest games were part of
ancient religious ceremonies that bound communities through common belief systems. Modern sports retain ritual parallels with religious ceremonies, while being influenced by Protestantism's cultural
logic. Sports events may be read, through Durkheimian optics, as
quasi-religious ceremonies. As 'civil religions', and often promoted
through 'myths of origin', sports can be viewed as stiffening organic solidarity within increasingly secular nations. However, rival
belief systems and identities can destabilize the social order or, at
the very least, reflect sport's complex structural relations to the wider
social system. The subsequent works of Parsons and Merton enable
fuller consideration of these problems within functionalist analyses of
sport.

Structural-functionalism: Parsons and Merton

Post-war American sociology took functionalist theories in two notable directions. The first, more prominent approach was pursued
by Talcott Parsons, the most influential English-speaking sociologist

until the 1960s. The second approach, of Erving Goffman, deployed Durkheimian themes to explain social interaction.

Parsons was not purely a follower of Durkheim – other major influences included Weber, Pareto and (in conscious opposition) even Marx. However, Parsons's 'structural-functionalism' substantially elaborated the Durkheimian imaginary by focusing on the social system's constituent parts and how social institutions sustain systemic equilibrium (Parsons 1951). For Parsons (1966), all social systems maintain themselves by meeting four 'functional prerequisites'; each is linked to the defining elements of particular structures. This model is captured by the acronym AGIL:

- Adaptation: responding effectively to the environment; linked to the economic structure.
- Goal attainment: using resources and establishing goals for system members; linked to the polity.
- Integration: establishing social co-ordination and cohesion; linked to socialization and legal authority.
- Latency or Pattern Maintenance: sustaining and transmitting cohesive values, such as through the generations; linked to community and culture.

Parsons shows how two, opposing categories of 'pattern variable' capture value differences between social systems. These oppositions are as follows: ascription versus achievement, diffuseness versus specificity, particularism versus universalism, affectivity versus affective neutrality, and collective versus self-orientation. The first kind of pattern variables prevails in pre-modern or mechanistic societies; the second kind reflects modern values. For example, modern working positions should be rooted in personal orientation, achievement, universalism (e.g. education certificates) and affective neutrality. Moreover, much of Parsons's thinking is highly evolutionist. He argues that societies pass through various levels to reach the highest stage, occupied by industrialized societies, featuring increasing degrees of social complexity and differentiation. Thus, in Parsons's schema, 'an idealized contemporary America marks the virtual endpoint of history' (Seidman 1994: 109).[2]

Parsons influenced many early sociologists of sport: notably Lüschen, Loy, Heinilä and Kenyon. Parsonian approaches examine *inter alia* the social integration of individuals within the sport system. The AGIL model and pattern variables assist in describing the maintenance of that sport system. Consider, for example, sport's national governing bodies: they must adapt to economic circumstances in budgeting and planning, consult members to clarify goals, promote cohesion by punishing offenders, and sustain common values and community standards like balanced competition and fair play. Through sporting competition, most modern sports bodies actuate more modern pattern variables: for example, sporting achievement, ranking of performances within the sport, the application of universal competitive standards using affectively neutral umpires and referees, and encouraging excellence through the personalized language of self-motivation rather than collective instruction. Finally, as sports develop, they become increasingly complex, involving more social agents and featuring functional differentiation of tasks through specialized divisions of labour.

Problematically, Parsonian thinking seems to assume, wrongly, that the social system functions effectively in its entirety. For example, sports governing bodies are often wracked by internal strife, and may even close for numerous reasons ranging from bankruptcy to loss of members. Merton's (1968) sympathetic modification of structural-functionalism involved a more cautious, modest focus, favouring 'middle-range' theories that explore, through research, the functional *or otherwise* aspects of specific elements within the social system.

Merton (1968: 105) differentiated the manifest and latent functions of social action. Manifest functions are intended by social actors to produce positive adaptation within the social system. Latent functions 'are neither intended nor recognized' by social actors. Dysfunctional actions harm the social system, although they may be functional for specific social groups. Eufunctional actions are neutral, and have no systemic impact either way. Thus, using sport to publicize anti-smoking messages has the manifest function of raising public consciousness about illness, the latent function of binding audience common identification, the eufunctional action of being meaningless to foreign visitors, and the possible dysfunction of feeding health neuroses or even putting smokers off sport.

For Merton (1938), disjunctures arise within social systems between cultural goals and social structures (or 'institutional means'). For example, poor communities may share the cultural aims of wealthy communities but lack the institutional means for achieving these goals. This thesis helped describe how, in 1920s America, Italian immigrants identified with American cultural goals (wealth creation) but lacked the structural means (education, equal opportunities in employment) to achieve those ends conventionally. Hence, many Italian-Americans turned to crime to render those cultural goals accessible.

Merton (1968) suggested that individuals respond in five ways to cultural goals and their institutional means. We may illustrate these responses with reference to American football: the sport is organized in high schools and colleges (social structures) to allow young males to toughen their masculine identity (cultural value).

1 *conformism*: individuals conform to specific cultural aims that are pursued through recognized institutions: e.g. playing American football in colleges in an aggressive, highly competitive manner.
2 *innovation*: individuals follow cultural goals, but employ their own means of attainment: e.g. playing other sports outside college in an aggressive, highly competitive manner.
3 *ritualism*: individuals lose track of cultural goals, and follow institutional rules out of blind habit: e.g. routine football team involvement and an intense knowledge of its rules and procedures.
4 *retreatism*: individuals reject both cultural goals and institutional means: e.g. abandon the sport entirely.
5 *rebellion*: individuals reject cultural goals and institutional means, replacing these with radical alternatives: e.g. playing sports without competitive emphasis, outside of educational institutions.

Conformism is the most explicitly functional strategy for sustaining the social system. Other strategies have clear functional characteristics for specific groups of individuals, despite being partly dysfunctional in terms of sustaining machismo within the American football system.

Merton's thesis allows for structural differentiation in modern society. He helps to explain deviations from functional roles, despite their dysfunctional potential for the social system. His caution regarding the application of theory is to be welcomed, since it allows for different circumstances. However, I doubt that Merton or Parsons do more than describe (rather than explain the underlying causes or social complexity of) social responses to particular structural and cultural circumstances. Moreover, their continuing functionalist emphasis on social order and social needs means that they both underplay conflicts between groups within the social system.

Goffman and the micro-social order

Erving Goffman advances an intriguing development of Durkheimian sociology. This appears strange, since Durkheimian approaches are largely macro-sociological, whereas Goffman was concerned primarily with social interaction. However, Goffman's sociology deliberately elucidates many Durkheimian themes, such as social order and ritualism in social life, albeit at the individual level (see Burns 1992: 361–2; Goffman 1967: 47). Goffman takes inspiration from Durkheim's own words on the individual: 'The human personality is a sacred thing; one dare not violate it nor infringe its bounds, while at the same time the greatest good is in communion with others' (cited in Goffman 1967: 73). For Goffman, 'the common official values of the society' are reflected in individual public 'performances'; performance is a kind of ceremony enabling 'an expressive rejuvenation and reaffirmation of the moral values of the community' (Goffman 1959: 45).

For Goffman, the 'face' of each individual is 'sacred' within modern society. 'Face' represents the positive respect claimed by individuals within social interchanges. The rituals of social interaction are therefore intended to allow individuals to maintain face. Positive and negative interaction rites serve to safeguard face. In analysing 'positive interpersonal ritual', Goffman (1971: 62–5) utilized Durkheim's conception of positive rituals to explore how individuals support each other's presentation of self during interaction. Positive rites include compliments, greetings and other 'access rituals' that establish and sustain favourable social intercourse (1971: 73–91). Negative rites include avoidance rituals, such as minimizing physical contact with strangers, or 'remedial interchanges' such as when people apologize automatically for bumping into each other in busy streets. Overall, Goffman's positive and negative rites fit with Durkheim's definition of rituals by providing rules of interaction regarding how individuals should comport themselves to protect each other's face.

Goffman (1959) employed a dramaturgical metaphor to explain social life. As social actors, we seek to present a particular self-image that convinces the audience; our social roles, performance scripts, props and general setting are all organized with a view to 'impression management', to sustain this social order. If we mess up our act, or the audience gains discrediting information about us, our veneer of sincerity crumbles, and the whole performance is jeopardized.

Goffman's theoretical framework invites application to microsociological studies of sport. In UK football, Goffman's 'impression management' thesis has helped explain social interchanges between different supporter groups and the policing of fans (Giulianotti 1991; O'Neill 2003). Ingham (1975) considered him useful for explaining occupational subcultures within sport, despite Goffman's failure to address their structural oppression. Goffman is also weak in ethical terms, since actors appear as self-interested players devoid of social sincerity.

Goffman's work can illuminate the social dynamics of sport celebrity. The faces of celebrity athletes are highly sacred; hence interaction with them is subject to numerous positive and negative rites. Sports interviewers, for example, greet and introduce athletes with effusive compliments and positive affirmations of high status. Negative rites are observed as interviewers or audience members (but rarely athletes) take apologetic responsibilities for any misunderstandings or confusions that disturb the interaction. Celebrities, meanwhile, carefully manage impressions, employing appropriate props (trophies or background photographs), dress (specific fashions, branded sportswear) and demeanour (politeness, responsiveness to questions) while protecting against discrediting information.

Birrell (1978, 1981) provides the most substantive sport-focused application of Goffman. For Birrell, sports events are ritual contests wherein individuals can aspire to heroic status by showing 'character' through a mixture of courage, gameness, integrity and composure (Birrell 1981: 365–72). Character constitutes the Goffmanesque capacity to 'keep one's entire competitive self in order and under complete control at all times' (Birrell 1981: 372). This is similar to the classic definition within sport, that greatness is revealed in those athletes displaying 'grace under pressure'.

Critical considerations: a qualified engagement of the Durkheimian approach

Evidently, Durkheimian approaches offer useful theoretical models for sport sociologists, focusing attention on issues of community, solidarity, integration, ritual and religiosity within sport. Sport's relationship to community is particularly germane for sociologists, while ritual and religiosity appeal especially to historians and anthropologists. Parsons encourages us to model the sport 'sub-system' as a totality, and to explore its functional relations with other sub-systems. The more nuanced thesis of Merton allows for dysfunctions in the social system, notably through tensions between cultural goals and social structures. Finally, Goffman complements other Durkheimian analyses by redirecting the notion of the sacred on to the individual within modern societies.

Nevertheless, I agree with five core criticisms of functionalism and its kindred theories. First, functionalist thinking presents an overly deterministic picture of social life; much social action appears as an internalized stimulus response to social circumstance, rather than as rooted in social actors' critical reflections. Even Merton's middle-range approach provides an over-socialized reading of social action.

Second, emphasis on systemic equilibrium ensures that there is an inherent conservatism within functionalist thought, especially in Parsons. Durkheimian pessimism assumes that only repressive forces can control the social antipathies of individuals (Coser 1964). Functionalist social research downplays social conflict. Yet violent disputes around sports events have sparked military conflicts, notably in Central America and the former Yugoslavia. For Vrcan (2002: 74), sport has two faces, designating the 'humanization' and 'brutalization' of social relations. Thus, while some analysts believe functionalism is theoretically radical, I consider it to be inherently conservative (Merton 1968: 93).

Third, much structural-functionalism contains an evolutionism and ethnocentricity that over-simplifies non-industrial societies against the assumed virtues of the modern (for Parsons, American) way of life. Neo-functionalists like Alexander (1992: 294–5) have similar problems when discussing the positive 'cultural codes' of democracy, rather than critically highlighting the actual lack of 'equality' and 'inclusiveness' within Western states.

Fourth, Durkheimian thinking requires more robust, critical theorizations of power. It is easy enough to criticize Goffman, given his focus on social interaction rather than generalized power structures. Durkheim at least appreciated that class conflicts arise as better occupations are dominated by elite groups. However, both Durkheim and Parsons fail to consider adequately how consensus or conformity in the social system is manufactured through power inequalities.

Fifth, Mills (1959) famously ridiculed the empty verbal formulae and studied opacity of structural-functionalism by translating some of Parsons's vast passages into short, simple statements.[3] The discursive complexity of structural-functionalism does promote social differentiation within the academy, since few specialists can discern its meaning. But if widespread knowledge of the social system is necessary for its survival, then Parsons's obscure language is surely dysfunctional *vis-à-vis* realizing that end.

These criticisms lead me to a qualified engagement with Durkheimian themes within sport sociology. First, most importantly, we need to explore how sports events and institutions serve specific communities, without necessarily assuming that smooth integrative functions are always the case. Second, sport's social facts can be more fully explored through quantitative research, to reveal how social structures pattern specific social actions. Third, we may elaborate and apply the separate metaphors that depict sports events as religious ceremonies or social theatre. Fourth, via Parsons's systemic thinking, a continuing sense of cultural totality is needed to explain sport. However, fifth, via Merton, we should adopt the open-mindedness of the middle-range researcher when examining specific aspects of sport and their relations with the wider social system. Sixth, and finally, Goffman's focus on social interaction fits well within a modern individualistic culture. He is correctly cautious regarding the fragility of the micro-social order, and this should be reflected in our use of more macro-social Durkheimian approaches when studying the uncertainties of sport or wider social life.

2

Weberian Trends: Meaning and Rationalization in Sport

A common complaint about modern sports is that they are losing their enchantment. Scattered, largely subjective evidence is often put forward: athletes are 'over-coached', teams 'lack heart', stadiums are 'soulless', play is 'too professional'. While these criticisms can romanticize the past, they do reflect widespread concerns about sport's modernization. The suspicion lingers that sport is overly rationalized, with the result that the social meaning and symbolic pleasures of play have atrophied.

Here, I examine questions regarding the meanings and modernization of sports, building in large part on two socio-cultural strains in Max Weber's thinking.[1] On the one hand, humanist *interpretivist* approaches explore social actors' meanings and motives. On the other hand, the *rationalization* thesis registers the disenchantment of cultural relations. The discussion contains three main parts. First, I set out the interpretative sociological standpoint and its relevance to sport sociology. Second, I address sport's rationalization and bureaucratization, drawing particularly upon Guttmann. Third, I explore Ritzer's McDonaldization thesis concerning the 'deep rationalization' of society, arguing that while interpretivist and '*shallow* rationalization' positions are highly insightful, they require stronger sociological critiques of power relations.

Interpretative sociology: grasping sport's meaning?

Interpretative sociology contains many conceptual branches, such as Weberian sociology, social phenomenology, hermeneutics, ethnomethodology and symbolic interactionism. Interpretative sociology

explores the interrelations of social action to status, subjectivity, meanings, motives, symbols, context, the self, roles, identities, processes
and social change. Interpretative sociology eschews positivist thinking: that is, the explanation of human groups through laws and generalizations as found in natural science. Instead, Weber (1968/1922:
12–13) employed the term *verstehen* to describe, with some appropriate ambiguity, the empathetic understanding that sociologists must
exercise to explain individuals and their actions meaningfully. Interpretative sociology is underpinned by qualitative methodology, involving relatively open-ended interviewing and ethnography of research
subjects.

Interpretative sociology posits that individuals develop meaningful
understandings of their subjective motives, of the actions of others,
and of their social contexts. Symbolic interactionists consider how
signs communicate meanings through spoken language and non-
verbal symbols like gesture or dress. Social interaction is typically
structured through sets of roles and identities that accord with the
social status of individuals. The self connects individuals to roles
and identities, germinating different role interpretations and performances and varied social identities. Thus, social action is viewed as
relatively dynamic. Social interaction is influenced by the 'looking-
glass self' that allows social actors to imagine how others see them.
Social actors are also influenced by the actual or imagined responses
of 'significant others' (such as cohabiting partners), or 'generalized
others' (such as a team of workmates or community of friends)
to specific actions. As noted earlier, Goffman (1959) viewed social
actors as relatively manipulative in their self-presentations before
'audiences'.

Interpretative sociologies facilitate fuller understanding of the social
meaning of sports engagement. Interactionist sociology advances concepts that underpin our understanding of sport (Fine 1987). Watching
park baseball requires spectators to understand players' status and the
meaning of sports symbols. Sport itself enables social actors to construct distinctive social identities within specific role systems (O. Weiss
2001: 400). Individual players are allocated sets of game roles and interpret these varyingly during play. How individuals play during games
is influenced by the anticipated responses of 'generalized others' (the
team) or 'significant others' (particularly the coach). George Herbert
Mead, the founder of symbolic interactionism, argues that game sit-
uations and team-based thinking illustrate how children acquire personality and become 'organic members of society', through taking the

attitude of the other to influence how they act 'with reference to a common end' (1934: 159).

Adler and Adler (1991) engaged in substantial fieldwork to examine the socialization of male athletes within a college basketball team. Using role theory and symbolic interactionism, the researchers revealed how their study group experienced 'role-engulfment'. Upon entering college, these athletes sought sporting wealth and fame, but not at the expense of other social identities. Sport competition and coaching soon dominated their time, actions and social circles, so that the 'greedy role' of athleticism inevitably conflicted with the 'academic role'. But athletes also embraced the 'gloried role', enjoying the addictive intoxication of public adulation through their athletic status. For some, the 'gloried self' became most prominent, despite the athletic role emphasizing self-denial. When college sports careers ended, the athletes adapted with varying success to civilian life; some remained within sports to sustain the gloried self. Upon post-college retirement, many reflected positively that they had been 'touched by fame in a way few experience' (Adler and Adler 1991: 230–1). However, college athletes, like many other professionals, are increasingly engulfed by specialist roles. The 'renaissance man', with rounded cultural interests and diverse roles and identities, is increasingly marginal (Adler and Adler 1991: 228). Although the authors refer to Durkheim's points on specialization to explain this trend historically, Weber's analysis of modern rationalization and bureaucratization, outlined later, is particularly applicable.

Social anthropologists have generic affinities with interpretative sociology's core arguments. Armstrong's (1998) long-term ethnographic study provides the most sustained and convincing account of the meanings and values of English football hooligans. Klein's studies of bodybuilding subcultures (1993) and Latino baseball (1991, 1997) deploy sustained ethnography. Dyck's (2000) important anthropological collection on sport is similarly ethnographic, while he rightly argues that more fieldwork should be undertaken into children's sport (2000: 137).

Geertz's (1973) study of the Balinese cockfight is undoubtedly the most famous interpretivist analysis of sport. Geertz (1973: 434) insists that 'the imposition of meaning on life is the major end and primary condition of human existence'. All human behaviour 'signifies', as symbolic action, and can be interpreted as a text. Borrowing from Gilbert Ryle, Geertz recommends that ethnographers provide 'thick description' of research groups by interpreting the complex, submerged and half-hidden knots of human communication and interaction.

Geertz provides a brief, rich account of the organization, events and gambling practices at Balinese cockfights, as well as interpretative detail on male relationships with cocks. But his study is best known for its concluding interpretations and generalizations wherein meaning, symbolism, status, subjectivity and interpretation come into play. Adapting Bentham, Geertz argues that, for the Balinese male, betting on cockfights is a form of 'deep play' in which personal status (more than money) is at stake. The cockfight 'talks most forcibly' about Balinese status relationships, as 'matters of life and death'. Geertz compares Balinese re-enactments of the cockfight to rereadings of *Macbeth*, to explain how the event allows the Balinese male 'to see a dimension of his own subjectivity ... In the cockfight, then, the Balinese forms and discovers his temperament and his society's temper at the same time' (1973: 451–2). The anthropologist must 'read' the cockfight as cultural text about Bali, but that reading can only be done 'over the shoulder' of the text's authors and active interpreters, the Balinese themselves.

Despite their rise in the 1970s, interpretative perspectives have had a relatively restricted impact within sport sociology, for several reasons. Time-consuming, expensive fieldwork is required for adequate interpretative readings of human groups. Theoretically, sport sociology has tended to favour Cultural Studies approaches against interpretative frameworks like symbolic interactionism. Moreover, many figures within sport sociology received interdisciplinary or alternative training – such as in political studies, kinesiology, Cultural Studies and sport studies programmes – and so may have been under-exposed to interpretative approaches.

Interactionist standpoints on sport often contain other conceptual baggage. Blending symbolic interactionism and Cultural Studies can add important, structural theorizations of power relations, notably in fieldwork studies of 'subcultures' (for example, see Sugden 1987; Foley 1990). Interactionist theorists might complain that Cultural Studies positions present human action as predetermined by social structures. Alternatively, post-structuralist theory allows for greater variability in the 'decoding' of signs and symbols, or in the negotiation of roles, hence is perhaps more attuned to interpretative sociology. The positions of Erving Goffman and post-structuralists like Foucault have been combined to examine how Scottish football supporters presented themselves in a friendly, anti-English way before different 'audiences' at the 1990 World Cup finals in Italy

(Giulianotti 1991). The supporters' expressive symbols (such as flags, dress and songs) were viewed as relatively malleable signifiers of national identity whose dominant meanings were contested by different social groups (supporters, media reporters, football and political authorities). This synthetic theorization implies that elements of the interpretative standpoint should be critically reinterpreted and selectively deployed to examine specific actions, symbols and identities within sport.

Rationalization and sport

While Weberian sociology's interpretative dimensions emphasize intersubjective social relations, Weber opened up more objective fields of sociological inquiry regarding social stratification and rationalization. Weber (1978: 48–56) explored how cultural and normative factors, as well as economic ones, generated social stratification and historical change. In addition to Marx's emphasis on class, Weber noted how status groups and party affiliations stratify people in complex ways. Status groups, for example, are 'amorphous communities' for whom property is often irrelevant to social hierarchies. For example, Weber noted that in American social clubs, it was unusual for wealthy members to display 'condescending affability' towards their poorer brethren.

Weber's focus on rationalization processes constitutes probably his strongest influence within sport sociology. For Weber, rationalization drives modernity. Social relations are organized ever more efficiently and instrumentally, founded on technical knowledge rather than political or moral principles. Bureaucracies possess 'purely technical superiority' to alternative organizational forms by affording 'precision, despatch, clarity, familiarity with the documents, continuity, discretion, uniformity, rigid subordination, savings in friction and in material and personal costs' (Weber 1978: 350). Yet bureaucratization constructs an 'iron cage' that imprisons humanity within a disenchanted existence. Sociologists influenced by Weber thus face the question of how rationalization impacts upon social actors' symbolic worlds.

Frisby (1982) applied Weber's theory of bureaucracy to Canadian voluntary sports organizations. She hypothesized that organizational efficiency was promoted by nine principles: formalized rules and procedures, decentralized decision making, impersonal working relations, professionalism in decision making, specialization, career stability, large organizational size, higher proportions of clerical staff, and emphasis on science and technology.

Allen Guttmann (1978) provides the most substantive application of the rationalization thesis to explain the process of *Versportlichung*, the modern 'sportification' of physical culture (Guttmann and Thompson 2001: 176). Guttmann identifies seven key aspects of rationalization, and these can be illustrated through contrasting modern, Western sport with the sporting pastimes of ancient civilizations:

1 *secularization*: modern sport is independent of religious institutions or belief systems. In pre-modern societies, sports and religious festivities were interrelated. For example, pre-Roman France played ball games during fertility rituals; Japanese sumo wrestling was often performed 'in the service of the gods' at temples and shrines until the late sixteenth century (cf. Guttmann 1994: 161). Conversely, modern sport is rarely attended by paeans to the Almighty.

2 *meritocracy*: sport promotes fair competition. Pre-modern sport was highly exclusive; among Greeks, it was closed to non-citizens, notably women and slaves. Conversely, the sporting trend is towards greater opportunities for disadvantaged communities (e.g. non-whites). The 'level playing field' ensures that independent referees and umpires judge actions according to rules rather than social status.

3 *specialization*: modern sport, like industry, possesses an increasingly complex division of labour. Athletes in team games have specialized roles to learn and perform. In pre-modern sport, participants had few specialist roles, contributing as they wished towards the collective 'goal'. Folk football matches in feudal England were riotous affairs as scores of men fought for the ball. For the elites, true sportsmen were versatile in 'blood sports' as well as cricket, athletics and lawn games. Conversely, modern team sports like American football possess specialisms whereby some players contribute only for a few seconds in each game.

4 *rationalization*: instrumental reason involves identifying the most efficient means available for achieving desired ends. Guttmann notes the rational thinking behind James Naismith's invention of basketball in the late nineteenth century, after the YMCA had set him the task of creating an indoor adult game. Naismith took logical steps regarding basketball's rules, notably in deciding the basket's height relative to the size of the average player (Guttmann and Thompson 2001: 78; Guttmann 1988: 71–2). Modern sport is

characterized by rationalized preparation, organization and competition, to maximize the athlete's chance of winning. Pre-modern sport was less rationalized, either in differentiating spectators and players or in the athlete's intensity of pre-event preparations.

5 *bureaucratization*: for Weber, 'the whole pattern of everyday life is cut to fit' bureaucratic frameworks (in Giddens 1971: 160). Sport is controlled by office-filled, committee-stuffed governing bodies at global, continental, national and local levels. Clubs possess management committees with numerous office-holders. Positions inside sports bureaucracies should be decided by objective, rational criteria (qualifications, previous experience) rather than normative, relative factors (such as personal charisma or nepotism). Referees and umpires are appointed on the grounds of competence, not connections, to govern sports events objectively. Pre-modern games lacked governing bodies, while sports contests were informally organized and judged.

6 *quantification*: statistical data measure and compare modern sports performances, often across generations, reducing complex events to intelligible, manageable information for mass audiences. Conversely, pre-modern games produced few historical records: nobody recorded the Green team's losing streak in ancient Rome's chariot races.

7 *The pursuit of records*: the modern Olympic legend 'citius, altius, fortius' (faster, higher, stronger) captures the athletic compulsion to win tournaments and break records. The modern sporting Valhalla is filled with athletes who have set new, measured standards of human achievement. Lacking modern time-keeping technology, pre-modern games concentrated instead on winning contests.

The rationalization thesis insists that all modern sports undergo rationalization. For example, consideration of judo's modernization suggests that Guttmann's taxonomy helps to explain the rationalization of non-Western sporting practices. First, judo is now far more *competitive* than its founder, Dr Kano, intended. Second, modern sport's *meritocracy* has fitted partially with Kano's belief that judo could integrate diverse groups, while women's judo has gained recognition. Third, fighters, teachers and administrators adopt *specialized* roles; more fighters now focus on specific moves, thereby ignoring judo's more traditional, holistic philosophy. Fourth, intensive training regimes *rationally* maximize the practitioner's competitiveness. Fifth, competitors, clubs, and tournaments are *bureaucratically* affiliated and authorized by governing bodies. Sixth, on *quantification*, contests are performed within set times, and judged through Westernized scoring systems. Seventh, competitive *records* are established, such as the quickest-ever contest or the longest-running champion (Carr 1993).

The rise of sport's rationalization and bureaucratization has a historical dynamism whose consequences are often impossible to resist, even by the most powerful social groups. For example, rationalization within the modern Olympics guaranteed that the old traditionalist philosophy and practice of amateurism, supported by aristocratic elites, was doomed. In emphasizing record setting and victory, a professional culture among Olympic athletes was inevitably established in regard to specialization, training and ultimately payment (see Heinilä 1998: 158).

Guttmann's Weberian typology is subject to critical theoretical, empirical and normative scrutiny. First, Guttmann adopts only a partial Weberian perspective: rationalization is interpreted as a worthwhile property within sport, hence Weber's pessimism about the iron cage is rejected. It would be better to combine Weber with Marx, to connect rationalization with human alienation (see next chapter) (Gruneau 1999: 18–26). Our achievement sports culture privileges results over enjoyment, just as work has been degraded; human life achievement is measured in terms of results, just as modernity measures individuals and societies according to quantitative data (IQ scores, GNP levels, etc.). Modern sports, like industrial societies, discriminate against and exploit women and children. Modern sports undermine fair competition by allowing the wealthiest nations to buy success – for example, through expensive training centres. Eichberg (1998: 105) appeals to democratic values, notably pluralism and multiculturalism, to challenge Olympic sport, such that in time, 'The masses in different cultures, nations and regions will have their own festivals revealing their own patterns, their own traditions, their own historical and future changes'. In sum, he argues for sport's re-enchantment through the abandonment of Olympian rationalism.

Such criticisms need to be balanced, in a middle-range way, by noting the extent to which an alienating rationalization arises within specific cultures. As I note in the final chapter, Guttmann (1994) recognizes that different cultures adapt (rather than blindly embrace) modern, rationalized sports. Moreover, as the natural scientist Stephen J. Gould (1997) indicates, rationalization of sport does not always entail disenchantment. Gould considers why, in baseball, there are no longer exceptional levels of batting consistency: no batter has attained the mythical batting average of 0.400 since 1941. Performance differences between players have also declined. For Gould, in diagrammatic terms, these facts mean that players have come much nearer the 'right wall' of maximum human achievement, yet no one can quite touch the wall by hitting 0.400 or higher in today's intensive competition. Role specialization in teams and the general excellence of play ensure that the wall remains intangible. Yet Gould is not disenchanted, but revels in the maximal, highly specialized beauty of contemporary play, while nurturing the faith that 'every season features the promise of transcendence' (1997: 132). Rationalization in baseball thus procures aesthetic excellence, and never negates the 'you never know' prospect of extra-ordinary sports performance.

Second, Guttmann's thesis may contain empirical weaknesses. We may take each rationalization category to explain:

1 *secularization*: religion still contributes significant practices to sport – for example, in pre-match ceremonies and prayers, and athlete charms and superstitions.
2 *meritocracy*: social stratification still largely determines access and success in sports. To pick an extreme instance, none of the world's major yachting competitions are dominated by teams of unemployed black African women. Moreover, limited standardization in sport can produce highly unfair competition – for example, in all skiing events, differences in ski preparation and quality can determine results (Loland 2002: 63–4).
3 *specialization*: in many coaching methods, such as Dutch football training, the positional versatility of athletes is promoted. In athletics, greatest superstar status is accorded to all-rounders like Carl Lewis who master several disciplines.
4 *rationalization*: non-rational factors often prevail in play. Office politics or bureaucrat career building can undermine the 'rational' organization of sport tournaments or the establishment of global sporting calendars.
5 *bureaucratization*: the business trend towards 'down-sizing' the number of white-collar employees has cut many sport bureaucracies. Powerful, charismatic personalities continue to dominate sport's governing bodies. Meanwhile, 'pre-modern' sports organizations survive under the control of their traditional, elite rulers – for example, the Jockey Club that controls UK horse-racing.
6 *quantification*: sport culture still focuses less on statistical detail and more on the social-psychological and aesthetic aspects of play.
7 *record setting*: despite focuses on record breaking, the autotelic pleasures of playing and winning still have major relevance to competitors and spectators.

Sport's modern features may be rejected or remoulded by counter-cultural movements. For example, 'extreme sports' may prioritize the corporeal pleasures of sports engagement over emphasis on ethics like record setting and specialization. Some educational philosophies challenge the modern rationales that channel team sports opportunities towards the able few to exclude most children (particularly girls) from participation. Alternative priorities centred on participation, social harmony, and the life-course benefits of exercise are advanced.

Third, the rationalization thesis normatively disregards intrinsic goods such as aesthetics, moral education and community building in sport (Loland 2000; Lasch 1979; Walsh and Giulianotti 2001). Like the performing arts, sport contains 'this element of moving, of improvisation, an element which pulls against the rationalised and the bureaucratised view of aesthetics' (Blake 1995: 201). As Gould earlier implied, sport seduces through the possibility of human transcendence. Loland (2000) recommends that sport should downgrade timing and record keeping, while enhancing meritocracy, playing to win, cultivating skills, and viewing athletes as persons (and not mere performance ensembles). These arguments remind us that sport is socially and culturally malleable; more prominent tendencies towards rationalization may be significantly curtailed.

Contemporary rationalization: Ritzer's McDonaldization thesis

Weber's rationalization thesis has been updated and reapplied in Ritzer's (1993) theory of 'McDonaldization'. For Ritzer, our rationalized modern society is encapsulated in the organizational logic of McDonald's, the American fast-food business chain. Four organizing principles define McDonaldization:

1 *efficiency*: speed and ease of service are optimized in 'the search for the best means to the end' (Ritzer 1993: 443). Highly rationalized divisions of labour and 'drive-through' windows facilitate rapid sales to passing motorists.
2 *predictability*: 'a world with no surprises' minimizes risk. McDonald's consumers safely assume they will receive the same products, services and sensory experiences in any franchise throughout the world.
3 *quantity over quality*: (large) size is emphasized over gastronomic value, complexity or distinction.

4 *automation*: wherever possible, human labour is replaced by non-
   human production, making the organization more efficient and
   reliable. At McDonald's, cooking is highly automated and requires
   minimal employee training.

The results are obvious: the rationalized production and retail of
fast food is enormously successful, establishing a paradigm copied by
competing companies. McDonaldization's organizing principles have
subsequently pervaded numerous other areas of modern life, from
financial services to higher education. In Weberian mode, rationalization processes have irrational consequences: 'they serve to deny the
basic humanity, the human reason, of the people who work within
them or are served by them' (Ritzer 1993: 121). McDonald's dehu-
manizes the dining experience while deculturizing the gastronomic
arts. Alienation within rationalized social systems has perhaps become
more prominent since at least the 1960s.

Ritzer notes that 'de-McDonaldization' is attempted by some organizations, as they coat products and services with a veneer of
enchantment. Yet this surface derationalization is itself assiduously
rationalized in the quest to retain consumers. There are parallels here
with the old arguments of Cohen and Taylor (1976) on the attempts of
modern individuals to escape from 'paramount reality', from the com-
partmentalized roles and routines that we fulfil every day. However,
sport, gambling, sex, violence, drug use, tourism and even fantasy
fail to deliver a satisfactory escape from paramount reality, becoming in themselves a source of ennui (1976: 222). Thus, our identity as
'sports fans' becomes one more role obligation in the prison of modern
leisure: the season-ticket condemns us to another year with the same
match-day neighbours, watching standardized players and opponents.

In chapter 8, I examine Ritzer's ideas more fully with regard to
North American baseball stadiums. We can apply his thesis to other
sporting domains, such as the long-term evolution of sports coaching.
Efficiency in service provision is facilitated by the rational division
of labour among coaches. Each coach requires qualifications to teach
specific techniques to particular athletic standards. On *predictability*,
similar divisions of labour and coaching techniques are found across
the world. *Quantity over quality* involves housing large pupil numbers
in sports clinics (promoting efficiency and fee income) and having individual athletes practise set moves constantly. *Automation* is apparent
in the gymnasium machinery employed by teachers and, more subtly,
the use of pre-set training programmes rather than informal expert–
pupil dialogue. 'De-McDonaldization' is suggested, for example, by

the transformation of some elite coaches into celebrities, or focus on top athletes with unpredictable styles. Yet even these latter talents are integrated within sport's complex divisions of labour; their value is still measured by efficient production of good results.

Despite its effective description of rationalization processes, Ritzer's model has substantial weaknesses. Ritzer's reference to 'McDonaldization' *and* 'de-McDonaldization' renders his arguments untestable and unfalsifiable: he cannot be proved wrong, but then he cannot be proved correct. Moreover, McDonaldization over-emphasizes the culture of rationality while underplaying its political economic roots: McDonald's rational organization has a profit-seeking *raison d'être*. Some institutions have the resources to implement McDonaldization more concertedly than their rivals. In sport, huge international inequalities exist, largely because the developed world can afford the most scientifically advanced facilities and personnel, to maximize athlete productivity.

McDonaldization has undeniable nefarious consequences, such as environmental devastation, reduction in food quality, and serious dietary and health problems across entire populations. To the corporation, these 'irrational' outcomes are secondary to the goals of profit, growth and shareholder reward. In sport, McDonaldization contains similar costs – notably athlete injury, environmental devastation, social exclusion of poorer communities – that are considered secondary to producing good results and generating profits. The 'irrationality' of rationalization, then, depends on who is making the calculations.

These critical weaknesses arise in Ritzer's suggested challenges to McDonaldization. To oppose our depersonalization by corporations, Ritzer advocates greater individuality in social relations rather than collective mobilization. In sport, this means that we should avoid automated ticket-lines; take pre-game meals and drinks at intimate hostelries, not fast-food chains; and applaud unpredicted, risky athletic manoeuvres and criticize predictable techniques. However, all these instances of individualistic, savvy consumerism lack a sufficiently collectivist approach that could effectively expose and challenge the rationalization of sport.

Finally, Ritzer's neo-Weberianism is far more pessimistic than Guttmann's approach. Ritzer sees rationalization entailing a cultural homogenization that can be offset only superficially by de-McDonaldization. Thus, principles of efficiency, predictability, quantity and automation come to dominate all sporting cultures. Guttmann is more cautious; as I note in chapter 12, he emphasizes that sporting disciplines are reinterpreted and often fundamentally transformed by their receiving cultures. Japanese 'samurai' baseball, Brazilian football, Samoan rugby, Balinese cockfighting and Trobriand cricket variously demonstrate that local cultures fashion distinctive aesthetic codes, social conventions and even rule changes within sports.

Otherwise stated, Ritzer identifies 'deep rationalization' occurring across cultures, whereas Guttmann provides a far more plausible, 'shallow rationalization' argument that emphasizes cross-cultural diversity. In nations like Brazil, for example, rationalization and modernization come into a complex, dialectical relationship with specific traditional values, to produce distinctive, synthetic kinds of sport. Thus, the culture of Brazilian football contains a 'double ethic' (Da Matta 1982). On one side, sport's modern values promote standardized rules, meritocracy and the role of performance over social status. Alternatively, 'traditional' values in Brazil privilege patronage, personal connections and the familial. Brazilian football and society are shaped by the interplay of these two cultural codes. Even when rationalization appears strong, hierarchical values find new forms of articulation (Da Matta 1991: 154–5). Thus, Brazilian football is notorious for its *medalhões* (big shots) and *malandros* (rogues) who bypass football's laws on and off the field to maintain social influence. Overall, the case of Brazilian football confirms the relatively shallow reach of cultural rationalization processes within sport, in this instance through sustaining pre-modern discourses and asymmetrical power relations.

Concluding comments: Weberian approaches and power

Evidently, interpretative standpoints help explain athlete socialization and cultural identities within sport. Guttmann provides an insightful, elaborate sports application of Weber's rationalization thesis, but it harbours theoretical, empirical, normative and aesthetic problems. Ritzer's McDonaldization thesis identifies a deep rationalization process within modern routines of production and consumption that invite application within sport. His thesis lacks sufficient focus on political economic factors or consideration of collective, resistant strategies. I have resisted Ritzer's implication that rationalization processes entail cultural homogenization. Modern rationalization processes within sport may be reinforced, challenged or forcibly fused to local cultural beliefs, traditions and values, giving rise to distinctive, hybrid products.

Focus on rationalization processes helps clarify sport's disenchanting dimensions. Undoubtedly one significant aspect of the globalization of sport has been our search for exotic play, albeit within Western sporting models. As Geertz indicates, one sociological fascination lies in how sport enables a rich, hermeneutic dialogue between the particular (Balinese cockfighting) and the general (Balinese male identity) within specific cultures. Nevertheless, the question of how power relationships shape identities and practices still lingers. Focus on social interaction illuminates the influence of generalized others in the construction of identities and actions; assessment of rationalization also indicates the possibility of irrational consequences. However, the socio-cultural perspectives discussed here do not proceed effectively to the next, more structural questions: which social groups can ensure that, when it matters, it is they that constitute the 'generalized others' in shaping social action? Which groups decide whether the 'irrational' costs of rationalization should be borne? In the following chapters, we consider rather more fully the arising issues of domination and subjugation within sport.

3

Marx and Neo-Marxists: Sport, Work, Alienation and Ideology

Sport's commercialization is increasingly apparent. More sports-related finance issues adorn the business pages of the world's press, while massive volumes of capital are entering sport, notably from media corporations. In the United States, the NFL began an eight-year $17.6 billion deal with television networks in 1998. The NCAA has a basketball contract with CBS for $6 billion over thirteen years. Around the year 2000, world football had an annual turnover of over £250 billion, equivalent to the gross national income of the Netherlands.[1]

Marxism provides the most deliberative sociological framework for analysing sport's commodity status. Here, I discuss Marxism and sport in four main parts. First, I outline Marx's social theory and his reading of capitalism. Second, I explore how specific neo-Marxists have utilized his thinking to explain modern sport. Third, I critically assess these neo-Marxist positions. Fourth, I discuss other neo-Marxist thinking on sport's commodification and professionalization. Overall, the discussion is concerned primarily with different neo-Marxist perspectives on sport, rather than on Marx's theory of capitalism *per se*. While neo-Marxist positions illuminate sport's penetration by capital, greater emphasis is required on social actors' critical reflexivity.

Marx and the critique of capitalism

Marx understood capitalism as an advanced, market-based system in which capital is employed to fund commodity production. The ruling capitalist class, the bourgeoisie, owns and controls the means of production (such as land or industrial machinery); the working class, or proletariat, has only its labour power to sell. The proletariat submits control over its industrial practices to capitalists. The capitalist owns the product, and derives 'surplus value' from the difference between the product's value and the capital expended in production. As a social system, capitalism foments 'alienation' across all social categories, as people experience productive labour, their fellow men and women, and their human potential as alien to them. In controlling the means of production, the ruling class dominates all other spheres of society. The State is merely 'a committee for managing the common affairs of the whole bourgeoisie', to dominate the proletariat (Marx and Engels 1998/1848: 44). Through ideological work, the ruling class shapes the dominant ideas within society.[2] While Marx viewed religion as 'the illusory happiness of men', he recognized that as 'the opium of the people', it facilitated 'an expression of real suffering and a protest against real suffering' (Marx, in Bottomore and Rubel 1963: 41–2). Capitalism produces a false 'commodity fetishism', projecting human qualities on to objects, thus hiding the oppressive social relations necessary to create these objects. Lukács (1967/1923) added the concept of 'reification' to explain how, under capitalism, exploitative social relations were presented falsely as thing-like entities.

Relations between the bourgeoisie and the proletariat are inherently antagonistic. Workers experience ideological controls, but antagonism towards employers intensifies as the proletariat grows, wages shrink, and education increases. Marx predicted that capitalism would buckle and collapse when the proletariat formed larger unions, to become a revolutionary class 'for itself'. Following the revolutionary overthrow of capitalists, the workers, he forecast, would seize the bourgeois State to establish a socialist 'revolutionary dictatorship of the proletariat'. Under communism, the State and bourgeois ideology would disappear, leaving a society founded on the maxim, 'From each according to his ability, to each according to his needs!'

Marx's theory has undergone substantial political adaptation and reinterpretation. Lenin (1998/1902) argued that the Communist Party drives the class struggle and is thus empowered to act in workers' interest. Capitalism is an imperial system, with the poorest nations harbouring most revolutionary potential (Lenin 1997/1916). Stalin remoulded 'Marxism-Leninism' to legitimize the Soviet State's totalitarian powers, and mask mass atrocities enacted in its name.

Marx is most commonly criticized on account of unfulfilled predictions (global communism never occurred), over-simplification of social stratification (class relations are more complex than dichotomous), and his 'economism', which viewed the economic base as determining all other 'superstructures' (cultural activities, for example, are not always commodified). Certainly, the Communist system advocated by Marx has never appeared. However, these criticisms over-simplify Marx's thinking. Marx does provide sophisticated interpretations of complex stratification and variable power struggles. In his analysis of Louis Bonaparte's seizure of power in France in 1848, Marx (1937/1869) evades the charge of 'economism' by placing human structures and social agency at the core of his philosophy: 'Men make their own history, but they do not make it just as they please; they do not make it under circumstances chosen by themselves, but under circumstances directly encountered, given, and transmitted from the past' (cited in Feuer 1969: 360). Thus, political, juridical and cultural superstructures do not merely correspond to their material base (S. Hall 1977: 60). In the sociology of sport, problems arise when Marx's erstwhile followers forget this point.

Marx, neo-Marxists and the Frankfurt School on sport and mass culture

How would Marx and Lenin have viewed sport in their time? The Marx of *Capital* would see sport as materially dependent, such that only Communist revolution would negate its commodification and alienation. Marx recognized that capitalism functioned more efficiently if rest and recreation replenished workers' energies, and that in leisure workers could feel 'at home' (Marx 1973/1844). Nevertheless, class societies stunt human advancement, hence bourgeois-controlled sport cannot facilitate our development. For Marx, under communism, recreation would be freely chosen and undertaken.

Unlike Marx, Lenin was a keen sportsman, mainly in skating, cycling and mountaineering, and extolled the developmental benefits of gymnastic exercise. Following the Russian Revolution, Lenin recognized more fully sport's state-supporting aspects in boosting military and industrial power (Riordan 1976). Soviet sport was controlled by the Communist Party and interwoven with Marxist-Leninist ideology. Sport advanced the international proletariat's struggle, challenging bourgeois norms and meeting Communist aspirations in health care, military training, female emancipation and political education (Rigauer 2001: 37). Under Stalin, 'mass sport' became a nation-building goal, while spectator sports were subjected to regular (if comparatively small) state interventions (Edelman 1993: 124).

Outside the Communist bloc, sport was an uneven forum for working-class organization and political mobilization. Europe's working-class sports movements expanded to counteract Fascist movements between the wars. The US Communist Party sponsored the Chicago Counter-Olympics in 1932, challenging the Los Angeles Olympics and the imprisonment of a trades union activist. The event attracted little attention or noteworthy athletic performances, but its prescient anti-racist policies were particularly commendable. In 1936, the People's Olympics were scheduled for Barcelona as a festival of peace, emancipation and anti-fascism, but the event was cancelled when the Spanish Civil War erupted (W. J. Baker 1992).

Sport's post-war functions did not always suit Marxist-Leninist aspirations. Soviet spectator sports were weak instruments for mobilizing citizen support for State or Party (Edelman 1993: 245). The Soviet Union challenged Western nations notably in football and Olympic events. While workers' sports organizations were harbingers of mass 'sport for all' policies in Western democracies, the professionalization and commodification of elite sport was normalized. Thus, neo-Marxist critiques of sport concentrated on elite, 'bourgeois' models.

The neo-Marxist sociology of sport

A diverse range of social commentators and scholars, deploying very varied levels of theoretical sophistication, have analysed sport from neo-Marxist standpoints. For the simplest perspectives, sport is an ideological tool, misleading the masses to sustain bourgeois control. Hoch's (1972) polemic argues that North American sports reflect sharp class divisions. For Rigauer, 'the athlete is the producer, the spectators the consumers' (1981: 68–9). As sports workers, athletes forfeit control over their labour power, and are forced to maximize productivity. The champion 'is totally governed by his trainer, a veritable foreman, whose sole aim is to increase the productivity of his athletes' (Brohm 1978: 105). Specialized divisions of labour force the sports worker to execute designated movements constantly, rather than to play creatively and experimentally (Vinnai 1973: 38). Self-development within elite sports is increasingly restricted, intensifying alienation. Commodification transforms athletes into advertising 'sandwich-boards' for major corporations.[3] While thankful for escaping other industrial work, 'in the illusory belief that he is free, the athlete locks the door of his cell' (Guttmann 1988: 183). Aronowitz's (1973: 410–11) more subtle analysis argues that, under modern capitalism, 'Spectator sports retain the alienated character of labour, but create the aura of participation for the observer'. So long as workers lose themselves in sports gambling or arguments over players, 'the system has a few years left'. He argues for a return to earlier forms of working-class leisure, notably bar-rooms where political discussions and local gossip combine with the reassertion of a fraternity that is otherwise denied in work.

Brohm asserts that the Olympic games are 'opiates' to keep the masses in stupefied happiness, securing 'class collaboration at every level' (1978: 108).[4] Sports tournaments enable televised 'brain washing' that 'aids the process of reducing the population to a servile mass' (1978: 114). Sport's talk of neutral refereeing, impartiality and cross-team sportsmanship merely mirrors the ideology of class collaboration regarding the 'partnership between capital and labour'. Brohm rages that the Olympics promote a national unity that is even backed by the French Communist Party. The proto-Fascist Olympics procure mass worshipping of the 'superman-champion', yet sport mutilates the body to create drug-fed athletic 'monsters', 'cybernetic robots', 'imprisoned, indoctrinated, regimented and repressed' (1978: 112).

What solutions are proposed? Hoch reckons we face a stark choice between 'socialism or fascism, global human liberation or barbarism' (1972: 212). The far more theoretically sophisticated work of Beamish (1993: 205–7) recognizes the complexities of class relations in sport. He notes, for example, that Canadian sport remains strongly influenced by old amateurist principles rather than employer–employee relations. Athletes lack basic industrial rights, and should turn to the courts to gain collective bargaining status, a minimum wage, overtime and holiday pay. Rigauer (1981: 103–5) proposes the most speculative neo-Marxist solutions to sport. He demands:

1 The removal of sport's work-like structures, repressive rationalization and achievement obsession.
2 The dissolution of conformism and promotion of democracy.
3 The overt politicization of sports, against the old fallacy that sport is 'free' of politics.
4 The removal of ideologies, to promote sport's liberal and educational aspects.

In later work, Rigauer (2001: 45) focused on how Marxist sport sociology might 'open and widen' its paradigm. In the main, he argued for greater critical openness and dialogue with other sociological paradigms.

The Frankfurt School

The pessimistic arguments of Brohm, Rigauer and Vinnai on sport are particularly indebted to the Frankfurt School of social philosophy that emerged in Germany in the 1920s, with Horkheimer, Adorno, Marcuse and Fromm among its prominent members. In establishing 'critical theory', the Frankfurt School combined Marxism with other intellectual disciplines, notably psychoanalysis. The Frankfurt School was committed to the Enlightenment principles of critical reason, intellectual and aesthetic progress, scientific advancement, and human emancipation. Modern capitalism was deemed to negate these principles, as scientific rationalization and 'instrumental reason' dominate human subjects (Adorno and Horkheimer 1979/1944; Poster 1990: 34–5). Capitalism's 'culture industry' 'impedes the development of autonomous, independent individuals who judge and decide consciously for themselves' (Adorno 2001: 106). Popular cultural products, in film, music and sport, are instrumentally standardized, pre-packaged as commodities with a 'pseudo-individualization' that distracts the masses from their 'unfreedom'.

For Marcuse (1964), advanced industrialism creates a 'one-dimensional' humanity. 'False needs' (such as in consumer culture) create 'euphoria in unhappiness', distracting the masses from critical reflection and emancipation.[5] Jameson (1979, 1981), a Marxist literary theorist, argues that mass culture is intrinsically ideological; it provokes genuine emotions and desires that cannot be met properly under capitalism's oppressive relations.[6]

The Frankfurt thesis partly parallels the highly elitist cultural theory of Arnold, Eliot and Leavis, who dismissed the unedifying mass culture of the working classes, bemoaned post-war Americanization, and lamented England's cultural entropy. Sport held an ambiguous status. 'Plebian' pastimes like wrestling were dismissed with disgust as inherently anti-intellectual. Elitist sports like cricket were venerated for their refined aesthetic and cultural codes.[7]

For Adorno (1982: 80–1), modern sports function to sustain industrial capitalism. They may 'seek to restore to the body some of the functions of which the machine has deprived it. But they do so only in order to train men all the more inexorably to serve the machine.' Physical exertion of labour is replicated in sport, becoming something people must 'learn to enjoy' (Adorno 2001: 194–5). Sport is 'pseudo-praxis', its rules resembling the market's brutal competitiveness. Athletes might learn some virtues through sport, but the 'powerless' spectators, the 'applauding hooligans', the 'howling devotees of the stadium' experience no emancipation (Adorno 2001: 91). Sports events are a 'model for totalitarian mass rallies' (Morgan 1988: 818) while also exemplifying the culture industry. Like Hollywood celebrities, many 'star' athletes obediently perform routine functions while being marketed as having pseudo-individualistic properties (like an unusual haircut or new romantic muse).

Neo-Marxist sport sociology: criticisms, but reapplication

Much neo-Marxist sport sociology harbours debilitating flaws, in particular a tendency towards crude economism (Jennifer Hargreaves 1994: 17). Hoch and Brohm formulate an erroneous 'left-functionalism', assuming that all social structures 'function' to preserve capitalism (Gruneau 1999: 140n). This ignores the varied socialization of individuals, their rational and critical faculties, interpretative diversity, and capacity to mobilize opposition. As the Marxist political historian Ralph Miliband (1977: 52–3) points out, one should not avoid serious thinking on sport simply by assuming, as some Marxists do, that supporting a sports team is incompatible with the development of class consciousness and participation in class struggle.

The Frankfurt School's critical status is more intriguing. Initially, they seem 'literally unable to imagine sport as something other than a complex of pathological attitudes and instincts' (Hoberman 1984: 244). However, their damning of the culture industry needs contextualization. Unlike Brohm and Rigauer, Adorno and Horkheimer could not access later sociological theories, such as semiotic theory, that would have enabled patient decoding rather than sweeping dismissal of popular media (Poster 1990: 34–5). Moreover, Adorno (2001: 195–6) did soften his position on consumerism, noting that people consume products and discourses 'with a kind of reservation' such that they are 'not quite believed in'.[8] On sport, the public's 'double-consciousness' combines enjoyment of rationalized fun with explicit misgivings. For Morgan (1988), Adorno understands sport as a form of *regression*: individually, as spontaneous, child-like play; in societal terms, as a return to when nature dominated humanity. Children's play seems infantile and silly, but its 'uselessness' and freedom from instrumental reason must be preserved. Sport should be no different from the classical arts: an end in itself, defined by standards of excellence that 'contribute to our self-understanding and self-mastery' (1988: 831–2). Like the arts, 'the usefulness of work' and 'the uselessness of play' in sport may be harmoniously and freely interwoven (1988: 833). Notably, many sporting heroes are celebrated for *playing* with a child-like absorption, with comparatively stronger self-expression and enjoyment of the occasion. Such athletes are typically contrasted in public discourses with well-drilled performers and team systems that produce highly rationalized but inherently dull spectacles.

Both the Frankfurt School and neo-Marxist sociologists underplay sport's aesthetics. Leading athletes like Rodman, Beckham or De La Hoya may be famous partly for their pseudo-aesthetic characteristics (stylish clothing, different haircuts), yet their sporting *raison d'être* is defined by their objective, competitive excellence and technical artistry within sport. It is hard to imagine these athletes being valued so differently within a post-capitalist society freed from instrumental reason.

More problematically, the Frankfurt School and neo-Marxist sport sociologists pay insufficient attention to critical action and interpretation among the 'masses'. These sociologists thus arrogate to themselves an unwarranted privileged epistemology, above and beyond the perspectives of ordinary social actors. Certainly, Western sports presentation is inherently ideological, but sport contains numerous illustrations of political dissent. Consider two cases of industrial action among athletes. In 1980, Mexican baseball players went on strike to improve their financial and political rights; modest benefits in pensions and life insurance were won. In 1947–8 in colonial Rhodesia (now Zimbabwe), African football clubs in Bulawayo boycotted their own football tournaments to prevent political incursions by white administrators. The boycott outlasted the general strike among African workers at that time, and saw off white encroachments (Stuart 1989). Neither the neo-Marxist sport sociologists nor the 'culture industry' thesis would explain convincingly the political agency behind these episodes.

Oriard (1993) notes these weaknesses when examining Jameson's neo-Marxist 'containment model'. Like catharsis theory, the containment model suggests that sport spectators undergo emotional release, thereby dissipating potentially harmful (or revolutionary) energies. However, sport generates (rather than dissipates) aggressive behaviour and dysfunctional emotions. Jameson claims that the masses have a child-like wish to experience culture repetitiously, with little variation and highly predictable outcomes. Oriard concedes that in popular music, fiction and televising of sports, the emphasis is on reproduction. But, with regard to American football, Oriard (1993: 6) argues that 'the games themselves as often as not resist such packaging': incidents and results are not so readily predictable. Equally, while mass culture's commodities may seem inauthentic, sport itself does possess authenticity. As a former professional, Oriard knows that the specific plays, hits and debilitating injuries of American football are all real experiences.

Overall, while neo-Marxist positions illuminate interrelations between class division, rationalization, ideology and commodification, their determinism underplays the political and aesthetic diversity within sporting practices. Moreover, these strengths and weaknesses, as Oriard indicates, become more apparent when subjected to closer assessment regarding specific sport practices and experiences. In the following section, I discuss the commodification of cricket before branching into other sports.

Sport, industrial production and commodification

Cricket, class and commodification

Cricket is the case study *par excellence* for exploring sport's class stratification. Created in England, cricket is founded upon class divisions; its numerous rules and rituals reproduce social stratification through play. The division of amateurs (aristocratic or bourgeois gentlemen) and professionals (more working-class players) originated in the early nineteenth century, ritualizing class stratification.[9] The two cricketer classes were allocated separate dressing-rooms and addressed differently during play – gentlemen by title, players simply by name.[10] Fitting imperialist ideologies, cricket club captaincies were reserved for amateurs: only in 1952 did Len Hutton become England's first professional captain. Off the field, inter-class fraternization was actively discouraged. The amateur–professional divide was formally abolished in 1963 for material rather than egalitarian reasons: fewer amateurs were sufficiently rich to play daily without pay. Nevertheless, English cricket has remained elitist and 'disproportionately upper class' in leadership, social codes and player background (Marqusee 1994: 134–5).

Marxist sociology encourages us to explain the cultural practices and aesthetic principles within sport according to the logic of capitalism. Harriss (1986, 1988–9) examines how cricket after 1918 lost aristocratic playfulness to become 'an efficient, scientific game based on cautious bourgeois principles' (Harriss 1986: 66). Australian Don Bradman is universally regarded as the world's greatest cricketer: his international batting average, compiled between 1928 and 1948, is 99.94, almost double that of the next best players. Bradman's calculated risk taking and machine-like technique personified the core values of a bureaucratized, rationalized modern capitalist world (Harriss 1988–9: 7). Yet, before 1914, pre-industrial values lingered strongly, and batsmen prioritized style, grace and risk taking in play. Jack Hobbs's career is indicative: before 1914, Hobbs was an artful, highly entertaining batsman who, in single innings, scored 200 or more on only one occasion; after 1918, as modern capitalism's instrumental reason took hold, Hobbs scored twelve double centuries and admitted to taking far fewer risks. Cricket bowlers underwent a similar rationalization of technique and performance: risk-takers like spin bowlers who lost runs to batsmen were replaced by artless performers adept at grinding out opponents.

From the 1960s onwards, cricket underwent further materialist transformation. Introduction of one-day cricket challenged the traditional, several-day format for matches. One-day cricket was marketed as involving spectacle, thrills and escapist consumption (notably all-day drinking). Compared to several-day cricket, 'postmodern' one-day games inspire commodity fetishism across their mass of consumers:

> While cricket in the era of modernity performed an ideological function in masking the contradiction and oppression inherent in the capital/labour relationship, cricket in the era of postmodernity performs a different ideological function, by presenting the act of consumption as though it were totally unrelated to the social relations of production. (Harriss 1990: 120)

Cricket's modernization and postmodernization were marked by intense class struggles. The traditionalist aristocracy and old-money classes clashed with modernizing forces among the new bourgeoisie over rationalized styles of play and the demise of amateur values. Latterly, the established bourgeoisie has regularly expressed antipathy towards one-day cricket's 'loutish', working-class appeal.

Harriss's overall argument is somewhat deterministic, and rather underplays the relatively autonomous cultural development of any sport's organization and aesthetics. One-day cricket may be television-friendly, but its public appeal and playing techniques have other causes besides global capital. First, it suggests a folk cultural return to cricket's *pre*-modern elements, when spectacle, risk taking and carnival excesses were prominent. Second, it sharpened many skills inherent to cricket: fielding, shot selection among batsmen, and bowler accuracy. These honed skills have helped improve standards at several-day cricket fixtures. Third, Harriss exaggerates the epistemological break between one-day and multi-day cricket; the two games, and their supporters, sit alongside each other.

Commodification, professionalization and sport's corruption

Other sociologists have borrowed from Marxism to examine sport's commodification. Andrews (1997) describes the NBA as a global 'commodity-sign' rather like Disney, Ford or Exxon; other sports governing bodies, such as the NHL, the NFL and Formula One, share this trademark distinction. LaFeber (2002) has detailed how 'the greatest endorser of the twentieth century' (a.k.a. Michael Jordan) helped build Nike and the NBA into multi-billion-dollar transnational corporations. Heinilä (1998: 162–3) notes sport's professionalization and commodification. Thus, elite athletes are on market-building missions when they salute crowds after victories or publicize sponsors' products during media interviews. Through the example of New Zealand's superstar rugby union players, Hope (2002) even anticipates the commercially driven transmutation of national sports teams into 'global corporate property' that is 'loaned' back to those national customers who subscribe to international pay-television corporations as the only way to watch these teams.

Of course, sport's professionalization and commodification are long-standing processes. The sport stadiums of the late nineteenth and early twentieth centuries were erected across Europe, North America and Australasia to accommodate more admission-payers. League competitions were organized by clubs to maximize revenues. Athletes have always been tied to other forms of consumerism, notably to the alcohol industry, product endorsement and the ghosting of articles for the popular press. In sports like tennis and track and field athletics, the athlete's struggle for professional status and paid reward lasted longer, but once successful, new off-field earnings soon appeared.

Professional sport has undergone exaggerated, more intensive commodification since the early 1960s. The 'hyper-commercialization' of Australian sport is viewed as originating in the 1970s (Stewart 1993). The 'hyper-commodification' of football in the UK and across Western Europe was wrought by massive, new capital injections from the late 1980s, specifically from pay-television stations, merchandise outlets and advertisers, and the sale of club equity on stock markets (Walsh and Giulianotti 2001; Giulianotti 2002). In the NCAA's 'amateur' sports, hyper-commodification has witnessed television contracts for basketball balloon from around $40 million in 1985 to $545 million per year fifteen years later (Sperber 2003: 36, 216). Some professional sports are now controlled by outside corporations. Rugby league in England and Australia is effectively owned and controlled by leading media corporations; leagues have been radically reorganized, and many clubs closed or forcibly merged, to accommodate new clubs in wealthier 'target markets'. Commodification thus engenders conflict-based relations of consumption, particularly when poorer sports fans cannot afford higher prices for stadium admission or pay-television subscription fees.

Recent commodification impulses have outmoded some earlier arguments surrounding sports clubs. Hardy (1986: 22–3) had stated that professional sports clubs were 'traditional firms' with 'a single unit or single office, with a single owner or small group of owners, with a single product line, in a single geographic area'; clubs 'have remained essentially local firms, even as their once strictly local markets have sometimes extended to regional or national dimensions'. Today, however, leading sports clubs like New York Yankees and Manchester United have diverse product ranges including clothing and textiles, insurance, perishable foods and tourism. In sports leagues organized as cartels, governing bodies (like the NBA, the MLB and the AFL) constitute umbrella firms sheltering club 'franchise' outlets. In controlling franchise allocations, the umbrella body can ensure that no unwanted market competitor arises within that sporting discipline. Conversely, while McDonald's authorize their own fast-food franchises, they cannot prevent rival companies from selling identical products at competitive rates.

Sport's integrity is corrupted by transformation into commodified, television-focused entertainment (see Lasch 1979: 106–7). American sports are littered with unnecessary play-breaks to accommodate television adverts. In televised snooker, tables are equipped with thinner cloths and wider pockets to increase artificially the pace of play and player scoring power. Overt corruption may arise when the uncertainty of outcome is commodified by match fixing and bribery. Many betting scandals originate in the relative exploitation of professional athletes by club owners and managers. Professional boxing has always had managers who fix fights by insisting fighters 'take a dive'. In the United States, 'amateur' NCAA athletes have accepted bribes to fix results, risking lifetime bans to win meagre earnings for their key roles in a billion-dollar industry. Globalization processes and the creation of illegal gambling syndicates, notably in Asia, have served to facilitate networks that corrupt matches involving international cricketers and some European footballers.

Marx predicted that the concentration of capital in fewer and fewer hands would destabilize and ultimately end capitalism. Marx did not live to see his forecast thwarted by imperialist expansion overseas (stealing resources from elsewhere), ephemeral improvements in the proletariat's quality of life (such as consumerism), and the increased ideological work of pro-capitalist forces (notably in media and education). In sport, the concentration of wealth and power among fewer clubs and nations can destabilize the system, as fixtures and tournaments lose 'uncertainty of outcome'. In sports like baseball and football, the richest clubs dominate competitions through their economic strengths in the labour market and corporate sponsorships (see Hall, Szymanski and Zimbalist 2002). The richest teams often employ large squads, ensuring that many highly talented players have to sit out numerous games or even much of a season. This perverts the participatory ethos of sports, depriving other clubs of access to these players while robbing audiences of the right to see the best talents on the maximum number of occasions.

The more pessimistic Marxists would argue that sport is restabilized by potent ideological messages projected through the mass media, to legitimize dominant cartels and to inculcate consumerism concerning these clubs' products. Fresh, if volatile, sources of capital injection are discovered, and new international alliances of sport's major clubs are formed. In baseball, in 1997, the Florida Marlins' owner, Wayne Huizenga, upset elite clubs by spending $80 million on top players to buy/win the World Series. After losing $30 million, Huizenga quickly traded away most of the champion team for the next season. European football's wealthiest clubs have formed the G-14 business club to advance their collective interests, thereby pressurizing Europe's governing body to reshape competitions in their favour. Overall, it is in examining sport's hyper-commodification that Marxist perspectives have greatest explanatory currency.

Concluding comments: determinism and commodification

Sociologists influenced heavily by Marx agree that under capitalism, bourgeois sport is suffused with alienation, ruling-class ideologies and commodification. For post-war neo-Marxist sociologists, sport (under capitalism *and* Soviet-style communism) is dominated by instrumental reason and needs to be reinvented as non-work freedom.

The arguments here contribute substantially towards an empirically grounded, critical sociology of sport. As the Frankfurt School indicates, sport as cultural practice is subsumed by instrumental rationalism, with technical efficiency and result achievement prioritized over subjective immersion in experimental play. Sport's contemporary hyper-commodification is categorically distinct from earlier periods of commercialization. Class conflicts erupt regarding relations of production, as industrial action among athletes testifies. Underlying antagonisms regarding relations of *consumption* are increasingly prominent, since commodification of sports goods exaggerates distributive injustices – for example, when poorer sports fans cannot afford stadium admission prices, club merchandise or television subscriptions.

However, much Marxist theory still over-emphasizes economic determinants inside sport. Some historical changes within sports like cricket are plausibly explained as outcomes of struggles over society's material organization. But economic reductionism does not tell all. Other structural influences, including those restricted to sport, impact upon the aesthetic codes, social organizations, and sport's broader cultural meanings and practices. Sport does not fulfil only the ideological needs of capitalism. It has many innocent attractions, most obviously its departure from much of everyday life (Morgan 1993: 44–5). For example, unnecessary obstacles are avoided or removed in ordinary life, but sport is full of contrived impediments (such as rules prohibiting ball handling or crossing lanes in races).

The most coherent neo-Marxist position must account for social actors' critical faculties and interpretive capacities. Many professional athletes are not passive cogs in sport's commercial wheel, but have won improved industrial conditions and often superlative financial rewards for their erstwhile commodification. We must also account for sport aesthetics; thus, Adorno's softer position, on sport's creative aspects, requires closer examination. Sociologists have barely scratched the surface in exploring sport's reflective and socially critical elements. Meanwhile, the goal must be to reclaim the more politically interpretivist aspects of Marx that had explained the complexities of French Bonapartism. To that end, the Cultural Studies approach discussed next is significantly more successful.

4

Cultural Studies: Hegemony Theory beyond Resistance

Interdisciplinary Cultural Studies is the most influential theoretical and research paradigm within sport studies. Cultural Studies was born out of social-scientific endeavours to explain the major cultural struggles of the post-war period, as advanced by black civil rights movements in North America, internationalist feminist movements, youth counter-cultures, rising environmentalism, and France's political uprisings in May 1968. Cultural Studies reworked Marxist theory to locate a 'cultural politics' in the leisure practices of subordinate communities stratified by class, youth, gender and ethnicity/race.

Cultural Studies' intellectual conception mixed British foreplay with Continental insemination. In Britain, Richard Hoggart (1958) and E. P. Thompson (1963) ignited intellectual interest in working-class culture. Raymond Williams (1961, 1975, 1977, 1981) published substantial Marxist studies of modern cultural history, despite still privileging high culture (notably the novel and drama) over its lower manifestations (including sport), and often ignoring gender, race and colonialism questions. The influential *New Left Review* was founded in 1960; and the Centre for Contemporary Cultural Studies (hereafter CCCS), established in 1964 at the University of Birmingham, came under Stuart Hall's guidance. Continental theories gained influence: from France, Louis Althusser's structural Marxism and Roland Barthes's semiotic theory; from Italy, belatedly, the visionary analyses of Communist leader Antonio Gramsci (1971), whose key thinking had been recorded while he was imprisoned by Mussolini.

Cultural Studies has mushroomed into a vast pan-disciplinary academic domain, encompassing sociology, political science, history, geography, literary criticism, linguistics and semiotics, media and communication, area studies and political activism. I do not have space for an exhaustive analysis of the significant theoretical and method-ological differences that inevitably arose across Cultural Studies. How-ever, I do note how commentators like Fiske, McRobbie and Willis emphasize the audience's critical engagement with popular culture, while others, notably Clarke and Critcher, and John Hargreaves, focus more on struggles within the historical reproduction of class domination.

For epistemological and pragmatic reasons, this chapter addresses Cultural Studies' core principles and issues. Later chapters highlight Cultural Studies' wider influences upon research fields like gender, eth-nicity and the body. While recognizing trans-disciplinary approaches on sport, I am concerned that too much contemporary work in Cultural Studies forgets its sociological roots in theory and method. Sociological commitments to balancing theory and evidence can be undermined if we embrace evidence-free 'theory' from disciplines like semiotics and literary criticism to ponder somewhat narcissistic life-style questions rather than analyse the position and practices of marginalized communities.

The discussion has five parts. First, I outline Cultural Studies' British foundation, in particular its debts to the CCCS and Raymond Williams. Second, I explore Gramsci's hegemony theory with regard to sport. Third, I assess the key theme of 'resistance' both conceptually and substantively. Fourth, I introduce the concepts of 'transgression' and the 'carnivalesque' to enhance the Cultural Studies framework. In conclusion, I recommend some areas for the redevelopment of a Cultural Studies approach within sport sociology.

Cultural Studies: foundations and core principles

Cultural Studies focuses on cultural struggles that arise between domi-nant groups (producing official culture) and subordinate groups (pro-ducing popular culture, including sport). Popular culture is defined as essentially contradictory and paradoxical: it can destabilize the social order, but is made by dominated groups from material and sym-bolic resources that facilitate domination. For example, sport spec-tators maintain the social order by paying admission, cheering the nation's athletes, and consuming merchandise; they undermine so-cial order through 'excessive' behaviour that offends dominant groups and by creating 'subcultures' that castigate sports authorities. Unlike much neo-Marxism, Cultural Studies analysts rework Marx to conceive of subordinate groups as active agents in shaping and reshaping identities and practices according to historical circumstance. As Grossberg (1988: 22) explains:

> Cultural studies is concerned with describing and intervening in the ways discourses are produced within, inserted into and operate in the relations between people's everyday lives and the structures of the social formation so as to reproduce, resist and transform the existing structures of power. That is, if people make history but in conditions not of their own making, cultural studies explores the ways this is enacted within cultural practices and the place of these practices within specific historical formations.

The CCCS pioneered this approach to analyse how youth subcultural styles appropriate and restyle everyday elements of modern material culture (Hall and Jefferson 1976). For example, bin-liners and safety pins became punk fashion accessories, to symbolize youth solidarity in escaping the boredom of modern education, industrial labour and pre-packaged leisure. For the CCCS, such 'authentic' styles represented 'magical', temporary solutions of young people to their collective structural problems, rooted in age, class, ethnicity and gender. For Hebdige (1979, 1988), youth subcultures are engaged in semiotic conflicts or sign warfare with the dominant social order; punk dress and music, for example, challenged conventional codes regarding acceptable attire and musical harmony. Of course, rebellious styles don't overthrow the dominant social order. Instead, entrepreneurs inside the dominant culture refashion authentic youth styles, 'defusing' their radical content for 'diffusion' as mass commodities (J. Clarke 1976: 185–9). Punk began as a nihilistic underground subculture, but its major acts and fashions were soon commodified for mass consumption. Some sport subcultures have endured equivalent changes. Snowboarding subcultures initially suggested youthful resistance to mainstream skiing, but its rebelliousness was soon commodified, rendering it financially and culturally inaccessible to the lower classes (Heino 2000).

Williams's reading of culture and society significantly influenced the CCCS. For Williams, 'culture' is not elite; it is 'ordinary', part of a 'common culture' deserving investigation. Willis (1990) developed the idea of 'common culture' to examine youth culture's 'symbolic creativity' and 'grounded aesthetics'. 'Symbolic creativity' captures 'the multitude of ways in which young people use, humanize, decorate and invest with meanings their common and immediate life spaces and social practices' (1990: 2). 'Grounded aesthetics' concern the selective construction of dynamic, aesthetic meanings for particular symbols and practices (1990: 21). Willis illustrated these terms through reference to the social relations within sports participation and the cultural meanings arising within football fandom (1990: 110–14).

Others have explored the creative semiotic engagement of social actors within popular culture. For Fiske (1987), pop culture is constituted by 'polysemic' texts, each containing multiple meanings that germinate diverse everyday interpretations. A sport celebrity like David Beckham, for example, transmits various textual meanings that are interpreted in diverse ways by actors from different social categories. Thus, Beckham may be a sex symbol for some women and gay men; for more traditionalist males, he embodies excessively feminine traits (Cashmore 2002).

Raymond Williams (1958) emphasized the importance of common culture in working-class communities. 'Deep community' is conveyed by the members' 'structure of feeling', as constituted by their beliefs, assumptions, styles of expression, manners of speech and behaviour, and senses of belonging (R. Williams 1961: 62–7). A structure of feeling defines a lived culture, binding community members and disclosing their antagonism towards the dominant culture; unlike an ideology, it is neither formal nor systematic (R. Williams 1977: 132–3). Sporting rituals and practices are often imbued with potent structures of feeling. Hoggart (1958: 85) noted how rugby league teams were 'an important element in the group life' of working-class districts. Robson (2000) demonstrated the structure of feeling surrounding Millwall football club in working-class south-east London. The concept carries serious methodological implications: social researchers must grasp empathically these distinctive structures of feeling to explain particular communities.

Williams also provides a valuable model for examining the politics of culture. At any historical juncture, various 'dominant', 'residual' and 'emergent' forces are at play. Dominant forces establish the most conventional forms of social relations and practices within society; residual and emergent trends respectively comprise past and future forces. The residual differs from the 'archaic': the archaic comes from the past and is knowingly 'revived'; the residual also emerges from the past but remains significantly involved in present culture (R. Williams 1977: 122–3). Similarly, the emergent is 'substantially alternative or oppositional' to dominant forces, whereas the 'novel' merely extends the dominant culture. Changes within the class structure help reshape these political relations historically.

The modern Olympics help illustrate Williams's model. The Olympic movement is an archaic nod to ancient Greece's athletic contests. The Olympics' dominant culture is modern, male and bourgeois, celebrating ideologies of nationalism, professionalism, corporate capitalism, competitive success and corporeal power. Residual Olympic culture reflects some older values and political influences, notably amateurism or insidious social links between Olympic officialdom and extreme-right movements since the 1930s. Novel aspects are found in new technical innovations, such as athlete drug testing or media presentation, or locating new national hosts (e.g. China). The emergent is found in new social forces that anticipate significant change (e.g. professionalism's wider entry in the 1980s, and tighter anti-corruption regulations). However, the Olympics' dominant culture will remain largely undisturbed without any radical transformation of class relations or capitalism (see Ingham and Hardy 1993).[1]

On commodification, Raymond Williams (1961) argued that individuals and social groups could hold three distinctive relationships to cultural institutions. 'Members' consider that non-economic reciprocity and mutual duties exist between the individual and the institution. 'Customers' are more utilitarian, remaining loyal to the institution but expecting it to meet particular needs. 'Consumers' are purely instrumental, and shop around institutional markets. Critcher (1979: 170–1) applied these classifications to explain English football spectator and player identities. He discerned a strong rise in 'customers' and 'consumers', and these inevitably side-lined (to a 'residual' position) the membership structure of feeling within working-class clubs. Alt (1983: 100) similarly observes that, in American football, supporter rituals of local team identification have given way to switching allegiances to winning sides.

Community as an ideal has come under particular political attack since the late 1970s. Across Europe, North America and Australasia, the New Right scorned collectivist thinking, notably through Margaret Thatcher's infamous maxim that 'there is no such thing as society', only individuals and families. This anti-sociological philosophy shaped state policies in resource provision and policing within sport through the 1980s and 1990s. More credible critiques of community recognize that structures of feeling also marginalize, exclude or victimize those who deviate in some way. This criticism does not abolish the concept of community *a priori*. Indeed, any Cultural Studies position must be critical of intolerant communities, and should envisage community forms that are enlightened, culturally diverse and tolerant. In sport, attempts to render communities more tolerant, to enlighten structures of feeling, have included local anti-racism initiatives among spectator groups.

Post-structuralist critiques of community indicate that Cultural Studies reads false levels of 'authenticity' into subcultural practices. Others argue that community traditions and identities are essentially 'invented' myths, just as African 'tribal' identities were invented by colonial administrators, and British national traditions are largely aristocratic inventions (see Hobsbawm and Ranger 1983; Nairn 1994). Two points follow here, however. First, the 'invention of traditions' argument is most effective when critiquing how *dominant* social groups seek to shape popular cultural practices. Cultural Studies should focus on how the specific meanings of community and tradition are themselves the contested terrain, involving different elements of dominant and subordinate groups. Thus, for example, in sport, the definition of the 'true fan' is a subject of much critical discussion, with different football authorities, media reporters, corporate sponsors and many kinds of fan group each inventing different historical variants of this mythical construct. Critical sociologists should examine how more powerful elements (notably sponsors, media and football authorities) invent the fan historically; sociological research should not be about disparaging the identities of supporter groups whose traditional practices (like standing during games, or swapping abusive comments with rivals) are subjected to prohibitions.

Second, 'deconstructing' all sports traditions and identities as 'invented' does not get us far. While all traditions are invented in some way or another, they are also lived: they are amended, reformulated and even discarded by social groups. There may be much 'forgery which goes into the "forging of nations"' (Ascherson 2002: 264), but senses of community and nationality are popularly perceived and experienced, and represent key referents in modern struggles for emancipation or independence. For example, in modern-day Zimbabwe, Ndebele tribal identity may have originated largely as a 'colonial fiction', but it has developed into a core cultural identity among the peoples of Matebeleland, as reflected in part through sport. Restricting analysis to the cultural invention of that identity is sociologically dull, and ignores how subaltern social agents mould and remould these constructions of community.

Hegemony theory

Gramsci and Althusser

Gramsci's concept of 'hegemony' is one of the most important within Cultural Studies. Hegemony describes the particular fluid power relationships, methods and techniques within a class society whereby dominant groups secure their control through the ideological consent, rather than the physical coercion, of the dominated group. The exploitative social order appears 'natural', or 'common sense', ensuring that the dominated group 'lives its subordination'. Dominant groups accommodate elements of the subordinate social class within the hegemonic bloc, however resistant counter-hegemonic formations arise. Hegemony is established within different societal domains (in politics, business and industry, cultural arenas) where various classes or class fractions enter into struggle, opposition, manipulation, compromise, negotiation and accommodation. Hegemony theory explains more effectively than prior 'ruling class' theories the modern realities of elective democracy, leisure and private life. It captures cultural traditions and practices 'as they are', in personal relationships, leisure, art and entertainment (R. Williams 1977: 110–11). However, we should avoid following some interpretations of hegemony theory into an 'overstatement of the ideological predominance of the "ruling class"'; such an overstatement underplays the diverse and continuous challenges to that state of domination (Miliband 1977: 53).

State and civil society relationships help shape hegemony.[2] In advanced states, civil society is a highly complex 'superstructure' comprising many organisms and associations that are not economically predetermined (Gramsci 1971: 235). States promote consent across civil society, but hegemony is always redefined and contested, partly via conflicts within associations and institutions. The related concept of 'national-popular' helps explain cultural connections between subordinate social classes, national ambitions and popular beliefs (Gramsci 1971: 421). Intellectuals produce and communicate ideas, beliefs and discourses that develop hegemony across civil society. Modern capitalism's intellectuals include lower-level functionaries and state administrators who merely apply hegemonic ideas and principles. Gramsci differentiated between 'traditional' intellectuals, who, rather idealistically, claim independence from class bias or location; and 'organic' intellectuals, who emerge from specific class locations, and thus in the case of subordinate classes, possess more progressive potential. For Stuart Hall, Cultural Studies should be practised by 'organic intellectuals' committed to movements of social emancipation (Bennett 1998: 31).

Despite Gramsci's far greater emphasis on the role of resistance and struggle within his notion of hegemony, his work does harbour some conceptual parallels with that of Althusser. First, for Althusser, repressive and ideological state apparatuses function to secure social domination (see Gramsci 1971: 12); ideological apparatuses include the educational system and mass media. Althusser (1971: 174) adds the concept of ideological 'interpellation', wherein people are 'hailed' as particular kinds of subjects, giving rise to particular identities. For example, televised sports are surrounded by advertising images that 'hail' us as consumers, and to which we respond in self-recognition. Sports commentaries interpellate divisive forms of identity, and thus 'hail' us as men (not women), Americans (not Australians), or whites (not blacks). Through interpellation, our recognized identities sustain a social order rooted in social division, efficient production and consumption. Second, to evade charges of 'economism', Althusser borrows a Gramscian phrase to argue that the political and ideological (or 'cultural') superstructures of society are 'relatively autonomous' from their material base. Thus, outcomes of hegemonic struggles inside sport are not predetermined by economic power. However, Althusser is overly concerned with how domination is secured, rather than practically contested. Thus, rather problematically, he argues that the economic structure *is* still determinant 'in the last instance' (Althusser 1971: 136).

Evidently, hegemony theory contains differences regarding issues of ideological determination and critical social action. It is most persuasive when evading determinism. Ideological interpellation is certainly utilized by dominant groups and institutions. But, as concepts like 'relative autonomy' and 'organic intellectuals' indicate, social actors do not necessarily internalize these messages whole-heartedly, or construct alternative world-views that reflect subordination. Cultural Studies' recognition of ordinary culture's legitimacy and its abandonment of economic reductionism are to be welcomed. Yet we should beware of overplaying popular culture's societal significance, or imagining cultural practices as sealed off from other structural forces.

Hegemony theory in sport

Hegemony theory has strongly influenced numerous analyses of sport. In terms of British sports' imperial diffusion, Mangan (1998a: 22) has argued that British headmasters were 'intellectuals' in 'spreading and legitimizing dominant convictions' concerning imperialism's benefits. Local pupils accepted this 'common sense' which established a 'national-popular', disabling dissent by making imperial dependence appear normal. For example, the British colonial state introduced cricket to West Indian civil society as an 'innocuous outlet for mass frustrations', reinforcing hierarchies of race, gender and class. A 'common sense' imbued cricket's conventions, enabling

> the transmission of values like respect for authority, especially that of Whites, deferred gratification, and team spirit; the inculcation of norms such as unquestioned acceptance of the decisions of authority figures, in particular Whites (this was embodied in the term, 'it's not cricket'), the use of myths such as the inherent superiority of the colonizer and inferiority of the colonized, and the utilization of the bat as a symbol of authority – this explains why Whites were expected to be batsmen. (St Pierre 1995: 79)

However, as Gramsci allows, subaltern non-white populations produced organic intellectuals like C. L. R. James to challenge domination within sport and civil society. The indigenous black population embraced cricket to signify (usually covert) resistance to oppression. Cricket remains an informal and anonymous niche within civil society, where whites and authority figures generally are derided, while heavy drinking and carnival atmospheres implicitly challenge the colonial value system.

A Gramscian framework is evident in Stuart Hall's (1978) reading of football hooliganism in conjunction with other work on social control (Hall et al. 1978). Hall (1978: 35) argued that media and state responses to football hooliganism reflected a rising right-wing populist ideology that victimized weak elements in the society. Ironically, later analysts drew strong connections between Margaret Thatcher's free-market individualism and jingoism and the xenophobia of some English fans at fixtures overseas (I. Taylor 1987; J. Williams 1991).

Clarke and Critcher (1985) engaged Williams and Gramsci to critique modern UK leisure. They argued that hegemony theory advances leisure studies in four ways, by recognizing cultural diversity, disclosing how cultures work together to establish domination and 'leadership', viewing cultural struggle as an ongoing, everyday process, and understanding how groups that avoid incorporation always threaten the social order (Clarke and Critcher 1985: 228). Constant struggles within UK leisure are registered by the attempts of dominant groups to repress and replace 'undesirable' free-time activity with more 'civilized', profitable recreation.

John Hargreaves (1986) has advanced British hegemony theory's most substantive, sports-focused elaboration. He argues that, historically, the mid-Victorian sports culture helped differentiate the bourgeoisie from subordinate classes. Mass sports participation arrived in the 1880s as the 'respectable' working classes gained greater resources (material, educational and temporal). Within the hegemonic bloc, upper-class gentlemen and 'more thrusting capitalistic elements' conflicted over amateurism in sport. Commercialism penetrated many sports, notably those with mass popularity, but gentlemen-amateurs retained influence so that 'the hegemonic structure remained intact' (Hargreaves 1986: 206). Subsequently, popular sports were redefined as commercial entertainment, thus 'encouraging the atomization of working-class clientele' into individual consumers. The State assisted business class hegemony by presenting sport as consumerist (notably through the public sector broadcaster, the BBC) (1986: 218). Meanwhile, mediated, elite-level, international sport helped forge the 'national-popular', diverting public awareness of class and other divisions, to sustain bourgeois hegemony.

Hargreaves recognizes that opposition and discontent recurred regularly. He rightly criticizes the British Left's failure to organize alternative, counter-hegemonic sporting institutions. Nevertheless, sport opened three counter-hegemonic 'fissures'. First, the British State's weak sports policies in impoverished neighbourhoods served to intensify rather than alleviate alienation and opposition. Second, a tension remains between sport's ludic and expressive dimensions, and its conversion into political ritual and commercial outlet. Third, the struggle for gender equity within sport continues; its conclusion will have 'almost incalculable consequences', particularly for the working class.

Almost three decades later, Hargreaves's 'fissures' require modification. First, despite Blair's window-dressing, sport provision in the poorest communities remains abysmal. Second, sport's hyper-commodification has entailed the greater dominance of more bourgeois and less participatory forms of spectator, further undermining the ludic elements of sport culture. Third, while 'more women in sport' is a State mantra, sport's commodification devalues their participation (as prize-moneyed athletes) and proscribes access for working-class women.

Hargreaves's analysis does highlight deterministic weaknesses in some hegemony theory. Sports history does not demonstrate that colonizers psychologically manipulate the colonized: 'Culturally dominated groups have often had sports imposed upon them; they have also – perhaps just as often – forced their unwelcome way into sports from which the dominant group desired to exclude them' (Guttmann 1994: 178–9). Hargreaves also overplays the hegemonic bloc's historical unity. In Britain elites were divided over sport's capacity to harmonize society, while sports professionalism and the survival of some pre-modern sporting practices show that working-class popular culture could evade 'wholesale submission to bourgeois values and fashion' (Tranter 1998: 49). These criticisms do not negate hegemony theory, only those inflexible applications that underplay relative autonomy and social agency within working-class popular culture.

Resistance

'Resistance' is a key concept within Cultural Studies, defining how subordinate groups challenge domination through cultural practices. Resistance may take physically active or more symbolic forms. Riots or civil disturbances feature regularly in sport's history and can reflect strong class antagonisms (see Jamison 1996: 38). Among athletes, violent resistance can be sublimated partially through competition. For example, at the 1956 Melbourne Olympics, soon after the Soviet invasion of Hungary, the Hungarian water polo team defeated the USSR in a bloody encounter that reflected anti-Soviet feelings (Rinehart 1996: 136). In Argentina, sports identities have symbolized united, overt resistance towards political elites and financial institutions during the economic crises of 2001–2. Many participants at street demonstrations wore the national football team's shirt, indicating that 'the only thing that has been left in Argentina is the football team' (Eduardo Archetti, quoted in *The Observer*, 10 February 2002).

Fiske (1989: 2–3) differentiates between 'resistance', involving confrontational semiotics, and 'evasion', involving more innocuous practices among subordinate groups. For example, at the 1994 Gay Games' opening parade through Manhattan, many participants were attired to celebrate their sexuality, thereby semiotically resisting heterosexual, patriarchal norms. Conversely, according to Fiske, the work-free hedonism of surfer culture 'evades' capitalism's disciplinary routines. However, this loose interpretation would allow us to read 'evasion' into any social practice, while ignoring how social actors themselves understand their activities. Nevertheless, evasion, as social *in*action, may signify cultural contestation, notably within mainstream and sporting politics. For example, in Chile, public disgust at Pinochet's rule was conveyed by mass refusal to visit Santiago's national stadium, where civilians had been tortured and murdered (Arbena 1986: 92). In Australia, a three-year court battle over the control of rugby league began in 1995, alienating many of the game's enthusiasts and resulting in smaller crowds.

In the West, sports resistance is mostly confined to cultural politics within the relevant sport (see Wren-Lewis and Clarke 1983). Resistance is articulated through generalized opposition towards sport's commodification, notably when competition, or even the right to compete, is defined by monetary and marketing considerations. In North America, some committed supporters of smaller clubs have protested baseball's domination by a few super-rich clubs.[3] In Australia in 2000, 80,000 people demonstrated against the exclusion of the South Sydney club from the National Rugby League (NRL).[4] After several court battles, the club was readmitted despite its weak market position.

De Certeau (1984) has explored how social actors' 'ways of using' products can create 'indiscipline' to 'lend a political dimension to everyday practices' (quoted in Edelman 1993: 16). He differentiates between two forms of resistance. The 'tactic' is 'an art of the weak', involving 'calculated action', played out on 'terrain' controlled by a 'foreign power'. The 'strategy' occurs in isolated places controlled by social actors themselves (De Certeau 1984: 35–7). Yelvington (1995: 44–5) employs this dichotomy to explain black resistance in West Indian cricket. Under colonialism, West Indian emancipation engaged with cricket tactically, since no alternative cultural spaces arose for a nationalist, anti-imperialist stance. After independence, cricket became a 'strategy' for refashioning and reinventing old colonial cultural forms to reflect distinctive West Indian identities.

La perruque ('the wig') is, for De Certeau, one notable tactic of the weak. *La perruque* denotes workers' evasion of work-place surveillance and discipline, such as by using employers' tools to make products, or by inventing less onerous working practices. *La perruque* designates how the weak use evasion and stealth to reappropriate, for their own ends, the dominant classes' political, economic and cultural resources. In sport, *la perruque* can be found among stadium spectators who sneak into better seating positions without paying, or drop banners of protest over advertising boards, or produce fan magazines (or 'fanzines') to sell inside and outside the stadium. Conceptually, *la perruque* is more persuasive than Fiske's concept of 'evasion' if only because its practitioners are conscious that their actions upset the social order.

'Resistance' theory is not without its problems. Some Cultural Studies analysts somehow identify covert resistance 'virtually *everywhere*' in popular culture (Gruneau, quoted in Donnelly 1993: 141). The concept's ubiquity feeds intellectual laziness; researchers, to put quick theory on their research evidence, will redeem the concept yet again. However, deciphering resistance in so much social action must forfeit the concept's powers of explanatory discrimination. If so many popular cultural practices are 'resistant', then the dominant social relations of production and consumption would have collapsed long ago.

One early sports application of resistance indicated its potential weaknesses. Ian Taylor (1969, 1970, 1971) asserted that English 'soccer hooliganism' embodied the inarticulate resistance of young, working-class males towards attempts by football club owners to commercialize their sport, and to attract new, bourgeois spectators. Taylor's admittedly speculative arguments traced the historical divisions and structural tensions affecting football, but his claims regarding football hooliganism were refuted by subsequent research (see Armstrong 1998; Giulianotti and Armstrong 2002). Explicit resistance is undeniable – for example, through political campaigns against sports tournaments or individual statements against racism. However, when sociologists discern latent resistance in actions like violence *between* spectators, then we grossly exaggerate our interpretative reach in explaining individual motives.

This particular weakness is further exposed in Castells's (1997: 8) analysis of identity within the Internet-driven 'information age'. Castells proffers three identity types. First, 'legitimizing identity' is formulated through dominant institutions and groups, to mould the actions and self-understandings of social actors. Second, 'resistance identity' emerges among dominated social actors as a survival or resistance strategy. Third, 'project identity' lends political coherence to resistant acts through new or alternative identities that challenge domination directly. Castells (1997: 357) recognizes that resistance identities do not result inevitably in project identities, but does not explain adequately why this transition may not occur. Such political inertia cannot be explained away by old arguments about ideological false consciousness. It is far more plausible to believe that social actors are consciously less 'resistant' than is presumed here; and even when resistance does arise, the content is not significant enough to become a political 'project'.

Taylor's and Castells's weaknesses underline the need for sociologists to continue to hear social actors' voices. As noted earlier regarding the interpretative standpoint, we need at least to gain detailed understanding of the meanings and motives attached by social actors to their actions. This should help meet Canclini's (1995: 180–1) criticism that hegemony theorists select data to fit (and thus confirm, rather than test or prove) the meta-theory. There is far more to popular culture than antagonism towards dominant social groups. Pleasurable and aesthetic dimensions in popular culture are themselves worthy of close sociological scrutiny (see Rojek 1995: 23–4).[5]

Cultural Studies allows us to explore how more obviously 'resistant' and 'protest' cultures within sport are neutralized and/or accommodated by the hegemonic bloc. Consider the neutralization and commodification of 'Olympic protest': images of the 'black power' protest by two African-American sprinters at the 1968 Olympics are now found in television commercials; at the 1992 Olympics, 'protest politics' among the US basketball 'Dream Team' consisted primarily of Nike-sponsored players covering the signs of rival merchandise companies (McKay 1995). This commodification of resistance mirrors CCCS arguments regarding the colonization of youth subcultures by entrepreneurs. However, the Cultural Studies position is less effective in explaining 'resistant' subcultures that actively *embrace* commodification, to function as niche businesses within the sport industry. For example, the 'Barmy Army' of England cricket supporters appears as a resistant subculture that criticizes English cricket authorities and shocks traditionalists with exuberant, raucous styles of support.[6] However, the Barmy Army is no commercially innocent, 'authentic' subculture, but a professional business organization: the founding members operate a tour agency and sophisticated merchandising machine under its trade-marked name.

Transgression and carnival

The anthropological concept of 'transgression' provides a persuasive alternative to resistance when explaining practices that apparently contravene the social order (Bale 2000: 154). Transgression involves boundary crossing, particularly breaching moral parameters or hierarchical codes. While resistance implies *intentional* social opposition, transgression focuses on *consequences* of actions, enabling sociological identification of how popular culture can break the dominant culture's conventions without inferring some latent intent behind social practices.

Cultural transgressions are often discerned in carnivals and folk culture's 'carnivalesque'.[7] Across European towns and villages, since at least medieval times, various folk carnivals have been held, usually controlled by local peoples and featuring a market-place culture of excessive behaviour and corporeal pleasure.[8] Social hierarchies are often symbolically transgressed or inverted, such as by electing boys as local bishops on the day, or creating grotesque representations of local dignitaries.[9] Some carnivals functionally reproduce the social order by ritually reinforcing social hierarchies or allowing people to let off steam in a controlled environment. Other carnivals carry more subversive subtexts. In Rhineland carnivals during the early nineteenth century, for example, the indigenous, largely Catholic populace employed pamphlets, songs and parades to mock their Prussian masters' militaristic, bureaucratic and censorious culture (Brophy 1997). I consider at least two aspects of carnival as politically unsettling. First, carnival always has the potential for social breakdown. Second, even if carnivals seem to promote the social order long-term, the mocking of powerful figures is a transgression that affords moments of popular empowerment.

Elements of the 'carnivalesque' – excess, inversion, laughter, transgression and the privileging of the lower bodily stratum over the upper body – are identifiable in sporting events. Historical connections link pre-modern carnivals and 'folk games' to contemporary sports. Horse-racing, cricket matches, wrestling and pugilism were often staged during folk festivals, and retained elements of that culture (such as heavy gambling) during modernization.

Sociological analyses of spectator cultures may deploy conceptions of the carnivalesque (Giulianotti 1991, 1995). During the early 1990s, the most dedicated fans of Scotland's national team were often highly intoxicated, and apt to express rather ribald criticism of the Conservative government or leading football officials. Popular players (or 'folk heroes') in football and many other sports possess reputations for excess: notably, spectacular and dramatic skills during play, and sexual adventure and intoxication outside the sport. Yet the modern carnivalesque is subjected to regulation and profit seeking by dominant groups and institutions. At international sports tournaments, so-called carnival atmospheres are manufactured by muzak over public address systems; spectator behaviour is closely monitored by private security or police officers, to eliminate public excess; public parties are permitted only within designated, highly commercial areas. Thus, in sport, the cultural politics of the carnivalesque involves underlying struggles between dominant social forces that seek to control and commodify 'folk' events and subordinate participants who wish to party more freely.

Concluding points: critiquing and refounding Cultural Studies in sport

Culturalism and social agency

Evidently, Cultural Studies has contributed substantialy to the sociology of sport. It has legitimized ordinary culture as a realm of scholarly inquiry, reaffirmed the value of community within social analysis, and recognized that cultural practices arise in relationships of relative autonomy *vis-à-vis* other structures. Some models of hegemony theory fail to capture the complexity of social relations within sport at any historical juncture, although Williams's model of historical change clarifies power relations within sport. Resistance certainly occurs within popular culture but sociologists must confer with social actors to obtain the meanings and motives behind social actions. Alternatively, the concept of transgression enables researchers to explain actions without imputing motives. Moreover, sociologists of sport should exploit anthropological themes relating to carnival and the carnivalesque, to illuminate the folk impulses within contemporary sports cultures and to explore how the corporeal aesthetics of sports are subjected to underlying conflicts.

While Cultural Studies should certainly purge any residual economism, it should not fall prey to a theoretical culturalism by exaggerating the cultural freedom of social agents. Cultural reductionism within Cultural Studies can entail omissions of the politics of culture. McChesney (2002) disparages contemporary Cultural Studies writers who cannot sustain the legacies of Hall and Williams. He claims that John Fiske and Angela McRobbie display 'stupidity' for their 'gross and callous mischaracterization' of the capitalist market-place, as a 'popular system' enabling contested relations without predetermined outcomes (2002: 85). McChesney insists instead that the market (including popular culture) is a 'mortal enemy' of community, producing 'abysmal' journalism and vapid public 'debate' (2002: 86). Though his language is a little purple, these points are valid.

Willis (1990) makes some of these misjudgements in his depiction of the radically fragmented power structures and cultural practices of contemporary society. He observes that there is no 'power bloc' that can control popular tastes and modern fashions; instead, divisions and disagreements arise among all political forces. The commercial sector is 'seething with anarchy' and incapable of predicting popular tastes and styles (1990: 156). Willis thereby forgets that the dominant business of contemporary politics actually involves building and rebuilding new hegemonic alliances. The exponential growth of marketing departments and advertising within sports clubs and equipment manufacturers shows that contemporary industries firmly believe in the manipulability of the market.

Latterly, post-structuralist and postmodern social theory have had mixed results within Cultural Studies. As I argue in later chapters, some post-structuralist theories provide important conceptual tools for examining power relations. For Bennett (1998: 62), Foucault, when compared to Gramsci, is better to 'think with' and 'do with', to explore the diffuseness of power and the subjective governing of human relations. The 'postmodern left' has embraced 'identity politics', relative to the post-industrial, post-colonial mixture of consumption, class, ethnicity, gender and sexuality (Eagleton 2000: 127–8). But again, the consequent emphasis on cultural identity and life-style politics can underplay structured inequalities while exaggerating the 'resistant' aspects of everyday cultural practices.

Moving forward: dietrologia, *structured polyphonic research and normative reinvention*

Briefly, I suggest four ways in which Cultural Studies perspectives can enhance their analyses of sport and popular culture. First, much of hegemony theory resembles what Italians call *dietrologia*, that is, the science of observing the unobservable, the discerning of hidden motives behind the actions and discourses of peoples. *Dietrologia* has critical sociological value for explaining the practices and interrelations of hegemonic groups. Indeed, it is a key hermeneutic component of many popular cultures, allowing social actors to discuss and speculate on the underlying mechanisms of power, whether in sport or in wider politics. However, I have major problems with *dietrologia* when it turns into a full-blown conspiracy theory. Typically, hegemonic groups operate in far more complex and less crudely collusive ways. A more serious problem arises when Cultural Studies writers apply *dietrologia* to subordinate groups, to discern a hidden 'resistance' in all kinds of cultural practices. As noted earlier, Cultural Studies needs to shake off this theoretical instinct. Instead, to blend Merton's methodological caution with neo-Weberian interpretivism, we need to adopt a 'middle-range' perspective; we need to deploy qualitative research that reveals the cultural values, meanings and motives of specific social actors and groups; and we need to relate those findings to particular frameworks of power.

Second, to remedy weaknesses in Cultural Studies readings of human agency, we can return to the CCCS's fieldwork commitments. Too many analysts avoid fieldwork by doing 'textual studies' that decode popular culture in *their* terms, rather than those of social actors. If fieldwork is undertaken, data are too frequently intended to fit pre-existing theories. Instead, Cultural Studies analysis should engage social theory that is 'radically contextualist' and 'prefigured on the uniqueness of any historical moment' (Andrews 2002: 113). We require a 'contextualist cultural studies' possessing a 'critical engagement with theory', *selectively* amending, introducing and discarding theories as context necessitates.

Third, via this 'theory-method', Cultural Studies analyses should produce what I would term 'structured polyphonic' research. The structured elements concern the social actors' circumstances, in particular their historical, structural and geographical location; their life-chances; and their material and symbolic resources, including the sources of, and dominant meanings attached to, these resources. The polyphonic aspects of research should capture the open-endedness of social action and cultural relations within this context and the reflective, dialogical manner in which these actors make sense of their immediate and structural circumstances. Through Bakhtin's understanding of the term, polyphony also encourages the reader of sociological texts to engage fully with the research 'characters' and the research analysis. Thus, 'structured polyphonic' research should not restrict the sociological text to a pre-defined plot, predicted outcomes or prearranged theoretical explanations (Morson with Emerson 1997: 258–60).

Finally, with Morgan (2002, 2004), we require a greater normative component within critical sociological analyses of sport. One way of achieving this is through fuller utilization of Jürgen Habermas. To justify this point, it is necessary to explain Habermas's position in a little detail.

While highly critical of modern capitalism, Habermas provides a more optimistic theoretical optic than his Frankfurt School predecessors. Habermas argues that the unfinished, historical 'project of modernity' is characterized by faith in progress, reason, rational reflection, enlightenment and human emancipation. He agrees that contemporary modern capitalism is marked by bureaucratization and the dehumanizing, disenchanting emphasis upon instrumental reason. He critiques the decline of the democratic 'public sphere', the political space for citizen debate. The 'lifeworlds' in which people explore and develop identities, norms and common understandings are being 'colonized' increasingly by rationalized 'systems' (like large bureaucratic corporations or political machines) that flex their power through money, status and votes. Nevertheless, Habermas reasons that the Enlightenment project remains capable of achieving what he terms the 'ideal speech community'. Within such a democratic community, all communication is 'distortion-free': sectional interests and ideologies are removed, and arguments are judged according to rational debate and reflection, rather than the speaker's status or wealth.

Morgan has demonstrated the relevance of Habermas's critical theory to modern sport. Sport has been badly served by the rise of instrumental reason over normative reflection and action, a process that leads towards violence and corruption among athletes, officials and supporters (Morgan 2004).[10] More generally, sport in liberal democracies is dominated by the instrumental media of money, departmental bargaining, opinion polls and voting patterns, rather than lifeworlds of popular participation, critical debate and moral reflection.

Morgan (1993: 234–7) adopts a highly Habermasian position when advancing his model of a democratic, enlightened 'practice-community' for sport's reform. In line with Michael Walzer and Cultural Studies followers of Raymond Williams, Morgan argues that community itself is an 'internal good' of sport. It must be shared by those within sport's 'practice-community'. Although Morgan tends to restrict membership of this practice-community to athletes, it should include non-players, particularly supporters, employees and officials (Walsh and Giulianotti 2001). The practice-community should constitute a highly mature public sphere wherein debaters 'come into the athletic forum armed only with their arguments, leaving behind all titles, goods, and vantage points that derive from their standing in other spheres' (Morgan 1993: 242). Morgan appreciates that 'rational authorities on the game', who stand in a master–apprentice relationship with relative novices, will have greater discursive powers within the practice-community. Morgan's Habermasian model provides normative principles for sport's reform. It extends Cultural Studies' concern with community, democratization and equality of expression and action. Compellingly, it encourages us to imagine how, within sport's cultural *politics*, we may begin to remedy the very structural and cultural inequalities that are analysed by the sociological core of Cultural Studies.

5

'Race', Ethnicity and Intolerance in Sport

Sport, like other domains of social life, has always been character-ized by racist social relations. Racism tends to focus on variable skin colour and assumed physiological differences between peoples, but historically the word 'race' has possessed diverse meanings. 'Scientific racism' originated in the mid-nineteenth century and classified peoples into typologies or 'species' (Banton 1988: 16–23). This 'race logic' fur-nished European colonists and white settlers with an assumed ideo-logical justification for the subjugation and annihilation of indigenous peoples across the world. Despite the post-war rise of human rights issues, the consequences of violent European 'civilization' remain in-escapable; fundamental inequalities in employment, education, social mobility and wealth remain between different ethnic communities. Though cruder variants are popularly discredited, racist systems of knowledge linger within cultural realms; sport is no exception. Race and Ethnic Studies (rather like Gender Studies) has become a rec-ognized academic discipline. However, unlike many critical studies of 'race' and racism, I emphasize the erroneous, socially constructed roots of 'race' *per se*.

Here, I build upon the critical insights of the opening four chapters, and in particular the discussion of Cultural Studies, to examine five broad issues concerning racism and ethnic intolerance within sport. First, I critique physiological arguments surrounding sports perfor-mance and 'race'. Second, I outline international histories of sport and racism within five key contexts: the United States, Africa, Australia, Britain, and former British colonies in the Caribbean and Asian sub-continent. Third, I discuss the cultural politics of racism relative to social segregation and anti-racism initiatives. Fourth, I explore the obduracy of racist discourses through analysis of sports aesthetics and black sporting 'role models'. Finally, I assess the sport position of different ethnic minorities through a broadened definition of racism.

'Race' and athleticism: from Social Darwinism to genetics

'Scientific racism' favoured the classification of humans into 'race' types. In the 1850s, the French Count Arthur de Gobineau advocated an influential thesis that depicted white 'races' as physically and intellectually strongest: 'The American savages, like the Hindus, are certainly our inferiors in this respect, as are also the Australians. The Negroes, too, have less muscle power; and all these people are infinitely less able to bear fatigue' (quoted in Miller 1998: 126). Darwin's theories of natural selection and the 'survival of the fittest', to explain evolution in nature, were bastardized to sustain social racism. Evolution, the Social Darwinists contended, obligated whites to conquer, subjugate and modernize other 'races'. Moreover, racial differentiation was not always colour-coded. In Britain, the Irish were presented as somewhere between 'negroes' and gorillas, or (along with Jews) as the middle-point in the evolutionary chain, with Anglo-Saxons at the top and blacks ('Hottentots') at the foot.

For British colonists, sport facilitated 'racial' development and the display of physical and moral superiority. Non-whites were racially excluded for lacking moral fibre and mental agility. When black athleticism was subsequently demonstrated, later racist thinking invented a pseudo-scientific, inverse relationship between physique and intellect. Anglo-Saxons were considered more advanced intellectually than physically; blacks were the opposite. In its crudest terms, this logic has lingered through such assumptions as 'It's either more brains or more penis: they can't have both' (Tatz 1999).

Other racist theories regarding black athleticism parody Darwinism. One post-war basketball coach claimed that blacks outran whites because in Africa 'the lions and tigers had caught all the slow ones' (Roberts and Olsen 1989: 45).[1] The 'Middle Passage' myth claimed that slavery enhanced black physicality, since only the toughest survived enslavement and transportation then mated to spawn a micro-race of super-slaves that later included black super-athletes (Hoberman 1997a: 78, 194–5). Even civil rights crusaders like E. B. Henderson were seduced by this myth (P. Miller 1998: 135). Of course, it ignores social reasons for black athletic successes, while there is no historical evidence that the strongest Africans were enslaved or survived transportation. Moreover, the myth conveniently excludes whites: for, surely, decades of international warfare would have procured a super-race of Anglo-Saxon survivors?

Sailes (1998: 190–6) outlines other, similarly misguided arguments regarding African-American athleticism.

- *Matriarchal theory*: 'absent fathers' in black families mean sports become outlets for male children's hostility and frustration; the sports coach becomes a surrogate father. However, research confirms that young athletes are suspicious of coaches, and often hail from two-parent families.
- *Mandigo theory*: according to sports commentator Jimmy 'The Greek' Snyder, blacks are physically advanced because 'the slave owner would breed his big black with his big woman so that he could have a big black kid' (quoted in Wiggins 1989: 179). However, the counter-evidence is overwhelming. Slave owners raped or otherwise sexually engaged slave women, while most slaves chose their own mates; by the early twentieth century, any gene pool rooted in slave breeding would have been lost.
- *Psychological theory*: African-Americans lack the intellect or emotional control required of sport leaders. However, this myth becomes a self-fulfilling prophecy: black players are excluded from leadership roles *because* it is accepted by white sports officials.
- *Dumb Jock theory*: African-Americans enter further education as athletes and cannot match non-athletes academically. Conversely, research indicates that student athletes marginally outperform non-athletes academically. Lower grades among some African-American athletes are mostly attributable to lack of resources in earlier education.
- *Genetic theory*: African-Americans allegedly have more white twitch muscle, increasing speed; whites have more red twitch muscle, enhancing distance running. This theory has weak research support, while long-distance African runners debunk myths regarding exceptional white stamina.

The Bell Curve thesis argued that high black fertility rates (possibly linked to larger genitals) were depressing US intelligence levels (Herrnstein and Murray 1994). African-Americans, it was concluded, should further their athleticism, to compensate for their genetically determined weaker intellect and to increase clan 'self-esteem'. This theory combined poor evidence and neo-conservative, racist assumptions (Hoberman 1997a: 3–4).

Jon Entine (2000), a television journalist, is the most recent protagonist of sports genetics. He posits that blacks comprise 12 per cent of America's population, but 85 per cent of basketball players and 70 per cent of NFL professionals. He claims that particular sporting excellence has specific geo-racial origins: athletes of West African origin dominate sprinting, East and North Africans dominate distance running, Eurasian whites excel in field and strength sports, and East Asians prioritize gymnastics. In elite athletics, Entine argues, minute physiological variations have genetic (not socio-cultural) causes and establish major competitive differences.

Certainly, we should protect true interdisciplinary studies, and ensure that researchers are not labelled 'racist' for considering all factors contributing to sports performances (Wiggins 1989: 185). Nevertheless, historically, the different physiological and genetic explanations fail to survive existing research. Genetic arguments require African-Americans to have implausibly high physical advantages over Caucasians; in basketball this comes to 27 to 1. Sports like basketball, baseball, sprinting, tennis, volleyball and baseball (notably pitching) all require similar 'bioenergetics', but African-Americans predominate only in the first three. These findings favour social rather than physical explanations for different ethnic, national and regional performances in sport (Hunter 1998: 97–8). Subsequent research by Glasgow University with Ethiopian athletes found a diverse gene pool, and no evidence to back the 'race genes' thesis (*Sunday Times*, 9 February 2003). Genetics arguments underplay the hard work and dedication of successful athletes, while the exclusivity of elite athleticism precludes strong generalization. As one American journalist explains, '*Every* individual who reaches the majors is already exceptional, so sorting out characteristics in this population should not have spillover ethnic connotations' (Koppett 1981: 205). Greater variations in athletic capability exist *within* each ethnicity than between elite athletes of different skin colour (Harpalani 1998: 118). Finally, as *The Bell Curve* unwittingly illustrates, any 'scientific' argument must be scrutinized for political influences.

To elaborate understanding of 'race' and ethnicity within sport, I turn now to examine specific international histories of racism, ethnic intolerance and cultural struggle.

Racism and sport: outlining international histories

The United States

Racist oppression of black people within sport began during slavery. Plantation owners promoted boxing among African slaves, with heavy wagers placed on fights. After the Civil War, slavery was abolished, but 'Jim Crow' laws reaffirmed racial segregation with inevitable sporting consequences. Many states segregated black Americans in recreational parks and sports stadiums. Organized sport was segregated, although baseball's 'Negro Leagues' show-cased black skills in spectacular games that drew 'mixed' crowds.

Historical study of black sports involvement enables fuller understanding of struggles among African-Americans for social equality and political emancipation. The black heavyweight boxer Jack Johnson became world champion in 1908. His later defeat of Jim Jeffries (the 'Great White Hope') undermined white supremacist beliefs and sparked riots across America against blacks (Harris 1998: 5–6). Johnson threatened the 'race' hierarchy; he treated whites as equals, owned night-clubs, attracted white women, and engaged in conspicuous consumption. During the 1930s, Joe Louis (boxing) and Jesse Owens (athletics) became the first black sports heroes for whites. Both athletes 'knew their place' in white eyes, and successfully represented America internationally. Owens dominated the 1936 Berlin Olympics, enhancing his popularity by defeating the representatives of Hitler's 'master race', but the athlete's life afterwards involved numerous financial struggles.

In team sports, black athletes struggled to break segregation. A few played American football professionally during the 1920s, but segregation was most symbolically challenged in 1947 when Jackie Robinson joined baseball's Brooklyn Dodgers. Though not the best African-American player, it was hoped (wrongly) that Robinson's military and college career would appease racist whites. Subsequently, African-Americans viewed sport as facilitating social mobility, and whites formulated ideas regarding inherent black athleticism. Through sport, African-Americans projected demands regarding civil rights and social democracy, to repay the patriotic sacrifices of black soldiers during the Second World War. Nevertheless, American sports institutions treated black athletes prejudicially in terms of inferior contracts and accommodation. Baseball's Boston Red Sox were the last major team to recruit a black player, in 1959 (Reiss 1991: 121). In basketball during the 1950s, white team owners introduced an 'only four blacks' quota that became inoperable, but all-white basketball sides still reached the NCAA finals until 1966 (Roberts and Olsen 1989: 39–45). In American football, some clubs refused to desegregate; Washington Redskins held out until 1962. At desegregated clubs, black players endured abusive testing by coaches, allegedly in preparation for mistreatment by opposing players.

Black civil rights struggles exploded into sport at the 1968 Mexico Olympics, when champion sprinters Jon Carlos and Tommie Smith gave the famous 'Unity' salute on the medal podium. Prior to the games, the Olympic Project for Human Rights, led by sociologist Harry Edwards, had divided African-Americans by demanding a black Olympic boycott. The project did succeed at least in publicizing black athletes' exploitation (Spivey 1985). Sport continues to have a highly ambiguous meaning for African-American communities. In some sports, notably basketball, black players' predominance promotes cultural pride and defiance (Boyd 1997: 132–3). However, talented black athletes remain undervalued compared to whites, while decision-making positions within sports organizations remain dominated by whites. Anticipated discrimination by large white audiences may persuade local teams to minimize black player recruitment, while the market prices for baseball cards typically discriminate against non-white players. Annual reports still highlight the inequalities experienced by non-whites and women in American sports, particularly in professional administration (Lapchick 2003). Meanwhile, the diverging life-courses of two leading black athletes highlight the increasing inequalities of class-defined African-American experience. Michael Jordan, of solid middle-class background, personifies the accommodative aspirations of 'buppies' regarding corporate America. Mike Tyson, by marked contrast, embodies the hardened, criminalized, social disintegration of many lower-class black communities within the harsh neo-liberal environment.

The sport–racism nexus ensnares other ethnic groups, notably America's indigenous population. For native Americans, European civilization meant systematic annihilation and annexation of their lands. Despite contributing the stickball games that became lacrosse, and embracing ice hockey in good numbers, native Americans in Canada have endured institutionalized racism that still undermines full sports participation. In the United States, native American symbols have been appropriated by major league sports teams like the Washington Redskins, Atlanta Braves and Cleveland Indians. Such crude signifiers demean native American culture, and reflect its custodians' subaltern position within American society (Bairner 2001: 106–7).

African trends

In colonial Africa, sports were part of Britain's imperializing mission. Christian missionaries helped inculcate the games cult, aiming to sculpt 'a universal Tom Brown: loyal, brave, truthful, a gentleman and, if at all possible, a Christian' (Mangan 1998a: 18). Other sporting proselytizers included teachers, soldiers and administrators, so that 'in the most bizarre locations could be found those potent symbols of pedagogic imperialism – football and cricket pitches' (Mangan 1998a: 43).

Thus, Africans' pre-colonial movement cultures were replaced by modern sports that were rationalized (measuring time, distance, performance), bureaucratized (accrediting sports officials and pedagogues) and 'civilizing' (in manliness, obedience and rule-following). In pre-modern Kenya, Africans had long practised running, throwing and jumping in competitions, dance rituals or everyday tasks; indeed, the Watussi people's jumping feats and the Maasai's distance running astonished early colonists. Organized sport was introduced to distract political unrest, dampen 'lascivious' local customs, and inculcate 'civilized' mores (Bale and Sang 1996). While some Kenyan and other African athletes have excelled in international competition, the annihilation of traditional body cultures and 'modernization' of local landscapes involved arguably greater collective losses.

Indigenous responses to sport varied by social stratification. White elites embraced sports more intensively than in Britain. Among African schoolboys, academic (not sporting) pursuits were favoured for social mobility and political autonomy (Mangan 1987: 164–5).[2] In African townships, sports like boxing and football gained greatest popularity (Ranger 1987; Giulianotti 1999: 7–8). Football lacked rugby or cricket's white ideological overtones and required little equipment. Subsequently, Africans in British and French colonies appropriated football to represent local forms of identity and independence from Church and State (Martin 1995).

In anti-colonial struggles, sport's role was most prominent in fighting South Africa's apartheid. Instituted in 1948, apartheid involved total systemic subjugation of Africans by whites. Sport competition was integral to white South African culture; hence post-colonial African governments and anti-apartheid groups exerted strong and successful pressure to exclude South African teams from all international sport (Guelke 1993: 152–3). 'Rebel' cricket and rugby tours, involving overseas teams, were organized by apartheid's officials and international collaborators, but disruption of games inside South Africa intensified

(Booth 1998). In the post-apartheid era, South Africa has struggled to make sport more equitable. In Natal, for example, white elites still control the finest resources (Merrett 1994: 115). The national sports teams may symbolize unity and reconciliation, but whites still enjoy superior coaching and education, thereby dominating elite sport, while racism remains in some sporting structures. Sport's commodification can undermine social reform. Cricket and rugby have introduced 'quotas', guaranteeing black representation in national teams, but this can weaken these sides' competitiveness and commercial appeal, thereby reducing money for township sports developments (Vahed 2001: 333-4).

Post-colonial African nations suffer the mass traumas of war and famine, the structured inequities of international trade, the imposition of free-market reforms by the IMF and World Bank, and corruption throughout the political classes. African sport is inevitably struck by these major problems (Armstrong and Giulianotti 2004). Sport certainly enables Africans to articulate senses of nationhood and cultural pride on the global stage. Yet the international sport system, notably its labour markets, locates Africans in a weak, producer position, to supply richer nations with cheap talent.

Australia

From the 1840s to the 1900s, Australia's colonial settlers systematically exterminated thousands of Aborigines. Yet, some exceptional Aboriginal groups played cricket, attracted mixed crowds, and even toured England in 1868. 'Protective' legislation and home 'reserves' later segregated Aboriginals from whites, although the Aborigine, Charlie Samuels, was Australia's leading all-round athlete of the nineteenth century. Between the wars, to enter sport, Aborigines could either disguise themselves (as Maoris or West Indians) or endure highly prejudicial and patronizing treatment by whites. Thus the brilliant Aboriginal cricketer, Eddie Gilbert, was denied competitive openings, and required a chaperone to travel among whites (Booth and Tatz 2000: 131–2).

In post-war Australia, state control over Aboriginals extended to the mass removal of children from parents to be placed with white guardians. Prominent Aboriginal athletes endured racist exclusion, although some entered athletics, rugby league, boxing and Australian Rules football. During the 1960s, some Aboriginal athletes (notably football's Charles Perkins) politicized racist experiences in sport, connecting personal troubles to civil rights issues. Political and material barriers to equality within sport remain huge. As recently as 1980, the Queensland state government passed draconian legislation to safeguard the 1982 Commonwealth Games from Aboriginal presence (Booth and Tatz 2000: 172–3). Planned Aboriginal protests at the 2000 Sydney Olympics were subjected to divide-and-rule pressures from Australian media and sports institutions (Lenskyj 2000: 77). In most remote Aboriginal communities, 'sports facilities' still comprise an unmarked dusty paddock to practise football or cricket (Booth and Tatz 2000: 202–3).

Britain

Widespread immigration of Afro-Caribbean and Asian people to the UK occurred after 1945, but hidden histories exist concerning non-European sports participation. Arthur Wharton, for example, was a champion sprinter and the first black professional football player in England during the mid-1880s (Vasili 1998). Asian cricketers have long represented England, notably Prince Kumar Shri Ranjitsinhji ('Ranji') in the 1890s. Since the 1960s, Afro-Caribbeans have become increasingly prominent, constituting around 20 per cent of English football professionals and dominating UK track athletics.

Inevitably, racism has permeated black and Asian sporting experiences. Sport spectators, notably through the 1980s, directed monkey chants and other racist insults at elite black athletes like football's John Barnes (in England) and Mark Walters (in Scotland). While such racism is now formally outlawed, institutionalized racism and structural exclusion remain. Few non-whites fill sport's coaching or chief executive roles. Racist stereotypes among teachers and coaches serve to channel particular ethnic minorities into or (in the case of football's Asians) out of particular sports. Meanwhile, sport's increasing commodification means that poorer communities (notably black or Asian) are less likely to connect with local professional sports clubs.

The cultural politics of 'race' have been particularly apparent in English cricket. The 1968 'D'Oliveira affair' provided a major impetus for anti-apartheid sanctions after England cricket selectors had initially bowed to South African racism by omitting a brilliant non-white cricketer from their English playing squad selected to tour the Cape. During the 1990s, non-whites endured racist sniping from politicians and some cricket analysts. The leading Conservative politician Norman (now Lord) Tebbit recommended a 'cricket test' for incoming immigrants: those cheering for their nation of origin, and not England, should be deemed unfit to stay (Marqusee 1994: 137–41). English cricket has a poor record in recruiting non-white players. Although thousands of Asian males play cricket across Yorkshire, the county cricket team still fails to recruit some to play competitively. Cricketers with Asian or Caribbean backgrounds who do play for England have been accused of lacking patriotism and effort (Henderson 1995). Such inherently racist arguments grossly misunderstand the complex, shifting nature of cultural identity. Like all ethnic and cultural identities, 'black' and 'Asian' identities are not set in stone, but are essentially changing and fluid.

The Caribbean: cricket and liberation

In sport, Afro-Caribbean and Asian identities are strongly enhanced by defeating the old colonial master, England, at cricket. The West Indian historian C. L. R. James (1963) pioneered the critical analysis of sport within a racialized society, by examining the social history, politics and aesthetics of cricket – an ironic subject given James's Marxist philosophy and the game's centrality to British colonialism. Prior to West Indian independence, cricket clubs were strongly stratified along race lines; black players' exclusion from the national captaincy alienated many, sparking nationalist rioting in 1960. As independence was secured from 1962 onwards, cricket came to symbolize post-colonial cultural empowerment. The West Indies' side dominated world cricket throughout the late 1970s and 1980s; after touring and defeating England in all matches, West Indian supporters would celebrate these whitewashes as 'blackwashes'. Players like Viv Richards symbolized the black post-colonial struggle, and competed with particular intensity on English cricket's hallowed grounds, notably at Lord's in London (Beckles 1998: 87). England's cricket establishment and media often disparaged these achievements, suggesting that the West Indies' use of four fast bowlers betrayed cricket's heritage, and banning the carnival culture of Afro-Caribbean fans from English grounds (J. Williams 2001: 131–4).

In the Indian subcontinent, Christian missionaries like Tyndale-Biscoe had worked assiduously to inculcate British games, notably among high-caste Brahmins (Mangan 1998a: 183). While 'muscular Christian' values within sports typically contravened local cultural traditions, such as Brahmin avoidance of strenuous exercise,[3] the missionaries retained an ethnocentric, imperialistic self-assurance in driving pupils on to playing fields. Through rising Indian nationalism, however, cricket became 'Indianized' as locals 'hijacked the game from its English habitus' to produce new playing styles, supporter cultures and popular meanings (Appadurai 1995: 46). Latterly, cricket has dramatized conflicting religio-national identities across the subcontinent (notably between India and Pakistan) while drawing huge commercial revenues (Marqusee 1996: 292). Conversely, unlike the subcontinent, post-colonial authorities in the West Indies (notably in Barbados) retained British political codes and cultural values, so that cricket's playing ethics sustain their English origins (Sandiford and Stoddart 1995: 56–8).

These brief historical portraits highlight the utility of Cultural Studies' focus on cultural politics, given sport's role in structuring racist social systems and in facilitating resistance among racially oppressed peoples. Evidently, colonized indigenous peoples have endured systematic enslavement and genocide in both human and cultural terms. The established colonial systems employed sport to bind and amuse the colonizing communities, and to negate the pre-modern movement cultures of the colonized. Legal prohibitions (notably apartheid or Jim Crow laws) and other structural factors (such as stark economic inequalities, or racist politics in team selection) excluded non-whites from full sports participation. Where participation is enabled, it has been typically inspired by policies of enforced cultural Westernization, or racist assumptions regarding non-white athleticism. Accordingly, minority communities have struggled to ensure that sport, like other cultural realms, does not merely reproduce social oppression. As West Indian cricketers and Aboriginal athletes have shown, oppressed communities may reinvent sport's symbols and meanings to reflect their cultural identity and political aspirations.

Sport, cultural empowerment and anti-racism initiatives

The brief histories above demonstrate that sport cannot be analytically dislocated from other domains of structured power (notably the economic dimensions of social systems). This means that we should not isolate sport analytically to the extent that (like Hoberman) we blame it for 'damaging' minorities, or laud it for providing an exceptional story of black achievement and social mobility, as *The Bell Curve* authors and Allison (1998) had assumed (Carrington and McDonald 2001: 12).

Since the civil rights era, sport's cultural politics of 'race' have involved non-white athletes confronting institutionalized racist abuse. Such assaults are not merely explicit or restricted to spectators; they connect also to sport's instrumental professionalization. For example,

Australian athletes often 'sledge' or verbally abuse opponents to gain competitive advantages, but the insults slip easily into racism. Thus, when an Aboriginal player is called a 'black cunt' during an Australian Rules fixture, he is deemed to have 'taken it the wrong way' if he demands an apology (Booth and Tatz 2000: 214–16).

Athlete challenges to such mistreatment are varied. In Australian Rules football, black players mounted an anti-racism campaign throughout the 1990s, inspiring the governing body to appoint a 'racial and religious vilification' officer. Nevertheless, some commentators dismissed the campaign as misunderstanding 'gamesmanship', while media invective is still aimed at politically vocal Aboriginal players (Nadel 1998: 241–5). Similarly, in UK football, anti-racism campaigns acquired prominence only when black players expressed collective disgust at racist treatment by supporters and officials. Today, football's Europe-wide anti-racism organization (FARE) functions to raise spectator consciousness regarding prejudice and intolerance. Such initiatives highlight how Cultural Studies arguments concerning social justice may fruitfully enter sports policy.

Some argue that the apparent over-representation of non-whites within many sports suggests that systematic racism has been eradicated. However, this argument is deeply flawed. First, many young blacks perceive sport as affording social mobility that is denied them in more orthodox employment spheres. Yet, in truth, professional sport delivers relatively few from social disadvantage, even in extremely stratified societies like Brazil (Evanson 1982: 403). Although they dominate the NBA numerically, young black males have only a 1 in 135,800 chance of making the grade (LaFeber 2002: 92). 'Scientific racist' myths regarding natural black athleticism underpin the institutional routine of transferring black students into sporting competition rather than academic subjects (Cashmore 1982: 98–109).

Second, ethnic differences in sports participation invariably reflect the intersections of class, gender and 'racial' subjugation. Sports like golf require relatively high economic and social capital from players, thus producing few black professionals. As sports like US baseball move from free-to-air to subscription television, fewer members of the black working class watch and practise these games. Additionally, non-white minorities can feel unwelcome in sports stadiums dominated by white audiences and cultural attitudes (Lapchick 1991: 290).

Third, the sport exclusion of ethnic minorities often connects to critical gender issues, notably the restriction of athletic mobility almost entirely to males. For black female athletes who do excel, if 'racial' prejudices are counteracted, other forms of symbolic domination are intensified. For example, as Florence Griffith-Joyner's ethnic identity became less apparent in media analyses, her sexualization expanded (Vertinsky and Captain 1998: 552–3). In some non-Western cultures, notably Islamic ones, women's sport tends to be proscribed, impeded by local male influence, or intensively regulated, notably in dress codes (Zaman 1997). This leaves Western sociologists with an interpretative problem: do they adopt a universalist, human rights critique to attack this social exclusion? Or do they follow cultural relativism to argue that such a Western critique is inherently ethnocentric?

Fourth, in team sports, black males are still segregated informally (or 'stacked') along racist lines. Stacking is defined as the placement of white athletes in central positions associated with intelligence, decision making, leadership, calmness and dependability and the location of non-whites in peripheral positions requiring explosive physical powers (especially speed), unpredictability and infrequent participation. Although some tinkering across sports is required to establish central/peripheral positions, the results appear compelling. Loy and McElvogue's (1970) pioneering US study found black athletes over-represented in baseball's outfield and in American football's defence and offence backfield. Aboriginals in rugby league and Australian Rules football are stacked in non-central positions (Hallinan 1991, 1999). In New Zealand rugby, Polynesians are deemed to lack mental coolness, inevitably affecting their positional allocation (Miller 1998: 138). In English football, black players were under-represented in central midfield, and featured particularly as attacking wingers, where pace and unpredictable play are prioritized (Maguire 1991). In Brazil, national team coaches have long been reluctant to select 'unpredictable' and 'unreliable' black players to play as goalkeepers. While some sports like basketball appear to have outgrown stacking, covert stacking still excludes non-whites from executive, managerial and coaching roles throughout sport.[4]

The obduracy of racist politics and ideology in sport

While different participation rates provide empirical indications of continuing sport racism, more subtle cultural prejudices arise in relation to sport celebrities and aesthetics. Many sports institutions put immense emphasis on 'role model' non-white athletes. The global celebrity of Tiger Woods (golf), Michael Jordan (basketball, not baseball), Rivaldo (football), Cathy Freeman (track) and Sachin Tendulkar (cricket) seems to suggest that elite sports have eradicated residual racism. However, three Cultural Studies arguments expose this assumption.

First, more 'enlightened' racism arises across white sports audiences (Jhally and Lewis 1992). By embracing some non-white celebrities, white audiences appear to negate racist cultural codes, but still interpret the 'failings' of other non-whites in distinctively racist ways, in terms of inherently weak personal characteristics rather than institutional barriers. Second, white corporations and audiences may decouple the public meaning of black athletes from *any* ethnic signifiers. For example, Michael Jordan has been effectively 'whitened', or at least abstracted from his ethnic location, partly to assist his advertising appeal among white consumers (Andrews 2001: 127).

Third, elite athletes are polysemous: as cultural texts, they facilitate different interpretations by different individuals. Consider Muhammad Ali: his refusal to fight in Vietnam, his championing of oppressed peoples, and his conversion to Islam all signified a personal confrontation with racial oppression. Yet, Ali transcends a single public meaning (Oriard 1995). Ali's moral courage is obvious; in the ring, he was remarkably (perhaps foolishly) brave. He was also sport's greatest self-publicist, brashly insulting opponents and embracing media communication. More recent criticisms emphasize Ali's political and business failings and his regressive gender politics. His boxing career was epic, ending in the tragedy of Parkinson's disease, but Ali remains a hugely popular public figure and humanitarian ambassador. All of this feeds inconclusive debates over the 'true' Ali, and his wider meaning in relation to American post-war history.

Aesthetic practices and traditions contain strong ambiguities regarding questions of ethnic empowerment or racialization. Sport's aestheticization among black Americans has often occurred within a broader transformation of black popular culture. In the 1920s, basketball's rising popularity was coterminous with the emergence of blues music and new evangelical religious services, each cultural form being characterized by a festive, community atmosphere. Meanwhile, playing techniques in baseball's Negro Leagues were notably spectacular and visually entertaining, while black styles now dominate basketball. In football, South Americans honed playing styles that differed markedly from European ones. In Brazil, the distinctive, 'mixed-race' 'Lusotropical civilization' that Gilberto Freyre (1967: 432; 1964) examined, also developed a special football artistry among working-class 'mulattos' that is pivotal to global imaginings of the 'beautiful game'.

However, sport's aestheticization is invariably influenced by racism's material and ideological dimensions. In US basketball, the 'racial hierarchy' was reasserted materially through the acquisition of black players to perform like 'magical minstrels' in white-controlled professional leagues (Gems 1995). In turn, the racist construction of black sport culture, as everything that white sport culture is not, is internalized as self-knowledge by the black community.[5] Thus black athletes employ self-racializing vocabularies to explain their 'prowess'. Consider this extraordinary self-portrait by John Barnes, a leading English football player, coach and television pundit:

> Coming from Jamaica, I am blessed with rhythm. My innate balance and agility meant I could jump over all tackles flying my way at Watford and Liverpool. Footballers from the Caribbean and other warm climates are far suppler than the English, who are notoriously stiff... It's too cold in northern Europe to possess the sort of physical flexibility... I once had. (Barnes 1999: 145, quoted in Carrington 2001: 120n)

The contradictions are succinctly contained in the double-edged meanings of 'cool pose'. For Majors (1990), black males employ 'cool pose' within an 'expressive lifestyle' that embodies pride in black masculinity. Cool pose 'transforms the mundane into the sublime and makes the routine spectacular' (Majors 1990: 111). It is a cultural strategy for negotiating structural impediments, particularly in entertainment, sport and religious services. Michael Jordan and Julius Erving embody cool pose, while Ali's apparent vanity and boasting personified its resistant elements. Yet cool pose appears to be anchored in the spectacularist, athletic discourses that racially construct black identity. Here we need to recall Cultural Studies' definition of popular culture as being fashioned by disadvantaged and oppressed peoples from the materials and symbols that mark their domination. Black sports aesthetics attract a relatively structuralist interpretation of that definition: despite the creative expressivity of 'cool pose', it is never quite disembedded from the racist (self-) knowledge inculcated by white-dominated institutions and structures.

Racism and ethnicity: cultural prejudices and intolerance

Historically, forms of 'race logic' have applied beyond those of African and Asian extraction to include many ethnic communities. In sport, for example, stacking's 'race logic' also applies to nationalities and continental regions. Scandinavians are typified as rational whites *par excellence*; southern Europeans and 'Celtic races' are deemed more fiery, temperamental and often physically courageous; Latin Americans are deemed to possess natural flamboyance; and the 'unscientific, irrational' nature of Africans is deemed to reveal itself through magical intuitive performances that lack coherent game plans. The international sports media simply reproduce cross-culturally these entrenched, racialized categories. Often, the local environment becomes a normative metaphor regarding intellect or athleticism (hence, the ice-cool Swedes out-manoeuvre the hot-headed Africans). Yet, if industrialization had occurred initially in the Southern hemisphere, rather than in the Northern, then environmental heat would carry positive rather than negative metaphorical meanings (O'Donnell 1994: 377–8).

We need to extend critical analysis of 'race' into fuller appraisal of intolerance concerning religio-national identity and ethnic difference. Racism is not simply dependent on 'colour-codes'. Hence, systematic discrimination and prejudice towards Irish Catholics, or those labelled as 'white trash', require historical investigation, particularly since there is 'an invisibility of race in Whiteness' (Finn 1999, 2000; J. Z. Wilson 2002: 398). In Northern Ireland, the maltreatment of Irish Catholics' sporting institutions (especially football clubs) reflected more deeply entrenched forms of religio-ethnic discrimination. In Scotland, the religio-ethnic football antagonism between the Glasgow clubs of Rangers (associated with the Protestant, British Unionist majority) and Celtic (with Irish Catholic origins) is routinely described as 'sectarianism', though for some the term camouflages rather than exposes anti-Irish racism (Finn 1990: 5–6). Sport, notably football, has been one domain through which Irish Catholic people have pursued competitive relations with the majority (Protestant, British) community while exploring 'dual identities' as Scots and Irish Catholics. For some analysts, anti-Irish songs and abuse by Rangers fans are archaic rituals of rivalry, in a society with no paramilitarism and low measurements of religious discrimination (S. Bruce 2000). Others argue that anti-Irish discourses disclose continuing, unrecognized problems in Scottish society (Finn 1994b; 2000).

In North America, sports have been viewed as functional with regard to the acculturation and Americanization of white immigrants – notably, Jews, Poles, Italians and Irish Catholics. However, media and public discourses within sport have portrayed significant levels of intolerance towards ethnic groups. During the 1920s, at Notre Dame College, Knute Rockne assembled a highly talented, multi-ethnic team of American footballers that was regularly disparaged by insulting nicknames like 'Fighting Irish', 'Horrible Hibernians' and 'Dumb Micks'. Sports journalists mocked the striking surnames of

Polish players, although many great coaches insisted that Poles were the very best American footballers (Oriard 2001: 261–7). Jewish and Italian athletes were subjected to explicit racist stereotyping, but their successes directly challenged such characterizations. Jewish-American newspapers argued that American footballers like Benny Fried-man and Sammy Behr refuted racist depictions of 'weak, cowardly Jews'.

Jewish athletes during the inter-war years were viewed by fellow Jews as symbols of anti-racist resistance. To the Jewish writer Meyer Liben, they 'represented us against the world, which, we were coming to know, was filled with enemies, threatening us for obscure reasons. These heroes were fighting for us – each hook, pass, basket was a kind of blow against oppression' (quoted in Levine 1992: 272). Yet sport was an ambiguous 'middle ground' for Jewish-American iden-tity construction. Sports participants shaped distinctive identities as Americans and Jews. Sports assimilated Jews into American culture and society while providing for distinctive ethnic identity and soli-darity. Second-generation Jews notably preferred a 'secular Jewish-ness', a dual identity supporting the US's political and economic system alongside Jewish cultural concerns for ethnicity, family, freedom and personal indefatigability. The public meanings of Jewish boxers and baseball players reflected these fused values. For example, the brilliant baseball pitcher of the 1960s, Sandy Koufax, was immensely popu-lar among fellow American Jews. Koufax quietly circumvented ethnic prejudices but refused to pitch on Yom Kippur even though he was not particularly religious (Leavy 2002).[6]

Concluding comments: expanding critical horizons

In this chapter, I have provided a critical sociological analysis of 'race' and racism within sport. It is simple enough to destroy the popu-lar modern myths that still circulate regarding black athleticism. The 'middle passage' and 'Bell Curve' hypotheses are the more elaborate, pseudo-scientific variants of these ideological constructs. Genetics-based arguments draw such volumes of counter-evidence that they remain highly implausible.

Short cultural histories of specific national and regional locations highlight the ethnocentric, imperialistic and racist roots of sport's di-verse inculcation across the globe. It would be tempting, but ultimately inadequate, to theorize 'race' within sport through detailed reference to a few individuals and their conjunctures. In the United States, we could advance Johnson, Robinson, Carlos, Smith, Ali and Jordan; in the UK, we might name Wharton, D'Oliveira and Barnes; in Australia, we have Samuels, Gilbert, Perkins and Freeman; and in the Caribbean, we could list the cricketers Constantine, Sobers, Richards and Lara. But an adequate sociology of race within sport requires more detailed socio-historical contextualizations to elucidate the cultural differences and continuities, for example, in the resistant strategies of specific collectives to their racialized oppression.

Sport's cultural politics are reflected by anti-racism initiatives and the advances of ethnically marginalized communities within sporting institutions. Yet racist social structures and cultural practices survive in relatively covert ways, such as through 'stacking' in sports teams, the 'enlightened racism' of popular culture audiences, and the semiotic 'whitening' of elite black athletes. Even black sports aesthetics harbours more problematic bases in racialized patterns of self-understanding.

The sociological reading of racism within sport needs to broaden its geographical and epistemological remits. Much sport sociology on 'race' retraces the Atlantic triangle that has connected the UK, the Caribbean and the United States since the earliest days of modern slavery – all the while, of course, largely omitting the continent that actually supplied the slaves in the first instance. The vast geographical and social expanses of Africa (excepting South Africa), Latin America, and both southern and eastern Europe are insufficiently examined. These lacunae ensure that much writing on race has restricted empirical and explanatory purchase. Additionally, we should reflect more deeply upon the ontological roots of racism, to explore how the core features of modern racism are not 'colour-coded' and culturally exclusive, but isolate other collectives for systematic intolerance and prejudicial treatment. Significant comparative work is waiting to be undertaken on the patterns of systematic, racist misidentification and mistreatment experienced by different minority communities.

Deeper empirical and theoretical analyses of 'race' would have the greater benefit of tackling more concertedly the social roots of racism. Such approaches move us beyond seeking merely technical, incremental solutions to racism, like arresting abusive sports fans or increasing the proportion of non-whites in 'central' playing positions. Instead, we need to confront the nature of race logic *per se* if we are to develop a robust, normative redefinition of sport as a cultural field free of racism, prejudice and ethnic intolerance.

6

Gender Identities and Sexuality in Sport

Modern sport has always been a crucial cultural domain for constructing and reproducing dominant, heterosexual masculine identities. Sports institutions at elite and grass roots levels still typically harbour formal and informal restrictions on women's full participation. Yet, as we shall see, historical, sociological and anthropological readings of sport highlight the critical agency of marginalized social actors, and women are no exception.

Here, I discuss gender issues in sport in four main parts. I open with a preliminary, historical discussion of the gendering of modern sport. Second, I advance a detailed social history and critical sociology of women's experiences and potentialities within sport. Third, I examine the sport position of gays and lesbians. Fourth, I address sociological issues relating to masculinity within sport. I argue that, while gender-based relations of power and domination certainly obtain within sport, we should avoid culturally reductive readings that underplay social actors' critical, interpretative capacities.

Making sexist sport: modernity and gendered leisure

Gender stratification within sport began early. Up to the late nineteenth century, raucous bachelor subcultures pervaded many pre-modern pastimes such as blood sports like 'ratting' and crude pugilism contests, within cultures of heavy gambling, camaraderie and routine violence (Gorn and Goldstein 1993: 70–5). In America, this 'fancy' comprised unattached, young working-class men, often of immigrant stock; as in Britain and Australia, rakish aristocrats or military officers also featured. In Britain, traditional masculine practices, like drinking, gambling, carousing and 'whoring', were not displaced from sport until late Victorian times (Brailsford 1985: 126). Early Australian sports were similarly raucous, though less violent than British or American equivalents, despite men's numerical domination within the penal colony (Cashman 1995: 206).

The rise of the British 'games cult' that transformed sports reflected precise gender norms containing strong class and imperial inflections. Late Victorian bourgeois imperialist ideology associated sport and exercise with the 'muscular Christian gentleman', and neo-Spartan virtues of 'stoicism, hardiness and endurance' (Mangan 1986: 147). New sport ethics sculpted disciplined masculine selves. Individuality was subordinated to the team cause. Across British schools and colleges, the most adept at games gained social recognition to aid their spearheading of Britain's industries and empire; for the rest, the sports field instilled generalized qualities of leadership and manliness (Mangan 1981: 129–30). Boys shirking sports were scorned and ridiculed; being overly bookish was associated with a sickly pallor, degenerate physique and effeminate character.

The myth of 'fair play' in sport was invented, promoting 'controlled confrontation' between boys that involved conformity, pack brutality and competitive violence. 'Fair play' helped to sustain international ideologies regarding English elite virtues and the civilizing benefits of British imperialism.[1] Before founding the modern Olympics, the Frenchman Baron Pierre de Coubertin visited several English educational institutions and was left convinced that, if introduced to the *lycées*, these games could reinvigorate France's 'effete' upper class schoolboys (Mangan 1981).

British ideals of 'muscular Christianity' spread across the Anglophone world. In Canadian schools, for example, the influence of these ethics 'cannot be over emphasized' (Metcalfe 1974: 69). Different football codes enabled local, creolized emphases on masculine norms to be expressed through play. In Australian Rules football, true men displayed 'courage'; critics of the game's naked violence were disparaged as 'cowards' or 'old women' (Booth and Tatz 2000: 68). Through rugby, the Afrikaaners of South Africa cultivated a distinctive masculine, nationalist identity that emphasized 'ruggedness, endurance, forcefulness and determination' (Grundlingh 1994: 186–7). In American football, leading college teams (Yale, Princeton and Harvard) presented the violent game as a crucial pedagogical instrument for those entering business and public sector leadership (Sammons 1997: 384). Baseball shaped a particular masculinity among the white industrial working classes, rooted in myths of female and non-white inferiority, political democracy and class mobility, thus sustaining the dominant social order (Kimmel 1990: 64–5).

Accordingly, women and sport participation was normally a *non sequitur*. De Coubertin, for example, insisted that sport engagement would breach women's 'fixed destiny' as mothers and men's companions. 'Respectable' women exercised in private surroundings like secluded tennis courts; noticeable female exertion was linked to sexual deviance. During the *belle époque*, for example, Frenchmen viewed female cyclists according to the 'madonna/mistress' syndrome: as asexual spinsters or 'half-naked, voluptuous and sexually available' (Holt 1991: 125).

These sexist discourses still possess contemporary exponents. The sociologist John Carroll (1985) has advocated women's removal from sport participation. Sport, for Carroll, is a great moral educator, and 'the living arena for the great value of manliness'. Through sporting heroism, Olympian men seek 'divine favour and grace'; by natural contrast, women are compassionate and tender, but graceless in physical exertion, and so must recover their 'provider', reproductive role. Carroll (1985: 93–4) postulates that 'the fundamental feminine anxiety is of inner barrenness, of being dirty, polluted or ruined inside. This anxiety is biologically determined, although its surface symptoms vary from culture to culture.' Re-acquaintance with domesticity helps women dispel this inner turmoil. Carroll complains also that women's encroachment within sport reflects a 'matricidal culture' that corrodes the male's provider role and emasculates the virility and nobility of men. Women's return to the kitchen, Carroll reasons, can repair this damaged culture.

Of course, Carroll's thesis is astonishingly archaic and sexist to the point of self-parody. His analysis succinctly reproduces the patriarchal ideology that excludes women from sport. He assumes fixed biological and psychological 'natures' for both sexes, when all serious sociologists would insist that such differences are, in the main, socially and culturally constructed.

Women in sport: history, sexuality and political transformation

Women and modern sport: origins to 1945

Women's struggle for sporting equality is a long and incomplete one. In North America, women's intensive demands for more active sports engagement extends back to the early nineteenth century (R. J. Park 1978: 32). However, in pre-Victorian times, more influential, middle-class women were least likely to seek participation, and actual sporting pastimes tended to involve traditional activities (like smock races) rather than serious athletic contest (Guttmann 1991: 83–4).

Subsequently, class divisions tended to divide Victorian women in modern sport. In Britain, the moderate, notable increase of women in sport 'was limited almost entirely to the middle class' (Tranter 1998: 80). In North America and Australia, light sports like croquet and archery were adopted before middle- and upper-class women played tennis and golf (Vamplew 1994: 15). Lower-class women's sports involvement was curtailed by lack of finance, social influence and energy (due to the daily grind of labour); and by the wealthier classes' regulation of bodily display and sexuality. In Canada, from the 1870s, the YWCA employed athletic associations to rescue working-class women from 'degenerate' poolrooms or dance-halls. Nevertheless, the Anglo-American games cult did not entirely exclude bourgeois women (M. A. Hall 2002: 34–5). In schools, if teachers permitted, sports like hockey were enjoyed, and facilitated the 'unladylike' pleasures of getting dirty, playing rough and competing strenuously (C. Smith 1997: 67).

Women's advances in sport were often controlled and curtailed by men in accordance with patriarchal norms. Specific 'feminine/diminutive' rules for basketball, restricting movement, were introduced, but often ignored, by female players (Dean 2002). High-contact sports, while prohibiting female players, attracted sizeable female crowds. As spectators and administrators, women contributed significantly to Australian Rules football. In some grounds, gender segregation of spectators was introduced to protect gentle women from expressive masculine behaviour, while the press derided the notion of women as players (Hess 1998: 102–4).

Victorian middle-class women were instructed in the medical model of the 'delicate female' (Jennifer Hargreaves 2002: 56–7). Medics recommended 'gentle exercises, remedial gymnastics, and massage' to strengthen without overtaxing the female frame and its vital reproductive functions. Gymnastic drill was introduced and remained the major regime of exercise pedagogy for young women across northern Europe and the Anglophone world. In the *Turnvereine* (gymnastic clubs) and schools of late nineteenth-century Germany, girls were instructed in free-standing exercises, studiously avoiding movements thought to endanger reproduction (Pfister 2002: 167).[2] In Britain, the Swedish physical trainer Madame Martina Bergman-Osterberg institutionalized the 'Swedish system' of calisthenics for girls during the 1880s. In accordance with dominant medical and social norms, these non-competitive exercises were intended to promote discipline, health, grace and reproductive powers among women. Bergman-Osterberg rather personified the contradictions of female participation in late Victorian physical culture. She may have been a 'committed feminist who laboured throughout her life to remove barriers to women's progress' (McCrone 1988: 109). Yet she explained her pedagogy in pseudo-Darwinian terms: 'I try to train my girls to help raise their own sex, and so to accelerate the progress of the race; for unless the women are strong, healthy, pure, and true, how can the race progress?' (Jennifer Hargreaves 1994: 77).

Women's greater entry into physical exercise occurred alongside wider legal, political and civil struggles. 'First-wave feminism' began as early as 1850 and lasted until the 1930s, and helped gain women political suffrage, educational and employment opportunities, and resistance to sexual subordination (Walby 1997: 149–52). Some early female athletes were inevitably connected to these struggles, but most were pragmatic in seeking to play games as they wanted.

During the inter-war era, women acquired more energetic roles as America's mass consumer culture promoted youthfulness and fitness, while women's crucial contribution during wartime remained strong in the memory. Women's greater political autonomy assisted their creation and control of separate sports clubs and associations, notably in the UK and North America, although many were dominated by the middle classes and inculcated bourgeois norms of female respectability among working-class members (Jennifer Hargreaves 1993: 138–9). Having allowed female participants since 1900, the IOC grudgingly recognized women's events in 1924. Female Olympians doubled numerically during the 1920s, reaching almost 10 per cent of all competitors in 1928, but distance running, equestrianism and hockey remained prohibited. Successful female athletes still endured conventional gender discourses within the public domain. The star American, Babe Didrikson, was subjected to constant 'tomboy' or 'muscled moll' jibes. Conventionally 'feminine' stars like tennis champion Helen Wills were depicted more favourably (Guttmann 1991: 144–52).

Cultural continuities and differences in the gender/sport relationship were highlighted by social systems outside of liberal capitalism. Socialist societies promoted women's sport alongside official policies of militarized nation building and female industrial equality. In China, the Communist-inspired Red Sport Movement was founded in 1932, and sought to produce more active identities, 'iron bodies' and fresh duties and responsibilities for women (Hong 1997). The Soviet state valorized female athletes with 'courage, grace, skill, even strength, in the sporting area, winning prestige for club, factory, farm region, ethnic group and republic' (Riordan 1991: 199). In paradoxical contrast, Fascist regimes favoured women's traditional domestication in social policy, while exploiting the national sporting successes of both genders. Germany's Nazi regime promoted female exercise to assist reproduction and racial health, but fielded a large and highly successful team of women athletes at the 1936 Olympics to abet state propaganda (Pfister 2002: 169–70).[3]

Post-war sport and women

During the Cold War, women's sporting participation and exposure increased steadily, albeit mainly in official 'amateur' sports. Limited corporate and media interest arose for commodifying women's team sport as entertainment. Politically, Western nations sought to challenge Eastern-bloc domination in (still amateur) Olympic competition, although that lead had been achieved partly by losing grass roots recreation, and by the doping of young athletes (Pfister 2002: 172–3).

Women's Olympic participation has increased slowly but notably. Of all Olympic competitors, women made up 12 per cent at the Melbourne Olympics in 1956, 20 per cent at Montreal in 1976, around 29 per cent at Barcelona in 1992, and 38 per cent at Sydney in 2000. The women's sporting programme has grown gradually, despite IOC and IAAF conservatism. Women's limited political voice in sport impedes reform. Older and upper-class men dominate sport's governing bodies, in part by building careers through women's exclusion from sports participation or decision making (see Jennifer Hargreaves 1994: 221–2).

At everyday level, women's sports-related involvement is typically domestic rather than competitive. A century ago, women were advised to gain physical exercise through household labour rather than riding bicycles (Lenskyj 1986: 62–3). Today, sport institutions habitually promote women's domesticity through gender-specific work roles. Women are typically allocated 'voluntary' domestic tasks within local sports clubs: preparing food, cleaning kitchens and toilets, overseeing small money pools, washing dirty sports kits, and assisting male sport officials (S. M. Thompson 1999). In professional sports, gender divisions can be equally stark. Partners of male athletes perform wifely, reproductive roles in running households, bearing and rearing children, tending to the husband's needs, and struggling to conform to dominant cultural definitions regarding youthful female attractiveness.

In North America, politico-legal challenges to male sport hegemony have been important preludes to notable advances in women's sport. In the United States, the 'Title IX' federal law was passed in June 1972, prohibiting gender discrimination within sports at colleges and high schools. In the same year, six female competitors at the New York marathon staged a successful protest against the barring of women from starting alongside men. A year later, Billie Jean King defeated Bobby Riggs in the 'Challenge of the Sexes' tennis match. In 1974, the Little League permitted girls to play baseball and softball. In turn, numerous other 'firsts' for women have been achieved: Janet Guthrie competed in the Indianapolis 500 motor race (1977); the NCAA authorized national championships for women in sports like basketball, golf, soccer, swimming, tennis and outdoor track events (1982); Gayle Gardner became the first female play-by-play commentator on NFL fixtures (1987); Judith Sweet became NCAA president (1991); Julie Krone won a triple-crown horse-race, the Belmont Stakes (1993); Kerri Ann McTiernan became the first female coach on a men's college basketball team (1995); Major League Soccer recruited two female referees (1998); women competed in the same number of team sports as men at the Sydney Olympics (2000); Ashley Martin played and scored in a Division 1 American football game (2001); and Annika Sorenstam became the first woman in 58 years to compete on the men's American golf tour (2003).

Title IX is a controversial piece of legislation. Males continue to outnumber females significantly in joining college sports teams, while colleges still spend lavishly on big-time male sports, mainly American football and basketball. To counterbalance the gender divide and conform to Title IX, colleges spend heavily to attract female athletes into sports; often, this means cutting funds for other, popular male sports activities. Thus, the political Right insists that Title IX must be repealed (Gavora 2002). Liberals insist that Title IX must be enforced whole-heartedly to destabilize long-term gender inequalities (Eitzen 1999: 164). However, the legislation cannot succeed without significant structural changes across education: college presidents must divert finance from American football, while women's sports participation must be nurtured assiduously in childhood.

The potential for gender reform of sport is still significantly hamstrung by class and ethnicity factors. Only soccer has recently achieved a rapid, mass popularization among young American women, notably white middle-class suburbanites (Andrews et al. 1997). Many private-member golf clubs still provide males, notably the business classes, with a self-enclosed, self-absorbed haven, discouraging female membership or use of facilities. The Augusta National Golf Club in Georgia, which hosts the Masters tournament, is notorious for still excluding women. Although it has grown steadily, the LPGA still advances a rather traditionalist image to avoid alienating television stations and sponsors. Women's golf has become increasingly exclusive too, as the community institutions and facilities that had enabled poorer white and black females to participate have gradually disappeared since the mid-1970s (Crossett 1995: 212–16). The results are evidenced in the restricted class and ethnicity of current American-born LPGA players.

Serious gender divides remain in sport's prize-money and sponsorships, reflecting male domination in sport spectatorship and marketing and the reproduction of patriarchal mores within sport culture. We may consider how unequal rewards connect to both human physiology and sport's objectives and aesthetics. Professional sports tend to prioritize limited-duration and record-breaking performances. Current physiological differences between the genders favour men in meeting these goals. Men are 50 per cent stronger than women in absolute terms, and 25 per cent stronger relative to size; greater upper-body strength assists male superiority in many sports, from weight-lifting to golf. Women are physiologically advantaged over men in less prestigious, long-endurance sports, like extended swimming or marathons (Guttmann 1991: 251–2). While some research indicates that strength differentials can be reduced to 5 per cent, it remains noteworthy that the biggest rewards are available in sports that exaggerate existent male physiological advantages. In golf, regression analysis suggests that earnings differentials between the sexes can be explained by men's higher achievement levels within the game's rules (Shmanske 2000). These inequalities can be challenged only by increasing women's cross-class sports participation, by redefining more fundamentally the objectives of sport beyond achievement principles, and by augmenting the social status of those sports that physiologically advantage women.

Women, femininity and sexuality

Strong patriarchal gender codes dissuade many women from sport participation. Physical exertion inevitably builds muscle, but traditionalist gender mores connect enhanced muscularity to 'masculinization'. Female body-builders have been prime targets for this discourse, but mixed ideological politics underpin attacks on other athletes. East

European track athletes (like Jarmila Kratochvilova) have long been depicted as insufficiently feminine by Western sports journalists in a blend of sexist, jingoistic and neo-racist comment.

Patriarchal gender codes and the female 'look' of consumer culture certainly objectify women, yet critical agency is still viable within exercise regimes. In women's aerobics, the idealized body-shape is 'firm but shapely, fit but sexy, strong but thin', thus fitting hegemonic patriarchal norms, but female aerobicizers display critical ambivalence towards this absurd ideal while enjoying the expressive, emancipatory aspects of meeting and exercising (Markula 1995; Real 1999). Women's exercise regimes have significantly stretched the boundaries of 'permissible' muscularity and female body 'hardness'. Some research suggests that females entering sports in childhood are more prone to pursue 'hard', gender-challenging athletic styles (Mennesson 2000).

Sport's paymasters, such as television networks and corporate advertisers, constitute formidable institutional structures in routinely reproducing patriarchal norms. Sports media focus heavily on attractive female athletes like Anna Kournikova (her constant losses notwithstanding), thereby trivializing woman's athletic achievements. Women's sport is thinly covered by television news, while actual stories tend to emphasize humour and women's objectification (Messner, Duncan and Cooky 2003). Sport's commodification packages female athletes, via off-court endorsements of perfume and underwear, for the heterosexual male gaze. Sexual metaphors and promises imbue sports packaging: for example, since the 1920s, men's golf vacations have been presented as opportunities to 'score' on and off the course. At sports events, voyeuristic camera crews pursue 'honey shots' of attractive, semi-clad female spectators and athletes. Male 'sports' magazines run 'swimsuit issues', and avowed soft-porn media like *Playboy* pay heavily for celebrity athletes to pose nude. Some female athletes (like the Australian women's football team, the Matildas) have posed nude to publicize their sport. Despite arguments regarding self-expression and choice, such measures reflect these athletes' weak structural position within sport: self-sexualization is a desperate strategy to generate male-dominated public interest and corporate backing. Women's objectification within sport extends to the institutionalized sex subcultures involving male athletes and female 'groupies'. In North American sports, 'completely asymmetrical' relationships arise as teams of male players seek no-ties sex with female followers (Gmelch and San Antonio 1998). Several high-profile rape and assault cases involving professional athletes suggest a hidden history of sexual abuse against female fans, and a morally corrupted subculture among many sportsmen (Benedict 1998).

Guttmann (1991: 258–65; 1996) provides a nuanced, critical historical assessment of sport, sexuality and eroticism. He dismisses determinist feminist arguments that sexualizing sports athletes causes general violence against women; such an argument simply reduces all males 'to the status of Pavlovian dogs' (1991: 264). Guttmann instead evolves a balanced analysis of 'eros' and sports engagement. As a medium of physical expression, sport's erotic component is 'ineradicable', but remains essentially 'sport-specific'. Thus, squeezing female athletes into lingerie trivializes their achievements and corrupts the eroticism within their athleticism.[4] Nevertheless, to market products, advertisers will inevitably employ attractive females *and* males (including celebrity athletes). Guttmann reminds us indirectly that such objectification within sport is tied to other historical processes outside pure gender domination, such as health consumerism and the disciplining of bodies through modern fitness regimes. Furthermore, Guttmann encourages more critical feminists to explore (rather than piously deny) the eroticism of sport in its own terms. Some female communities have adopted this more open-ended approach towards sports eroticism. For example, the thriving lesbian carnival around some LPGA tournaments suggests that eroticism and consumerism around sport can move beyond heterosexual male interests. Such practices confirm too that diverse subordinate communities can engage in cultural practices that transgress their structural domination.

Manufacturing contentment: sports policy, gender reform and pro-feminist politics

Without denying women's critical agency within a historical context, women's sporting experiences would be transformed by the structural reform of sport institutions. This involves following the Canadian strategy of moving from sport 'equality' to 'equity'. Equality policies open doors to disadvantaged groups, including women. Equity policies restructure the sport system *per se* to ensure sport experiences are qualitatively similar for men and women (M. A. Hall 2002: 203–4). Implementing equity, of course, is highly problematic. Would it suit those grass roots female sports groups that thrive on informality and their members' peculiar sporting passions? And what of those major sports institutions that instinctively resist pro-feminist, equitable reforms (McKay 1997: 139)?

This leads us to consider what kinds of sports reform women might favour. Jennifer Hargreaves (1993) outlines three political strategies for women inside sport. First, *co-option* involves women 'catching up with men' in male sporting domains, taking on more of the roles that men have created and still control. Co-option is advocated by 'liberal feminists', and its implementation tends to be measured quantitatively. It rejects conservative claims that biological differences or traditional gender values prevent women's sports participation. However, by focusing naively on equality and constitutional reform, co-option fails to tackle more fundamental problems in sport like masculine norms that promote violent play and discursive sexism. Co-option also puts women on the defensive, forcing them to meet males on male ground and join male sporting rituals. Unless those rituals are radically redefined, women will continue to 'seem out of place' (see Novak 1994: 208–12).

Second, *separatism* involves women's 'self-realization' by organizing sports tournaments or associations independently of men. Separatism is advocated by 'radical feminists', and would enhance women's sports participation while exploring emotional intimacies in sport that masculine values suppress. Separatism politicizes personal life, but crudely attributes sport's problems simply to gender inequities. Moreover, radical feminism slips into essentialism and ahistoricism when it theorizes gender identities in terms of innate norms and inclinations, rather than socialization and cultural difference. Finally, separatism harbours reactionary elements, since it rejects a dialogical sporting model involving both men and women.

Third, *co-operation* between men and women helps establish new sporting models that negate gender differences. Co-operation is advocated by 'socialist feminists', recognizes the heterogeneity of social struggles (to include 'race' and sexuality, for example), and is geared towards liberation. This philosophy assumes that men are not inherently oppressive, but are socialized into assuming and reproducing oppressive roles and practices that damage men as well as women. Co-operation requires feminists to explore sport's possible experiences and meanings for women before developing a radically reformed sporting model. Hargreaves advocates co-operation and identifies implicit support from Paul Willis (1982) and Michèle Barrett (1982) *inter alia*.

While they are categorically distinct, impulses of all three strategies arise within specific sport struggles for women. In Canadian sport during the inter-war years, for example, liberal (if maternal) impulses arose in institutions like the Hamilton Olympic Club, championing women's greater participation while eschewing any appearance as 'man-haters'. Separatist impulses were prevalent among Toronto Ladies, who sought to remove all men from women's sport; other women pursued 'girls' rules' for specific sports, or introduced college 'play days' to assuage the competitiveness and divisiveness of male-defined sport. Elements of a historically specific co-operation strategy might be located in the emergence of joint sport practices among men and women: for example, regular travel and social contacts through sport were experienced as relatively liberating occasions during that period (Kidd 1996: 111, 120–42).

Evidently, the co-operation policy is the most practically and theoretically sophisticated. Its Cultural Studies influences ensure that it critiques the hegemonic marginalization of women within sport. Such a perspective also enables effective critique of the commodification of women's sport, notably how 'post-feminist' marketing messages still present female physical engagement as essentially passive (Lucas 2000).

Open play? Homosexual cultural politics and sport

The weaknesses of the liberal feminist, co-option strategy are particularly stark in respect of the sports experiences of gay people. For Lenskyj (1995: 47), 'the situation for women, especially lesbians, in mainstream sport has remained stubbornly woman-hating and homophobic'. In Canada, homophobia and 'dyke bashing' have intensified alongside elite sport's commodification (M. A. Hall 2002: 199–200). Griffin (1998: 55–63) has isolated several myths that serve to demonize lesbians within sport:

- Lesbians participate in particular sports (like golf, tennis and basketball), thus tarnishing those sports' image.
- Sports promote lesbianism by isolating young women within all-female settings.
- Lesbians are sexual predators among young athletes in locker rooms.
- Unwholesome and immoral lesbians constitute bad role models for young women.
- Lesbians are unfeminine, and so have unfair advantages in sport; thus they should compete with men.
- Lesbian cliques control some sports (like softball or golf) and discriminate against heterosexuals.[5]

Unsurprisingly, most gay professional athletes and administrators endure self-estrangement by disguising their sexuality to maintain careers, endorsement contracts and supporter loyalty (Booth and Tatz 2000: 206–7). Sport tournament directors and fellow players can pressurize gay athletes to remain in the closet. The LPGA, for example, works assiduously to present players as traditionally feminine. Openly gay players are presented as endangering the golf tour's finances, and thus the livelihoods of other golfers (Crossett 1995: 181–2). In women's ice hockey, elite players counteract possible 'butch' or mannish (and therefore 'lesbian') images to please image-conscious club managers and national selectors (Theberge 2000). Gay athletes use 'ironic gay sensibility' and other everyday strategies to make their secret identity bearable (Pronger 1990). Lesbian physical education teachers typically 'pass' as heterosexuals to protect their employment (G. Clarke 2002). Fear of the 'lesbian' label dissuades heterosexual women from sports participation. Parents seek to protect their daughters from 'preying lesbians' in sports teams, although male coaches are far more likely to abuse students (Brackenridge 2001).

Some athletes (notably female tennis players like Navratilova, King and Mauresmo) 'come out' often after years of gossip that lead to 'confession'. Perhaps the most prominent gay male athlete has been Australia's Ian Roberts, one of the world's top rugby league players during the 1990s, who received strong personal support from many fellow players and media commentators (Freeman 1998). The UK's most prominent case involved the late footballer Justin Fashanu, who committed suicide after being indicted in the United States for sexually assaulting a teenage boy. However, gay male athletes are much more likely to come out *after* retirement. It remains far more common for other athletes (like football's Graeme Le Saux or baseball's Mike Piazza) to formulate public denials of sports gossip regarding alleged homosexual inclinations.

Media and public discourses on HIV-positive athletes further marginalize gay athletes. The basketball star Magic Johnson and, to a lesser extent, the boxer Tommy Morrison were depicted as men who had been infected by following natural heterosexual instincts and 'accommodating' (in Johnson's phrase) multiple female groupies. Despite lengthy reports regarding their peripatetic sexual histories, surprise was constantly expressed towards their HIV status (Messner 1994: 123). Conversely, when the gay diver Greg Louganis's HIV infection was announced, the media expressed no 'shock', and did not go into exactly how the disease had been contracted. The homosexuality–AIDS couplet remained unchallenged, and served 'to perpetuate the assumption that gay bodies are inherently diseased and immoral' (Dworkin and Wachs 2000: 58).

Gay athletes can employ radical, self-empowering political strategies both within and outside modern sport to advance their interests.

Griffin (1998: 222–7) advocates the public openness of more gay and bisexual athletes and coaches.[6] She praises 'key agents of social change' who have pursued social justice by confronting sport's sexual politics. Griffin insists that all women are in a common struggle, hence unity benefits everyone.

Some gay athletes have formed their own sports clubs, leagues and associations. The 'Gay Games', first staged in San Francisco in 1982 with 1,300 participants, expanded to 3,400 participants in 1986, and 7,200 in 1990. In theory, the Gay Games embody separatist, radical politics; they secure equitable yet distinctive sports participation through celebrating sexual difference. However, the Games neither directly challenge nor resist dominant sports institutions and structures, though they show-case different sport values, identities and associations (Messner 1992: 159). More critically, Pronger (2000) indicates that the Games's sexual dimension and thus their radicalism have been suppressed. The 1998 Amsterdam tournament was presented as mainstream; sexuality and desire were replaced by the banal theme of 'friendship'. Less credibly, Pronger advances more speculative, essentialist claims concerning the sexual dynamics of sport *per se*. Exploring the psychoanalytic extremes of 'queer theory', Pronger's (1999) essay, entitled 'Outta my endzone', brings a whole new meaning to sporting clichés about 'backs to the wall' defending. He argues that contemporary sport contains an emotional logic that is 'phallically aggressive' and 'anally closed': consider, for example, how American football is founded upon violent penetration of the opponent's spaces while rigorously protecting one's 'home' space.

Pronger rightly critiques the attempted normalization of the Gay Games, while his psychoanalytical speculations stretch hermeneutic boundaries within sport sociology. However, his analysis lacks sufficient evidence and plausible sociological theorization. Indeed, we could argue that heterosexual unions (rather than homosexual ones), in sport or elsewhere, reflect more positive emotional relationships since they embrace (rather than exclude) the opposite sex. More seriously, Pronger grossly exaggerates sexuality's role in explaining sport's symbolism. Sport is more than a mass exercise in subliminal gay-bashing. Sport does provide for idioms of comparatively intimate, emotionally charged interaction with fellow males (hugging, kissing) that are otherwise proscribed. Nevertheless, it would be wrong to slip into another post-Freudian trap that depicts such interaction simply as the expression of repressed homosexual desire (Rowe 1995: 127).

Moulding men through sport: hegemony and diversity

Hegemonic masculinities

Academic critiques of masculinity within sport have concentrated upon how physical culture sustains heterosexual, male domination. Historically, sport's idealized masculine codes have deep affinities with the 'martial masculinity' cults of twentieth-century fascism (Mangan 1999: 7–9). Sport's restrictive masculine norms victimize many 'deviant' others, including women, effeminate or gay men, the old, children and the disabled (Ingham (and friends) 1997: 171). Moreover, sport's masculine mores often cripple men physically, socially and psychologically. Sports media disseminate dominant masculine norms among boys and young men through a 'television sports manhood formula' built around themes of gender, race, militarism, aggression, violence and commercialism (Messner, Dunbar and Hunt 2000).

Pro-feminist sport sociology is heavily indebted to the Australian social theorist, R. W. Connell (1987, 1990, 1995, 2000). Through his neo-Gramscian concept of 'hegemonic masculinity', Connell indicates that strong cross-gender consent is established for dominant masculine identities. Hegemonic masculinity constitutes the 'culturally idealized form of masculine character', centred on 'toughness and competitiveness', women's subordination, and 'marginalization of gay men' (McKay 1997: 17). Yet among all men, hegemonic masculinity may be neither the commonest nor the most comfortable of masculine identities (Connell 2000: 10–11). It is a 'relational', not fixed, identity, disclosing social hierarchies and connections between men and women. Thus, historical and cross-cultural variations arise regarding hegemonic masculine ideals.

Hegemonic masculinity features in numerous sociological studies of sport–gender relations: for example, in critiques of *Sports Illustrated*'s 'swimsuit issue' and the damaging consequences of violent masculinities within sport (Davis 1997; Messner 1992; see Connell 2000: 11, 188–9). Klein (1993) adapted Connell's thinking to expose the 'femiphobia' inside body-building subcultures. 'Femiphobia' emerges from 'the fear of appearing female, or effeminate'; it 'fuels hypermasculinity, homophobia, and misogyny', and is manifested through hyperconformity to masculine norms (Klein 1993: 269–73). Body-building is an obvious refuge for young men who seek to manage their masculine hyper-conformity and subjective insecurities through this 'comic book masculinity'.

Latterly, Connell has built his gender perspective upon a four-fold analytical structure. First, gender *power relations* enable study of patriarchy's survival despite its contestation by various movements. Second, the *production relations (division of labour)* of modern capitalism remain gender-specific, directing women into different labour as and when required. Third, *cathexis (emotional relations)* concerns the politics of desire in defining gendered objects of pleasure and in the distributive justice of pleasure. Fourth, *symbolism* concerns human communication's role in reproducing the gender order.

Each analytical structure can be applied to explain some core aspects of sport. First, modern sport's dominant mores regarding toughness, aggression and competitiveness have promoted patriarchal hegemony, to exclude or undermine women's participation. Second, women's labour has been engaged gender-specifically in (typically unpaid) domestic or clerical work to support male-dominated sports clubs. Third, modern sport advertisements typically objectify women as sexually available. Fourth, males define themselves through tough play or post-match rituals against symbolic others (women, homosexuals).

However, rather than fit sport into Connell's four existing structures, it would be better included within a new, fifth structure that explicitly concerns *leisure (consumption) relations*. This new analytical structure would reflect leisure relations' centrality to gender in postmodern culture and contemporary capitalism. Gender divisions in leisure relations share significant parallels and interconnections with those in production relations. Women's improved labour position provides greater disposable income that can be partly directed into sport-related consumption. As in work, women are channelled into gender-appropriate leisure practices, notably fitness regimes like aerobics. During economic booms, women function as a 'reserve army of labour' without overturning their domestic roles; in sport, women become a 'reserve army of leisure' to fill expensive stadium seats, sit in 'family ends', or purchase children's merchandise (Russell 1999). Meanwhile, as in work, most women are drawn into male-dominated leisure spaces, rather than creating radically different physical cultures.

Appealingly, Connell's thesis is receptive to theoretical elaboration, and can explain the empirical complexity of hegemonic masculinity. Unfortunately, Connell himself is inclined to adopt an inflexible model of 'hegemonic masculinity'. Two cases from Connell's (otherwise regular and important) perorations on sport illustrate this point.

First, Connell (2000: 157–60) argues that, for boys in education, there are three 'vortices of masculinity formation': discipline, boys' subjects and sports. Using Foley's (1990) study of Texas high school football, Connell argues that sport socializes boys into violent and aggressive behavioural codes, establishes male hierarchies, and constructs female cheer-leaders as mainly unobtainable objects of desire. Other contact sports in Canada, South Africa, Australia and the UK 'play a similar cultural role' in constructing equivalent gender patterns (Connell 2000: 159). However, this loose cross-cultural claim underplays significantly the major identifiable differences in school sports across regions and nations. For example, UK football rarely features cheer-leaders, and ritually represents community in different ways to US college sport.

Second, in his most detailed empirical study of sport, Connell (1990) examines how a professional tri-athlete (Steve Donoghue) lives 'an exemplary version of hegemonic masculinity'. Steve is young, physically fit, aggressive in competition, actively heterosexual, committed to earning money, and lacking gay friends or feminist inclinations. Through interviews with Steve, Connell depicts the athlete in highly pejorative terms. He chastises Steve's 'impoverished social and cultural life', his 'slightly unstable' self, his 'slightly childish language', his 'bleached, featureless world', and the 'pleasure and complacency' with which he accepts 'the cash and the sex'. Connell does not seem to dialogue with Steve or allow his subject to respond to this characterization. He does not interview Steve's coach or sponsors, but accuses both of manipulation; in Steve's answers to questions, 'the coach's presence is clear' alongside the 'borrowed language' of sport psychology (rather than the 'borrowed language' of Cultural Studies). Overall, rather than deploy ethnography to reveal the subtleties of hegemonic masculinity, Connell resorts to simple *dietrologia*: hidden voices and forces control Steve to the extent that one wonders why Connell bothered to interview the athlete.

While the outcome here is flawed, Connell's 'life-history' method has real potential for explaining masculinity's construction. It requires the researcher to explore how gendered agencies are experienced and constructed in relation to social structures. Unfortunately, the life-history method can degenerate into a kind of self-analysis that confuses authorial masculine *angst* for sociological insight. The otherwise excellent analyses by Messner and Sabo are indicative. For example, Sabo (1994: 161–2) discusses his participation in arm-wrestling contests with Afro-American prison inmates, but slides into a confessional series of liberal-bourgeois clichés. Somewhat absurdly, Sabo claims that each bout 'suspends the hierarchical distinctions between free man and inmate'. In the clench, his 'manly juices start flowing again', although 'I want to learn that it is OK to be vulnerable to defeat'. As Messner and Sabo show elsewhere, critical sociological readings of masculinity can advance without this self-absorption. Sociologists need to find a way between those polarized perspectives on men and sport that incline towards either a fixed identification of hegemonic masculinity or a subjectivist slippage into asocial solipsism.

Masculinities: historical and anthropological perspectives

Historical and anthropological perspectives serve to reveal the cultural pluralities and contradictions of masculine identity. Historical approaches disclose the critical reflexivity of social actors in constructing nationally diverse masculine mores within sport. In different football codes, these various masculinities are often articulated through nostalgic discourses. For example, just after each World War, American football facilitated displays of heroic, tough masculinity that challenged the 'feminizing' of society, while 'anti-modern' mythologies constructed old 'giant' players as larger than life, inherently tough, and less technically accomplished than their modern peers (Oriard 2001: 332). South African rugby is imbued with a traditional, conformist culture, facilitating white father–son bonding and typically excluding women (Grundlingh 1994: 197–200). In white New Zealand, rugby was originally a social and pedagogical bulwark against 'effeminacy' among white colonists, while contemporary discourses play nostalgically on the idyll of a unified nation, embodied by tough rugby-playing farmers and workers (Phillips 1994).

Anthropology facilitates understanding of how popular cultural rituals connect to nationality and masculinity. In southern Europe, where traditional masculine values relate to machismo, courage, honour and shame, male sexuality must be publicly 'achieved', while female sexuality is deemed to be innate or 'ascribed', thus requiring careful control (Marvin 1994: 143–4). The British anthropologist Pitt-Rivers (1984) interpreted the Andalucian *corrida* (bullfight) as a gendered allegory: the *torero* (bullfighter) enters as a feminine figure, but his masculinity is retrieved by defeating and killing the bull, to acquire its procreative powers. Without advocating a culturally and historically closed reading (MacClancy 1993), women's participation as *toreros* would require the *corrida*'s symbolic reinvention.[7]

Thus, anthropology helps to disclose the complex and diverse ways in which gender mores are reshaped by modernity, resulting in different forms of masculine identity. In revolutionary Cuba, Castro's government engaged sport to produce a 'new man' personifying the socialist virtues of 'modesty, brotherhood, internationalism and a cooperative spirit' (Pye 1986: 122). In Mexico, the 'traditional' Latino 'macho' culture displays many forms of behaviour (such as public displays of warmth and affection, and indulgence of children) which are otherwise associated with 'femininity' in North America. Moreover, contemporary machismo must accommodate a domesticated masculinity due to structural changes within labour markets and education (Klein 2000a: 70, 83–4). However, institutional and structural forces do not simply determine specific cultural forms of masculine identity; rather, these forces are negotiated in social actors' gender identity. For example, in Chile during the 1930s and 1940s, working-class males were associated with weak family responsibility, rowdy behaviour, heavy drinking and strong subcultures. Different social forces sought to forge a new kind of masculinity, partly through sport. The State envisioned a fitter, more orderly male identity to suit nation-building purposes. Employers sought reliable, fit workers to reduce absenteeism. The political Left favoured sport to advance class solidarity and political education. Yet Chilean males actively controlled the behavioural influence of these institutional forces: typically, after playing football matches or attending union meetings, the men went drinking (Rosemblatt 2000).

Eduardo Archetti (1998, 1999) has skilfully explored the complex anthropology of sport's masculinity–nationality relationships. Archetti (1999: 216) argues that the 'idealized masculinity' of elite athletes 'is not just about men, it is a part of a cultural system for producing differences'. He compares, for example, the popular representations of the skiers Vegard Ulvang and Alberto Tomba at the 1992 Albertville Winter Olympics. Ulvang was depicted as 'very Norwegian', undemonstrative, serene and close to nature, whereas 'Tomba La Bomba' became the boastful urban playboy, expressively Italian (loving pasta), and inspiring a new, football-type skiing fan.

More expansively, Archetti (1998) examines how different idioms of Argentinian masculinity are articulated relationally within physical culture. He compares football (involving man–man relations), tango (man–woman relations) and polo (man–animal relations). In exploring the competing, hybrid masculinities in Argentina, he rejects 'ideal typical' notions of masculinity and assumptions that singular gender identities dominate specific settings. The dominant playing style in 'gaucho' polo is 'manly' and risk taking, in contrast to more conservative, English styles (1998: 96, 104–5). In tango songs, alongside the dance's vivid eroticism, gender relations move outside bourgeois domains, reflecting the uncertainties and dilemmas of Argentina's inter-war period; a 'doubting masculinity' in relations with 'powerful women' is revealed (1998: 155–7). In football, the *criollo* Argentinian playing style promotes individual expression, creativity and technical skill – thereby inverting the modern European values of will-power, organization and courage (1998: 70–2). According to male Argentinian folklore, the *criollo* style is embodied not in the physically large, mature male hero, but in the boy (*pibe*) who possesses a small body, high skill levels, a character filled with cunning, creativity and vulnerability, and a disorderly, risk-taking life-style (1998: 182–4). Diego Maradona is the *pibe par excellence*.

Maradona has some cultural meanings that are uniquely Argentinian, but he is viewed by millions of fans *world-wide* as the greatest-ever football player. His dominant, masculine identity, as a great player, centres on his peerless technical skill and artistry. This popular aesthetic meaning of Maradona stands in strong contrast to sport sociologists' emphasis on the hegemony of violent, aggressive masculinity. This latter emphasis becomes even more misplaced when we survey the most lionized males in different sports histories. The greatest heroes are not the violent 'goons' (in ice hockey) or the destructive 'hammer-throwers' (in football). They are the 'artists' who (like Maradona) are often small and seemingly vulnerable in stature. In football, Maradona is joined by other technical talents like Zico (Brazil), Baggio (Italy), Platini (France) and Best (Northern Ireland). In rugby union, great half-backs like Cliff Morgan, Barry John, Phil Bennett and Jonathan Davies (all Wales) excited the crowds. In ice hockey, Wayne Gretsky is 'the great one'; and in American football, favoured talents will always feature spectacular quarter-backs (like Marino, Montana and Namath) over thunderous scrimmage players. Through sporting dramas, these brilliant players outwit and deceive tougher opponents; physical power and aggression are disarmed, becoming handicaps rather than pre-conditions of successful masculinity in play. Analysis of these popular, gendered aesthetics inside sport helps us to extend beyond the exaggerated emphasis on aggression and violence in masculinity. Such analysis helps us to consider the cultural complexity and aesthetic richness of popular masculine mores inside sport.[8]

Concluding comments: towards the critical reinvention of gender in sport

While modern sporting practices have been significant tools in the systematic reproduction of gender domination, sport is not a cultural zone of functional patriarchal closure. Both men and women critically interpret conventional gender roles and norms, to establish fresh gender identities and diverse aesthetic codes within sport.

Elite groups have sought historically to construct sports cultures in accordance with conjunctural patriarchal and capitalist mores. Women's exclusion from sport has given way to their inclusion as consumers, notably in enhancing their attractiveness before the male gaze. Yet, as a leading authority observes, we should not 'reduce the complexity of history to a monotonously doleful tale of man's oppression of women' (Guttmann 1991: 105). Moreover, there is no single 'shared experience' of women regarding gender roles and identities (Jennifer Hargreaves 1994: 288–9). Female sports contain diverse politico-cultural dimensions: some are regressive, some negotiate class and gender hierarchies, and some are significantly more radical. Bourgeois women's historical role in policing the physical cultures of lower-class women is indicative of the intra-gender contradictions that typically arise under capitalism.

Sexuality in sport generates one sociological space for recognizing the cultural politics of sporting practices. Certainly, the 'making of men' through games was intended, in part, to dissolve auto- and homo-erotic impulses within confined institutional settings. Women's exclusion from strenuous or combative sports represents one cultural extension of men's broader policing of female sexuality. Sport's competitive ethos emphasizes that men in play should 'not be gay', as one of Connell's (1990: 94) respondents put it. Sporting females are always liable to receive lesbian-baiting labels, particularly if they play competitively, show musculature, and engage primarily in high-contact games. Nevertheless, gay men and lesbians have deployed various formal and informal techniques to sustain their sports participation, to realize alternative interpretations of sports disciplines, and to challenge dominant gender codes. The Gay Games are one illustration; so too the growing presence of 'gay and lesbian studies' within sport studies and further education in general.

The poverty of reductive, gendered readings of sport is highlighted when assessing the position of males. Connell's notion of hegemonic masculinity can, if used flexibly, capture the contradictions and pluralities of masculinities within sport. Aesthetically, different masculine identities are favoured, most notably among 'artists' who transgress the dominant male mores by displaying grace and skill rather than toughness and power. Overall, I favour a critical, empirically informed cultural perspective that pursues justice within sport. Egalitarian policy measures, such as Title IX, have not gone far enough in realizing equality, never mind equity. Our first task is to formulate a balanced historical, anthropological and sociological understanding of how social actors construct different gender roles within sport. The structural reform of sport, favouring co-operative strategies, would enhance gender equity, enabling disadvantaged communities to realize their human potentials within play. This necessitates clear acknowledgement of the interconnections between gender and class, focusing particularly on structural measures that systematically exclude women with working-class and/or ethnic minority backgrounds. It also requires challenging the cultural centrality of achievement sport. Less focus should be accorded to sports that reproduce male power by their prioritization of upper-body physiological strength over restricted temporal and spatial durations. Once the forces of domination are fully exposed, we might manufacture a cultural context that substitutes inclusion for achievement, and allows for marginalized groups, particularly women, to experience greater bodily transcendence within sport.

7

The Body: Discipline, Conduct and the Pleasures of Sport

Since the mid-1980s, 'the body' has become a major domain for sociological inquiry. French social theorist Michel Foucault was crucial in diverting sociologists to matters corporeal. Global heavyweights like Bourdieu and Elias, and renowned sociologists like Featherstone, Hepworth and Turner, have written substantially on the subject. In consequence, sociologists have helped to deconstruct many taken-for-granted body assumptions. Thus, embodiment is conceived sociologically in terms of practices and meanings in relation to specific configurations of power.

Here, sport is theorized as a sociological domain *par excellence* for examining human embodiment; indeed, the body is sport's *sine qua non*. The discussion is divided into four main parts. First, I explore Foucault's seminal contribution to the sociology of the body, and assess his sporting relevance. Second, I address bodily 'risk' within sport with reference to violence, pain and injury. Third, I examine the construction of bodily pleasures with reference to social psychology and the sociology of consumerism. Fourth, I advocate a dialogical understanding of the body, with particular reference to Eichberg.

Foucault, discipline, conduct

Analysing the body

Foucault placed the body at the heart of his later, 'genealogical' theoretical framework. Following Nietzsche, Foucault posited that power and knowledge are not mutually exclusive, but interdependent; thus, we should chart the emergence and diffusion of new systems of thinking alongside struggles for power. The body is the crucial locus for those modern 'political technologies of power' that examine, regulate and control citizens (Dreyfus and Rabinow 1983: 114).

Foucault's analyses emphasize the fundamental shifts between 'epistemes' – that is, systems of knowledge and representation that define historical epochs. Modernity involved the transfer of power from old sovereigns (royalty, the Church) to new institutions (the State, bourgeois professionals), resulting in new political meanings and uses for the body. Modern professionals, especially physicians, 'gaze' upon the body as object and explain its pathologies through scientific 'discourse'. The 'bio-power' of modern experts produces docile, disciplined bodies; in prisons, for example, inmates undergo daily regimens of exercise, labour, feeding and rest (Foucault 1977). Disciplinary regimes construct a 'carceral archipelago' across entire populations; people become embodied objects to be known, administered, 'normalized' and governed by state institutions like the police and welfare services.[1] In turn, populations examine themselves routinely. Each individual becomes 'his own overseer', producing social order with maximum efficiency at minimal cost (Foucault 1980: 155).

While docile bodies (objects) are moulded among the lower classes, making modern confessional bodies (subjects) helps to pattern bourgeois conduct. Confessional bodies reveal their 'innermost selves' (for example, in sexual identity), employing particular 'technologies of the self' (like self-help magazines) to assist their self-analysis and quest for self-improvement. Senses of liberation may be experienced, but professional experts still play crucial guiding (or governing) roles. The concept of governmentality, adumbrated by Foucault in his final years, has been utilized increasingly by social scientists to uncloak this 'conducting of conduct'. Governmentality captures power as operating 'at a distance', through active (not docile) bodies (Rose 1999: 3–5; 1996: 43). Foucault wrote little on how commercial (rather than state) agencies governed conduct, but his ideas beckon a particularly cultural application to include consumption within leisure, life-styles and sport. Self-help manuals, diet plans, celebrity chef cookbooks and general leisure magazines are all life-style pedagogies that conduct our conduct within consumerist milieux.

Governmentality enhances Foucault's claim that power is not simply a negative force; rather, 'power produces; it produces reality; it produces domains of objects and rituals of truth. The individual and the knowledge that may be gained of him belong to this production' (1977: 194). More vaguely, Foucault argued that power is everywhere, not simply in institutions. Resistance to discipline or government always arises, often locally, for example, when old and new systems of knowledge clash, or when particular bodies and selves refuse to be disciplined or enter self-analysis (Foucault 1983: 208).

Notable conceptual continuities arise between Foucault and other sociologists. Although his post-structuralist theorizing builds upon Durkheim, Foucault's pessimistic reading of knowledge and rationalization is closest to Weber and Adorno. Corporeal discipline aids industrial capitalism, although (reversing Marxist positions) Foucault prioritizes the former over the latter. As we shall see, Elias's 'civilizing process' traces the modern cultivation of manners through body etiquette and emotional management, while Foucault's relational critique of power's exercise is more incisive. Bourdieu (see chapter 10) advances a more orthodox sociological argument connecting body cultures to social stratification. For Bourdieu, through sport and other cultural practices, dominant groups construct the 'legitimate body' in contradistinction to the bodies and practices of the lower social orders. Thus, until the late 1980s, winter sports and pastimes in North America focused on the embodied discipline of skiing; new pastimes like snowboarding were often banned from ski slopes because their techniques deviated from bourgeois visions of the 'legitimate body' (Humphreys 1996: 7–8).

Foucauldian sport

The Foucauldian imaginary invites sociological application to sport *disciplines*. As Bourdieu (1990a: 167) explains in Foucauldian terms, the 'secular ascesis' of modern sports training obtains from the body 'an adhesion that the mind might refuse'. Modern coaches *qua* accredited experts reduce player actions to routinized tasks, to be practised until the body repeats these manoeuvres intuitively. Sports pedagogy classifies and distributes bodies according to biomedical discourses that link physical characteristics to sporting aptitudes – for example, racist and sexist assumptions debar young girls from contact sports and black children from water sports. Body-size homogeneity becomes more likely in sport; coaches and medical staff may exclude expressive and diverse bodies, in favour of disciplined and strong bodies connoting dependability. Professional athletes are segregated into the 'carceral archipelago' of the modern sports club: exercise, diet and rest are rigidly controlled, and each individual is examined by medical specialists for physical flaws and 'character defects'. Meanwhile,

sporting populations are administered and governed through om-
nipresent sports bureaucracies and ruling bodies.

Foucault's concept of the episteme illuminates historical shifts
within movement cultures, notably between pre-modern (folk) and
modern sporting forms. Pre-modern festivals or carnivals were popu-
lated by 'dialogical' and 'excessive' bodies, diverse in shape and size,
given to intoxication, nakedness and self-decontrol (Bakhtin 1984).
Modern sports, as we have seen, cultivate disciplined bodies among
athletes, spectators and officials. However, Foucault grossly exaggerates the sudden, complete switch from one episteme to another,
thus underplaying the survival of (what Williams terms) 'archaic' or
'residual' cultural practices. Eichberg's 'trialectical differentiation of
body cultures' helps to illuminate this point. Eichberg argues that
three kinds of physical culture produce three separate kinds of corporeal understanding. First, the *streamlined body* is sculpted through
result production in 'achievement sport', such as the Olympics. Second, the *straight, healthy body* is shaped by socially hygienic fitness
regimes of 'disciplination', such as in gymnastics. Third, the *grotesque
body* communicates dialogically as an element of 'popular movement
culture' and features dance and laughter; pre-modern folk games like
the three-legged race are illustrative, as is traditional wrestling (Barthes
1972). Categorical differences between these body cultures are highlighted through their different understandings of 'stumbling'. The first
two categories are solemnly modern, hence stumbling is anathema to
appropriate corporeal comportment. The third, pre-modern category
embraces stumbling as part of the game and as a source of laughter,
such as in sack races or the tug-of-war. In recognizing the continuation of folk body cultures like the Breton games, Eichberg implies
that we should reject Foucault's indications regarding the absolutism
of modern sport. A significant (if suppressed) residual folk impulse inhabits all sports, surfacing when streamlined or disciplined bodies are
suddenly, incongruously, made to stumble or appear clumsy, generating audience amusement. It surfaces too among spectators at modern
sports festivals, when different bodies from various regions, nations
or continents intermingle.

Foucault's epistemic thinking is best restricted to explaining the
dominant cultural logic within particular historical epochs. Modern
sport's dominant cultural logic blends discipline and government, as
illustrated by gender issues. Early modern sports enabled physicians
and educationalists to objectify and control bodies according to sex.
Sport carried militarized meanings for men, whereas female physiology was considered unfit for vigorous exercise. Since the 1960s,

greater governmentality conducts male and female conduct in sport. Women's aerobics put to work the 'confessional self' (e.g. fitness as a personalized desire) with the aid of various 'technologies of the self' (e.g. personal work-out videos, health plans), thereby reproducing the jurisdiction of professionals (e.g. medical judges, fitness judges) through the language of personal liberation ('Look good, feel good!'). However, most sports pedagogy now moves discursively between stricture and freedom, discipline and government; the hierarchical power/knowledge relations between coach and athlete remain (Johns and Johns 2000: 231–2).

Foucauldian arguments illuminate the mass media's role in constructing corporeal government within sport through the logic of voyeurism. Sport's media voyeurism operates in vision, through the 'gaze' of televised sports, and in sound, through the confessional logic of sports interviews. Modern films build narratives by having audiences adopt 'voyeur' positions – for example, to witness 'secret' events that expose hidden selves (Denzin 1995). Televised sport employs this voyeuristic positioning in capturing and replaying, in intensive detail, moments of emotional intensity: the athlete celebrating victory, the pain of an injured athlete, the physical confrontations between competitors, and (most invasively) spectator grief when the contest is lost. In interviews, individual athletes are asked, not to explain their sports techniques, but to confess inner feelings. The new tennis champion is asked not, 'Why did your backhand return of serve improve?' but 'How do you *feel*?' or 'What does this victory mean for you as a person?' A burgeoning genre of confessional sports writing by players or fans has emerged to feed the tutored voyeurism of sports audiences; Fred Exley's *A Fan's Notes* and Nick Hornby's *Fever Pitch* are paradigmatic.

Not all sport populations are disciplined or have their conduct effectively governed. In the UK, successive legislation has sought to pacify spectators (notably football fans) through prohibiting 'hooligans' or certain actions (such as on-field supporter protests or, more nebulously, behaviour that 'alarms' fellow fans). Sports and public authorities have sought to conduct the conduct of supporters *qua* active subjects. For example, sports authorities seek to stage-manage 'carnival' atmospheres through hiring musical bands or playing music over public address systems; or advertisers present images of 'true fans' consuming products while having scripted fun. Yet, some bodies refuse to sit, but move around or stand during contests, and others consciously produce their own patterns of conduct that transgress new behavioural codes.

Among non-white or 'disabled' peoples, the body becomes a site of sporting struggle. In African societies like Kenya, pre-colonial movement cultures were 'exterminated' after colonization and then exotically 'museumized' to suit the 'gaze' of Western tourists (Bale and Sang 1996: 169–70). However, colonial sports still constituted a somatic space for constructing opposing selves and alternative patterns of conduct. Bodies that transgress discipline and government can acquire critical meanings for other oppressed peoples. For example, when assessing the cricket style of the West Indian Gary Sobers, C. L. R. James stated that his 'command of the rising ball in the drive, his close fielding and his hurling himself into his fast bowling are a living embodiment of centuries of a tortured history' (quoted by Stoddart 1989: 144).

Modern sports have provided one key cultural domain for distinguishing the able-bodied (participants) from the disabled (excluded). Early organized sport for disabled people was heavily influenced by medical discourses that favoured exercise to 'rehabilitate' the newly disabled (like those suffering from spinal injuries as a result of military conflict). Separate competitions for all disabled people grew internationally, enabling the Paralympic Games to open in 1960 and in every Olympic year since, under direction of the International Paralympic Committee (IPC). The Special Olympics for mentally retarded people now provide a world-wide, year-long programme of sporting events. The para- prefix in Paralympics is now interpreted as meaning 'parallel', asserting through nomenclature the different-but-equal politico-medical classification of populations now defined as 'physically challenged'.[2] Thus, the administrative segregation of disabled athletes is contested. The 2002 Commonwealth Games was the first major tournament to interweave disabled and able-bodied competitions. In turn, sport for disabled athletes has become more rationalized and achievement-orientated. Some Paralympians are overstating disabilities, removing body parts or using illegal stimulants (eleven doping cases arose at the 2000 Sydney games) to enhance competitiveness (Baudrillard 1998: 48). Classificatory logic now reverts to excluding the able-bodied: for example, Adam Sadler, a British wheelchair racer was banned by the IPC in April 2002 when his full mobility was revealed.

From this, it should be apparent that I consider Foucault's theories of discipline, governmentality, carceral archipelago and confessional selves to be extremely useful and applicable to the sociology of the sporting body. Foucault's 'epistemes' over-emphasize the radical historical ruptures that exist between pre-modern and modern cultural forms, including sport. As Eichberg indicates, we may identify

important residual elements of pre-modern folk culture in sport's contemporary, dialogical body cultures. In the following, I examine the
relationship of sporting discipline to the objectification of the body;
to violence, pain and bodily risk; and to the production of corporeal
pleasures in part through consumer culture.

Bodily discipline in sport: fascism, fighting and corporeal risk

Corporeal objectification: fascism

Before Foucault, critical analysis of the body in sport focused especially on anti-intellectualist, Fascistic impulses. Segel (1999) argues
that sport's cultural rise reflected modernity's broader turn towards
physical expression, thereby germinating militarism, war and Fascist
ideology. Nazi physical culture had three core elements: the ethos of
racial supremacy, the health of the people (*Volk*), and the body's military education. German men exercised 'steel-hard muscles and firm
flesh' to embody heroic Aryanism and defend the *Volk* in the perpetual
racial struggle (Hoberman 1984: 162–5). Pessimistic Frankfurt School
Marxists understood sport as a 'complex of pathological attitudes and
instincts' that simply sustained the Nazi body cult (Hoberman 1984:
244, 245). Despite the defeat of Nazism, Tännsjö (2000) argues that
adulation of sporting strength retains 'fascistoid' elements. Sport in-
duces mocking of the weak that can legitimize their extermination.

Corporeal objectification can substitute athlete individuality for the
'national interest'. Olympic sport pivots on the national (not personal)
identity of each athlete, as defined by kit colour and allocated number;
opening ceremonies are no more than orchestras of mass regimenta-
tion before a global audience's critical gaze. However, I would suggest
that such depersonalization is not Fascistic *per se*, but rooted in the
underlying interconnections of capitalism and rationalization.

Violent bodies: boxing and cultures of quasi-violence

Boxing, rather than fascism, provides a more fruitful domain for examining sport's corporeal objectification. Loïc Wacquant has produced several outstanding ethnographies of American pugilism that
utilize Foucault and especially Bourdieu. The objectification of boxers
arises in part through transforming their 'bodily capital' into 'pugilistic capital' to win fights, titles, status and wealth (Wacquant 1995b:
66–7). Their corporeal exploitation by managers is captured by boxers

through three self-descriptions (Wacquant 2001). As *whores*, boxers sell their bodies to profit the pimp/manager. As *slaves*, boxers are pushed to extreme violence, or wrapped in contractual bondage, by promoters.[3] As *stallions*, boxers are fed, housed, cleaned, exercised and farmed out to fight at the manager's or trainer's pleasure; their 'bones are picked clean' when profits are scented. Pugilists acknowledge their professional routine of corporeal damage, leaving 'bits and pieces of their body in the ring', constantly fearing the brain-scrambling or face-destroying potential of a single punch (Wacquant 1995a: 522).

Yet boxers retain self-integrity through alternative, if ambivalent, systems of corporeal self-knowledge. They deny that they will join the ranks of damaged fellow pugilists (Wacquant 2001). Climbing through the ropes, rolling punches, engaging opponents in intense combat, and embracing rivals at the end are experiences often described in highly excited terms by pugilists. Risk taking is understood as empowering, particularly given boxers' exploitation in all walks of life. Pain, injury and corporeal deterioration are intrinsic to boxing, yet fighters 'construct a heroic, transcendent self' within the 'skilled body craft' of their 'sweet science'.[4]

All other contact sports carry violent playing strategies and techniques. Injuries are inevitable, since 'The body as weapon ultimately results in violence against one's own body' (Messner 1992: 71). Sportive violence is not inherently individual, but a product of socialization. For Finn (1994a: 102–5), football players and supporters are socialized into a 'culture of quasi-violence' that stresses *different* values from those of everyday life. This culture 'accepts aggression and violence as central to the game but accompanies this acceptance with all manner of inconsistencies, uncertainties, qualifications and disagreements'. The culture of quasi-violence highlights the 'ambiguous and ambivalent' condition of sport's moral code, sparking irresolvable debates over the legitimacy of injurious acts during play: are specific actions that give rise to injury possibly illegal but tolerable to players, or categorically unacceptable (Finn 1994a: 103)? These vagaries, I would add, frequently allow violent athletes to evade legal proceedings.

Public and political pressures can persuade sporting disciplines to 'stamp out' (note the violent vernacular!) dangerous play. Rule changes can soften (rather than eradicate) cultures of quasi-violence. For example, in American football during the late nineteenth century, the highly effective 'flying wedge' playing formation, devised by a military strategist, was responsible for routine serious injuries and several deaths. Although its masculinizing effects were advocated,[5] the wedge was banned, yet coaches exploited rule loopholes to create similar strategies. Injuries abated only when a rules committee legalized the forward pass, prompting a radical shift in strategy and playing techniques that assuaged rather than eradicated the sport's injurious culture (McQuilkin and Smith 1993). Serious, debilitating injuries in American football remain common, and are rationalized through quasi-violent masculine discourses. For such cultures to be challenged more fully, the *moral* components within sport need critical reinvention (Morgan 2004).

Risk and bodily injury

We can conceptualize athletes' physical injuries and harm through Beck's (1992) theory of the 'risk society'. Beck's risk society is characterized by 'reflexive modernization' whereby social agents are increasingly knowledgeable, critical and participant in shaping social structures. Unlike the routine and seemingly unavoidable dangers of traditional society, modern society has produced 'risks' that agents reflexively identify, measure and minimize. Beck's arguments on modern technological risks, like radioactive pollution, do not transfer easily to sport, unless we consider the ecological devastation caused by cultivating sporting landscapes like golf courses. Risk's cultural, political and social aspects are highly relevant. Different 'risk positions' produce winners and losers, but a 'boomerang effect' strikes those who profit initially. Thus, risk society possesses different social cleavages from the class and nation divisions of modern capitalism. Contemporary political participation depends on risk knowledge, procures new public issues, and transforms political authority.

Beck's theory invites application to body risks in sport. In the UK, for example, all participants face the annual risk of joining the close to one million people who suffer sporting injury (*The Times*, 24 May 2000). 'Reflexive modernization' in sport involves isolating, minimizing or removing the causes of physical injury and pain, while retaining sport's integral techniques and strategies. Risk knowledge, particularly via scientific research, informs debate. For example, if neurological tests demonstrate that serious brain injuries result from heading balls, football's rules, playing techniques and equipment face juridico-political scrutiny. However, *pace* Beck, I do not agree that the 'risk society' transforms social stratification. In American sport, for example, suburban middle classes positively risk-assess football against more injurious sports like American football, while the lower classes still endure the riskiest sports like boxing. Beck's boomerang effect works only partially in sport. For example, boxing promoters are mildly 'hurt' by occasional bad publicity, and coaches often emerge from a painful period in the ring, but the greatest risks are always those taken by pugilists themselves.

Despite growing reflexivity regarding health questions, athletes are still coached to ignore the risk-signs of pain that signify physical break-down. Breaking 'pain barriers' has long been presented as 'manly' or the mark of 'true competitors'; 'hurting' during play confers social distinction. The athlete's capacity to ignore acute discomfort, to make the body 'invisible', is integral to sports professionalism (Howe 2001). Discussions within many athlete subcultures can serve to render mundane the risk of injury; ignoring this everyday hazard becomes a means for claiming subcultural membership (Albert 1999).

Risk awareness concerning the physical exertions of children has an ancient history. Aristotle (1981: 460) observed that 'it is rare to find the same people successful in the Olympic games both as boys and as men: their severe gymnastic training as boys has caused them to lose their strength'. Today, national labour laws and criminal codes, and international treaties such as UNICEF's Convention on the Rights of the Child (which only the United States and Somalia have not ratified), establish protective standards for children. Yet sports like gymnastics continue to engender acute pain and chronic injury among children, particularly girls (Ryan 1996: 11).[6] Legal, political, pedagogic and aesthetic measures would reduce children's bodily risks within sport. Full sports implementation of child labour regulations would criminalize coaching infringements. Sport's governing bodies contribute significantly to children's charities, but children require stronger formal representation inside sport. Coaching of children and adults within sport should substitute the 'culture of instruction' for a more dialogical relationship, enabling performers to discuss freely their physical conditioning with coaches. Finally, the reform of playing rules, corporeal techniques and aesthetic codes should minimize physical risks. For example, in judging gymnastic performances, reducing the scoring significance of the dismount (a particularly dangerous routine) would reduce injuries (Ryan 1996: 42–3).

Body risks: medical science and sport

Risk theory helps to disclose public reflexivity regarding chemical hazards. Here, I consider three risky chemical interventions faced by the modern athlete: legal medication to maintain performance, drug-taking occupational subcultures among sports people, and the illicit 'doping' of athletes.

Bodily risks concerning medical malpractice are most obvious in high-contact sport like American football. Around half of NFL players require club-prescribed pain-killers or anti-inflammatory drugs each season (*Sports Illustrated*, 27 May 1996). Club medics are pressurized to patch up injured athletes, rather than allow proper healing, thereby increasing risks of long-term damage. The players' occupational subculture also promotes the pained body's disappearance, with pain-killers freely used to continue participation, sometimes with extreme consequences. The injury-ravaged 1995 NFL MVP, Brett Favre of the Green Bay Packers, became addicted to pain-killers, resulting in a physical seizure and his entry into the NFL's substance abuse programme.

Injured athletes are afforded little institutional support. The NFL's mandatory stipulations regarding payment of injured players are short-term and ignore medical or coaching malpractice.[7] The NFL's Players' Association annually handles 30–35 player grievances against clubs. Several famous cases have arisen from the practice of injecting athlete limbs and joints with cortisone and other crippling drugs.[8] However, professional risks dissuade most players from pursuing cases: court defeat may occur, particularly through lack of club medical documentation, while NFL clubs effectively blacklist recalcitrant employees. Completed lawsuits are often settled outside court once the club's legal liability has been exposed. Clubs can reduce liability by contracting players' medical care through local health institutions.

The occupational subculture of elite athletes can contain significant off-field biological risks connected to life-style. HIV infection is more apparent in the developing world; in southern Africa, infection exceeds one in three among young adults, hence many athletes have died before their careers would otherwise finish. Magic Johnson's retirement in 1992 signalled the potential for HIV infection to threaten North American athletes' safety, but safe sex practices and anti-viral drugs have controlled AIDS levels among his peers.

In northern Europe and the old British colonies, drinking is pivotal to sport's popular culture, from post-match beers at local rugby clubs to sponsorship packages from the world's biggest drinks corporations. Alcoholism has blighted the lives of some great post-war UK footballers, like George Best, Jim Baxter, Jimmy Greaves and Paul Gascoigne. In North America, illicit drug use dominates some athlete communities. Around 70 per cent of NBA players were cocaine-users in the early 1980s, and in 1986 four of the top seven draft picks lost their careers (and in Len Bias's case, his life) to the drug. Positive cocaine tests and criminal indictments of players like the NFL's Lawrence Taylor and David Boston, and the late Darrell Porter and Darryl Strawberry in baseball, confirm that other American sports are affected. High percentages of black users reflect the increasingly depressed condition of black American youth (Guttmann 1988). Yet the global dimensions of illicit drug use are reflected by international football's list of known users, including Diego Maradona, the prospective coach of Germany, Christoph Daum, and England's Paul Merson.

Sport authorities have poor, if improving, rehabilitation records. At its peak during the 1980s, American athletes' cocaine culture was ignored to protect media contracts, attendance figures and endorsement deals. Player associations have since helped to prevent demonization of users by connecting drug sampling to confidentiality and rehabilitation. Test-failing players must enter rehabilitation programmes to resume playing. In other international sports, players failing recreational drug tests are treated inconsistently and often harshly.

Sport authorities have focused primarily on athletes' use of illegal, performance-enhancing substances.[9] The risks are serious and potentially fatal. For example, in female gymnastics, drugs administered to delay puberty can damage reproductive organs. Among bodybuilders, anabolic steroids can cause vital organs to collapse. More generally, steroids can produce infertility and aggressive behaviour; among women, they promote facial hair, deepened voice, liver damage and an enlarged clitoris (Klein 1993: 183).

Athletes have always used stimulants. Ancient Olympians consumed herbal confections to enhance competitiveness. In modern sport, many athletes (notably the 1904 Olympic marathon champion, Thomas Hicks) have taken stimulants like strychnine and amphetamines. In 1967, the British cyclist Tommy Simpson collapsed and died during the Tour de France after taking amphetamines. A year later the IOC established a list of proscribed substances and athlete testing. From the late 1980s onwards, rigorous testing has exposed many doping offences.[10] Athletics and cycling have attracted particular scrutiny. At the 1998 Tour de France, police raids netted large hauls of illegal substances and drug-taking paraphernalia, resulting in three cycling teams' competitive expulsion. A year later, the Olympic movement established WADA (World Anti-Doping Agency) to police international sport.

All sport systems are implicated in doping. While Eastern Europe was extraordinarily successful in identifying and nurturing sport prodigies, numerous athletes and coaches from former Communist nations have been exposed for doping, or have attacked the old national sports policies of institutionalized drug taking. In July 2000, two leading East German sport officials were convicted of causing bodily harm to young athletes through enforced doping. Yet Western sport systems are not innocent, and have even recruited successful but guilty coaches and athletes. Fifteen years later, it was revealed that 19 American athletes (including Carl Lewis) had won medals at the 1988 Olympics only months after failing drug tests.

Anti-doping policies struggle to combat five particular sport problems:

1 *testing procedures*: athletes employ 'masking agents' or break doping schedules to pass tests.
2 *establishing* mens rea: numerous athletes attribute positive tests to poor sampling, innocent medication (like nasal decongestants), or sabotage. Athlete legal proceedings against doping bans can financially ruin a sport's governing body, as the British Athletics Federation discovered in the mid-1990s.
3 *regulation differences*: sports governing bodies often disagree over the substances to ban, or the penalties to be imposed on offenders. In North America, basketball and American football prohibit and test for steroid use; until recently, baseball did neither. Inconsistencies undermine the credibility of sports performances and anti-doping initiatives.
4 *commercial imperatives*: doping enhances athlete performances, thereby increasing sport revenues. For example, after the 1994 player strike, American baseball regained public and corporate appeal through spectacular batting performances; several leading players attributed these feats to drug taking.
5 *political challenge*: some sports personalities advance pro-doping arguments. For example, Ron Clarke, a former top middle-distance runner, argues that doping can reduce advantages held by athletes from high-altitude nations.

To conclude, the risks of violence, pain and injury, and physiological damage through drugs and doping, all highlight the continuing importance of bodily objectification within sport. Through a Foucauldian optic, we can see that sport pedagogy and science discipline athletes into taking acute bodily risks, most obviously the weakest groups such as child gymnasts and lower-working-class boxers. Both cultures of quasi-violence and discourses regarding pain management can be seen as modes of governmentality that conduct conduct within sport.

Both enable sports participants to negotiate, suppress or even celebrate injury, violence and pain, according to context. Beck's 'risk society' thesis illuminates our greater reflexivity regarding sport's body risks, reflected in part by more dope testing and substance rehabilitation programmes. However, the power to act reflexively remains heavily tied to long-standing frameworks of institutional and social domination. Thus, a lower-working-class, male identity ensures that boxers interpret their highly dangerous sport as an extension of their risky urban milieu. Similarly, sports authorities prioritize doping offences rather than overall athlete health, thereby reflecting greater concern with institutional (not human) profitability.

Future debates regarding corporeal manipulation in sport will focus on genetic engineering and prosthetics. Both scientific procedures confirm the hegemony of expert systems via the body's initial objectification, yet their practice is subject to increasing public reflexivity on risk. As body modification has become intrinsic to consumer culture, so the rise of sport prosthetics may ensure that the cyborg athlete is not simply an invention of science fiction.

The pleasures of sport: flow, the self and consumer culture

We have noted Foucault's later interest in corporeal pleasure, primarily in late modern confessional discourses regarding sex. I elaborate that discussion by exploring sporting pleasures from two perspectives: the social-psychological aspects of corporeal arousal and the interdependencies of corporeal pleasure, the self and modern consumer culture.

Social psychology

For sport psychologists, the term 'intrinsic motivation' registers the personal gratification and pleasures that sport can provide. Apter's (1982) 'reversal theory' postulates two basic social-psychological states for individual arousal. 'Telic' individuals pursue rational goals, so high arousal is stressful but not enjoyable; conversely, 'paratelic' individuals are playful, fun seeking and enjoy high arousal. Intense sports arousal can engender 'peak experiences' that are marked by the athlete's detachment from consciousness (as a kind of disembodiment), ecstasy and euphoria, temporal confusion, increased energy and physical power, and sense of environmental unity (McInman and Grove 1991; Lyng 1990: 882). Csikszentmihalyi (1975; Csikszentmihalyi and Csikszentmihalyi 1988) uses the term 'flow' to describe such psychological states. Flow experiences are maximized when skills and challenges are both high. Skill/challenge imbalances precipitate other cognitive responses: if the individual's skills far exceed the challenge, boredom results; if the challenge is too high, anxiety results; if skill and challenge are both low, apathy results.

Phenomenological approaches are particularly germane for assessing intense corporeal experiences as lived, embodied practices, rather than in Cartesian terms that separate the mind and body analytically. Husserl's phenomenology, for example, has continuities with the hermeneutic and interpretivist traditions in promoting the researchers' attempts to bring out the lived experiences, and the meaning of these experiences, for the individual actor (Kerry and Armour 2000). Often, the 'practical consciousness' of immersion in sport exceeds athletes' explanatory capabilities; hence athletes commonly resort to comparisons with other forms of intense experience (such as drug intoxication, or sexual arousal) to describe their sporting flows.

Social-psychological and phenomenological accounts can neglect the structural and cultural factors that intensify experiences. Corporeal pleasures are *socially constructed*: people are educated into recognizing the psychological or emotional effects of the leisure experience, and into understanding those effects as personally pleasurable (see Becker 1953). Moreover, individuals play with psychological barriers and risks to experience flow, but such rules and conventions are *socially constructed* and imposed through social stratification. Consider, for example, the pleasures of transgression enjoyed by young women who play games that breach gender codes, or by beach sport pioneers who revel in bodily display. Finn's (1994a) 'societal psychological' analysis of violence and hooliganism within sport (in his case, football) connects flow experiences to psychological, historical and cultural factors. He explains that some spectator subcultures emerge partly to offset the boredom within sport, to generate new peak experiences.

Extreme sports illuminate the interconnections of psychological, phenomenological and sociological dimensions. Regarding sports like long-distance jogging, the triathlon, mountain trekking, rock-face climbing and parachute surfing, social-psychological perspectives reveal how (paratelic) participants withstand pain, fear and anxiety: 'the more intense the suffering, the more the achievement has a reassuring personal significance, the more fulfilling the satisfaction of having resisted the temptation to give up' (Le Breton 2000: 1). Dancing with death in many extreme sports can produce phenomenological moments of trance-like immersion and self-revelation. As one participant noted, shortly before attempting a fatal, trapeze-like manoeuvre across two gliders: 'I only feel right when I have goose pimples running over my skin. It's a gut need. It's a sort of drug. In fact I have to frighten myself' (Le Breton 2000: 8–9).

Lyng's (1990) study of 'edgework' among sky-divers advanced similar findings. Edgeworking involves the possible crossing of categorical boundaries, and requires 'a general ability to maintain control of a situation that verges on total chaos' (Lyng 1990: 871). More sociologically, edgeworking appears as a partial 'escape attempt': evading the routinized everyday world still depends upon reflexive modernization (Cohen and Taylor 1976). Participants spend more time preparing than playing; checking equipment, the local environment and weather forecast are critical, 'risk assessment' preludes to pursuing the peak experience (Lyng 1990: 874).

The self and consumer culture

More theoretical standpoints – as advanced by Merleau-Ponty, Goffman, Giddens and Bourdieu – provide fuller appraisals of the interrelations between embodiment, self, socialization and practical corporeal techniques. The body is no external 'thing', but intrinsic to composing self-identities and relationships with the outside world. Sport participation enables children particularly to improve motor skills and develop self-understandings as embodied social agents. Body management, control and regulation are pre-conditions of competent social action and effective self-presentation before specific 'audiences'.

Modern sport connects the embodied self to approved forms of self-identity. In the first half of the twentieth century, bodily exercise conjoined religious, imperial, sexual and racial identities. Consumer culture has long aestheticized the fit, tanned, healthy body – ideals endorsed by athletes throughout the world. Acquiring 'the look' involves intensive body maintenance *qua* corporeal asceticism and ceaseless consumption. Constant gym work-outs tone the muscles; slimming and dietary regimes preserve health; health foods, beauty products and cosmetic surgery enhance appearance (Featherstone 1991a: 182–7). Consumer culture also promotes a reading of the 'inner self' through bodily appearance. Thus, life-style products adorning the body become signifiers of the consumer's all-important 'individuality' (Featherstone 1991b: 86). Mass production and consumption confirm how spurious are claims that sports commodities bestow unique personal qualities on individuals.

The body cultures of contemporary sport indicate broader cultural embracing of hedonism over asceticism. 'Californian' sports – like surf-boarding, wind-surfing, hang-gliding and roller-blading – involve less rigorous training than older sports. Even in Japan, where collectivist, self-disciplining values are more entrenched than in the West, the disciplinary regimes of rugby and baseball are losing favour to pastimes like surfing that mix pleasurable engagement with consumerism (Guttmann and Thompson 2001: 227–8).

Consumer culture is constructed from the interplay between disciplined/objectified and governed/subjective bodies. On the one hand, measuring sports performance reduces athletes to statistical entities, as in baseball's batting and pitching averages. Children endure this to the point where sport success or otherwise becomes 'a statement about the total worth of the child' (Lithman 2001: 171). On the other hand, through conversion of adult athletes into celebrities, and the commodification of sports charisma through merchandise endorsement, sport moves away from the impersonality of athletic strength (as exemplified in Fascist sport), and towards the commodified personalization of sporting performance. For example, most team sports now carry the names of athletes emblazoned across their shirts, enabling fans to 'consume' this identity through buying and wearing 'replica' jerseys. In the most advanced cases of personalized sportswear, the sign values of athletes and corporations become interchangeable, as with Michael Jordan and Nike.

Concluding comments: promoting dialogue, andragogy and trans-disciplinary work within sport

In this chapter, I have made particular use of Foucault to examine the sporting body. Foucault illuminates the early modern disciplining and classification of bodies within sport, and the move towards corporeal government through confessional bodies and pleasurable, sport-related consumption. However, Eichberg's trialectic of body cultures reminds us that residual elements of a dialogical, folk culture still linger in contemporary sport.

I have argued against identification of a wholesale nexus between modern sport and Fascist ideologies of embodiment. In boxing and other contact sports, 'expert systems' discipline and objectify bodies, but athletes too are socialized into discourses of self-mastery in managing and distributing pain. Beck's theory of 'risk society' is useful for explaining rising reflexivity about dangers in sport, as evidenced in 'risk management', but fails to reconcile the distribution of risks to existent inequalities and stratification. The drug-related dangers faced by athletes are indicative: sports authorities prioritize doping, to protect their industry's image rather than athletes' welfare.

I favour analyses that connect wider historical, social, political and cultural forces to the phenomenology of 'flow' and 'peak experiences'. Consumer culture is integral to languages of pleasure within sport and popular culture generally. One future domain for the sport–consumer culture interplay is in body modification, germinating new forms of sporting participation and deeper changes in senses of the embodied self.

To conclude, I advance three arguments. First, developing earlier comments concerning violence, we need to reflect on sport's normative component. Such reflection is required within the sport system, and in the everyday practising and discussion of sport among players and spectators at all levels. Fresh moral discourses are needed to challenge the instrumentality, notably in achievement sports, that can engender explicitly violent play. Other disciplinary and empirical concerns arise. We need, for example, richer comprehension of athlete and spectator subcultures, to explain risk taking, pleasure, injury and violence in sport, and to disclose how these sporting processes are shaped by psychological, structural and historical forces. Such an approach requires a dialogical, investigative approach within sport, rather than an imposition of pre-ordained normative precepts upon social actors.

Second, I advocate a dialogical sociological model of the body. Following Eichberg, I am empathetic to the expressive, carnivalesque elements of the communicating body within folk physical cultures. This is not an anti-modern or regressive argument but one founded on critical, moral, dialogical precepts that should shape play in new ways. A dialogical body model requires sports science to be transformed by learning from critical advances in educational theory. We need to move from *pedagogy* to *andragogy* within sport science. Pedagogy is a predominantly monological mode of communication, entailing a one-way instruction in sport from coach to athlete. Andragogy is less authoritarian; it assumes that the learner needs to understand the value of what is being learnt and builds learning around experience. Although andragogy is usually associated with adult learning, it can be employed with any age-group. The fact that it is learner-focused ensures that andragogy entails a dialogical learning experience for both educator and learner (see Knowles 1973).

Third, body dialogue within sport has additional epistemological and methodological ramifications for what Foucault termed the 'human sciences'. Over 40 years ago, the British novelist and scientist C. P. Snow (1959) complained that modern Western intellectuals had divided themselves into two cultures, centring on the liberal arts and the natural sciences respectively. Dialogue across this divide has tended to fall on deaf ears and be mutually destructive. While a significant proportion of sociology employs the positivist methodologies of the natural sciences, its practitioners remain intrinsically more comfortable in communication with 'cognate' disciplines like history, anthropology, political science and literary criticism. Elias (1991: 103–7) insisted that sociology must dispense with false dichotomies, including the natural/social division. Unfortunately, throughout his long and ultimately powerful career, he showed little personal inclination to work whole-heartedly with systems of knowledge within physiology, psychology, neurology and other medical sciences.

This innate conservatism and defensiveness is particularly disappointing for sport sociologists. Many do not work in physically segregated arts or social science facilities, but are housed instead in research units, departments and faculties that employ biomedical scientists and their kin. Moreover, the human body provides sport sociologists with a study focus that positively demands integrated, trans-disciplinary research frameworks if it is to produce adequate explanation. Sport sociologists commonly grumble that their work is not treated seriously by peers in other substantive domains, such as religion or area studies. Fair comment; and one way to challenge such judgements is not through a retreating wave of disciplinary credentials, but through an enlightened, open-ended research dialogue with other disciplines that focus on the body. Building such a trans-disciplinary project is obviously beyond the possibilities of this short chapter. But, in the longer term, a trans-disciplinary analytical framework would advance better explanations of the body in sport. Sociologists of sport may even surprise themselves by pioneering methodological innovations and research insights on the human condition that are adopted by the human sciences in general.

8

Sporting Spaces: Valuing Topophilia

On one of his numerous come-back albums, Frank Sinatra crooned a poignant personal tribute to his old baseball team, the Brooklyn Dodgers, and their Ebbets Field stadium. The song – written by Joe Raposo and entitled 'There used to be a ballpark right here' – recalled the sounds and smells, the crowds and occasions, of sunny summer days spent spectating at Brooklyn's grand ground. In 1958 the Dodgers' owner moved the club to the more lucrative environs of Los Angeles, signalling the final curtain for Brooklyn's team. Ebbets Field was demolished two years later, but, as Sinatra's lament confirms, vivid personal and collective memories remain of the club, its community ties and its stadium. The Ebbets Field episode underscores how we generate particular emotional and popular cultural ties to recreational landscapes. Yet, as Brooklyn duly discovered, leisure is commodified, so that in a purely free-market context, money trumps sentiment. Unlike Ol' Blue Eyes, there was to be no come-back for Brooklyn's team.

Here, I examine the major sociological questions surrounding sport's spatial dimensions. First, with particular reference to Bale, I discuss people's emotional attachments to specific spaces. Second, I assess the political economy of sporting landscapes, notably stadium building and club relocation in North America. Third, I explore Ritzer and Stillman's three-phase historical model of sporting spaces. Fourth, via Foucault, I address social control within sporting spaces. Fifth, via Hannigan and Baudrillard, I examine the postmodern features of sports landscapes. I conclude by interrelating these different arguments, to suggest how sport's postmodernization may be experienced in an open-ended way.

Sporting spaces and emotional attachment: topophilia, patina and topophobia

John Bale has been sport geography's leading figure.[1] Adapting Bachelard (1969) and Tuan (1974), Bale deployed the term 'topophilia' to describe the affective ties of people to the material environment, to capture their distinctive 'love of place' (Bale 1994: 120). The sport setting's special qualities and characteristics help nourish topophilia, connoting a 'sense of place' to its habitués.

Bale (1991) indicates that sports topophilia is experienced in various ways through his deployment of five metaphors to capture the heightened public meanings of football stadiums. First, the stadium is a 'sacred place', projecting a particular spirituality among its 'congregation'. Quasi-religious events often occur in stadiums, like the scattering of deceased fans' ashes. Following the 1989 Hillsborough stadium disaster in Sheffield, at which 96 Liverpool fans were fatally injured, football fans brought offerings of football memorabilia as well as wreaths and flowers to stadiums in both cities (I. Taylor 1991: 4–5).[2] Second, the stadium may have 'scenic' qualities, providing athletes and spectators with distinctive visual pleasures. 'Complex landscape ensembles' promote individual enjoyment of the event, as opposed to functional, placeless settings lacking distinction (Raitz 1995: 28–9). For example, some English cricket grounds have local cathedrals as striking backdrops, or unusual ground features like the old lime-tree at Canterbury's cricket ground (Bale 1995: 81). Third, the stadium as a 'home' to players and fans grants psychological advantages over visiting opponents during sports fixtures. If the club seeks to move home, supporters often resist. Fourth, the stadium may be a 'tourist place', a heritage site, where visitors receive guided tours. Fifth, the stadium may engender deep local pride; the team constitutes 'a focus for community bonding and the source of "reconstruction" of some former *Gemeinschaft*' (Bale 1991: 135). Even in contemporary times, civic leaders still seek financial and political help to protect clubs endangered by falling support and indebtedness.

The concept of 'patina' helps to explain how old sports stadiums acquire added value for spectators (Ritzer and Stillman 2001). Patina designates the value-giving age signs that an object accumulates. It denotes how long individuals or communities have kept the object, and is an important referent for sustaining collective memory. Marks and colour changes are part of the object's informal text, signifying the imprints of those who have shared in its past. The 'patina' of old public spaces contains traces of prior users. Idiosyncratic marks – fading graffiti, rough footpaths, creaky wooden seats – can be central to the stadium's charm for regular spectators. These objects may signify dilapidation to outsiders, but they are material referents that help construct personal biographies (as long-standing supporters) or collective discourses linking different generations of supporters.

The obverse of topophilia is 'topophobia', whereby the landscape possesses negative emotional meanings (Bale 1994: 145–6). The 'sounds and smells' surrounding particular sport settings may generate hostility. Class-based factors are often prevalent; residents of wealthier suburbs can object to lower social classes using local 'public' spaces for sports purposes. 'Spillover' problems from stadiums may affect local businesses and residents. Many UK football grounds were built in relatively populous localities before 1914; some local residents have long contended with the stadium's 'negative externalities', like raucous singing, drinking, urinating, vandalism and fighting among fans (Bale 1990; Mason and Roberts 1991). More vulnerable potential users experience the greatest physical dangers relative to sporting landscapes. For example, some women or elderly people may avoid sports centres near poorly lit streets or neighbourhoods with reputations for crime.

Political economy and sporting landscapes: enclosures to mega-events

While emotional investments in sporting landscapes may intensify over time, political economic factors underpin their usage. In market-based societies, nearly all sport spaces are what Reiss (1991: 4) calls 'semipublic sports facilities': privately owned (whether by individuals, private associations or local authorities), where the public are charged admission fees.

Large stadiums were constructed to enclose sport, turning games into profitable spectacles that individuals paid to watch. Gate-money professionalized sports via athlete payment. The stadium began to mirror the socio-spatial distribution of city populations through division into class-based 'segments' or 'molecules' (see Sennett 1977: 135). More expensive, seated areas were reserved for the bourgeoisie; larger, standing terraces were dominated by working-class spectators. In the United States, numerous racecourses and baseball grounds were built during the sports boom of the 1870s to the early 1900s. Property and lease regulations forced some club relocations; the Chicago White Stockings baseball club, for example, inhabited six different 'home' grounds from 1870 to 1894. Rich, politically connected sports entrepreneurs gained urban locations for stadium development. By the 1920s many baseball clubs were settled in large arenas, and most urban Americans could attend some sports events, regularly or otherwise. The stadiums then acquired culturally democratic meanings, as semi-public spaces 'belonging' to all (Reiss 1991: 227–8).

The building of American stadiums with taxpayers' money generates strong public debate. By building stadiums, local authorities hope to dissuade sports clubs (or 'franchises') from moving to other cities, thus protecting local sports-related jobs. Sports teams are also said to boost the local economy (Euchner 1993: 68–70): the club's annual turnover should be multiplied by between 1.5 and 3.2 to calculate its 'multiplier effect' on the local economy – for example, in consumer expenditure on city food, accommodation and sports ephemera. Local authority 'boosterism' strategies deploy stadium investment to gain spin-off benefits from hosting sports 'mega-events' like the Olympics or American Super Bowl. Local politicians who retain or attract sports clubs and events for their city gain positive publicity. Symbolically, the major sports clubs may be 'civic flagships', presenting their home as a 'major league player' in American business and culture. Hence, during the 1990s, $11 billion of American taxpayers' money went on new sports arenas.

Numerous sports economists argue that the financial costs of stadium building typically exceed their benefits (Noll and Zimbalist 1997). One survey of 37 North American locations found that sports environments had reduced real per capita income, while team owners profited by playing the 'stadium gambit' and threatening to relocate (Coates and Humphreys 2000). Club owners and employees are often granted expensive concessions, like prime office space, tax allowances and expensive practice facilities. Euchner (1993: 185–6) found 'overwhelming evidence' that sports franchises did little to revitalize local economies. In Baltimore, sports fans and architects acclaimed the new Orioles' stadium as money well spent, but economists calculated that the $200 million public investment brought only $3 million annually in jobs and taxes (*The Australian*, 22 April 1999). Pre-construction 'estimates' and actual costs can differ wildly; the Louisiana Superdome was priced at $35 million but eventually soaked up $163 million (Anderson 1997: 107). Idealistic, post-Fordist claims – that stadium building can regenerate deprived locales – lack moral and financial support. In effect, the poor are asked to pay for stadium construction, and are priced out of entry upon completion, save for employment in low-wage seasonal jobs. Spending $800 million on a new stadium blasts a vast hole in city budgets for key social services, such as education, health and transport. This was precisely Mike Bloomberg's point upon inheriting stadium-building deals from his New York mayoral predecessor, Rudy Giuliani.

Sporting capital projects in Europe often benefit the power elite, while procuring questionable civic returns. Close political and social ties between Real Madrid football club's officials and local authorities freed the club to construct four new skyscrapers on its former training ground. The deal, agreed in summer 2001, earned the club around $420 million, thus clearing debts of $170 million. In France, the show-piece Stade de France, built on Paris's outskirts for the 1998 World Cup finals, was financed 53 per cent by private sector money and 47 per cent by taxpayers. The stadium's long-term financial legitimacy was undermined by failure to attract a major football club to this 'home'. Paris's main side, PSG, was reluctant to leave its home, while no new resident club could be established (Dauncey 1998: 116–19).

North American sport's unusual 'franchise' system allows clubs to relocate to new cities and stadiums. The political economy of American stadium relocation witnesses the abandonment of 'traditional publics' as new capital (civic or private) is embraced (Schimmel, Ingham and Howell 1993: 230). For example, in 1984, the Colts football team's move from Baltimore to Indianapolis was driven by Indianapolis's 'progrowth' and 'boosterism' strategies, to attract external capital and mould civic (but class-based) ritual within sport. Yet, even a winning local team will not by itself redefine a city's image or refound its economic basis (Rowe and McGuirk 1999).

Franchise relations are marked by serious structural inequalities. Schimmel (2001) suggests that, in North America, the era of 'fan as victim' may be closing. For example, in 1996, Cleveland Browns fans organized to block the club's move to Baltimore, while other cities have taken legal action to challenge relocations. However, these manoeuvres do not invert the hierarchical relationships between the NFL, club/franchise owners, local politicians and subordinate fans. If local peoples are committed to safeguarding the teams and stadiums that are precious to their 'structures of feeling', then franchise owners and associated corporations ensure they pay heavily for the privilege. (Cleveland's citizens paid $1 billion for capital projects to retain major league sport.) Indeed, struggles to protect local clubs against 'franchise flight' can have national dimensions. For example, Canadian team owners in the NHL have been courted assiduously by large, rich US cities. Given the particularly strong cultural and national symbolism of ice hockey within Canada, the gradual loss of NHL franchises to American cities confirms the general primacy of economic issues over public and cultural interests.

Similar problems arise for sporting 'mega-events' like the Olympic Games. Event planning and management are often autocratic, promoting senses of disempowerment and alienation among local people. Job and revenue benefits must be counterpoised against the higher local taxes necessary for capital projects, local people's voluntary work in running the event, and the fact that many cannot afford admission costs (France and Roche 1998). Environmental issues enter the political equation. The 1972 Munich Games did respond in part to the early rise of environmentalism, becoming thematized as the 'Green Olympics', and featuring some landscaped and *faux* greenery in and around the new stadium. The striking impact of buildings was softened by complex vegetation while even metal partitions were painted green (Eichberg 1986: 111). The 2000 Sydney Games were presented by the organizing committee in similarly verdant vein (Cashman and Hughes 1998). Some 'green' criteria influenced stadium planning, and germinated the unlikely hope that other capital projects might be similarly greened (Prasad 1999: 92). Yet many locals complained about the event's environmental impact, particularly at Bondi beach, where a temporary 10,000-seater stadium was erected to host the beach volleyball competition.

Overall, political economy perspectives are pivotal to the sociological analysis of sporting spaces. Discussion of sport fans' topophilic relationships to stadiums helps to articulate how social actors interpret the material environment in culturally rich, particularized ways. The construction of those complex meanings, however, is inevitably structured by and through power relations. Where capital links effectively with public elites, corporations possess the ultimate power, to close the stadium and destroy the intense symbolic system surrounding it, by shifting sporting tenants to new locations. Alternatively, as I discuss in the next section, the rationalization of the stadium to enhance its profitability can also have serious impacts upon the positive spatio-cultural experiences of sports spectators.

Rationalization and re-enchantment: historical categories of sports stadiums

I discussed in chapter 2 Ritzer's neo-Weberian 'McDonaldization thesis'. Ritzer and Stillman (2001) apply that thesis to baseball grounds, to argue that ballparks have been commercially 'McDonaldized', thereby alienating consumers. Attempts to 're-enchant' (or 'de-McDonaldize') ballparks have been relatively superficial, since instrumental profitability still underpins stadium designs. To elaborate, Ritzer and Stillman periodize ballparks' historical development.

Early modern ballparks were built during the early twentieth century, notable examples including Boston's Fenway Park and the Bronx's Yankee Stadium. Five particular qualities promoted these parks' enchanted, topophilic meanings among spectators: comparatively small size, allowing good views and intimacy; quirky individual features, like unusual wind channels that influenced play; iconic features like distinctive walls or vegetation that inspired fan affection; urban location; and playing host to epic moments in baseball history, thereby inspiring nostalgia.

Late modern ballparks were erected from the mid-1960s to the late 1980s, notable examples being Houston's Astrodome and Montreal's Olympic Stadium. These parks are highly McDonaldized in four definitive ways (Ritzer 1993). Efficiency is reflected in multi-use stadium design, to maximize extra-baseball revenues. Predictability is promoted by fixed roofs to control playing conditions, and by artificial turf to ensure surface consistency. The stadium emphasizes quantity over quality, through high seating capacities and multi-use design; quality is undermined by poor viewing angles. Workers' replacement by technology is evidenced by electronic ticketing machines and food kiosks that employ only sales people. These soulless stadiums evidence the 'irrationality of rationality', since they 'lose the magical qualities that attract consumers' (Ritzer and Stillman 2001: 100), thereby contributing to declining baseball attendances.

Postmodern ballparks have been constructed since the early 1990s, notable examples being Baltimore's Camden Yards and Atlanta's Turner Field. They feature 'simulated de-McDonaldization' that softens stadium rationalization, to re-enchant supporters in subtle ways. Some park owners stage 'extravaganzas' with little game relevance to attract and distract supporters: for example, scoreboards are increasingly high-tech and entertaining; firework displays or rousing anthems greet good plays by home teams. The stadium houses new means of consumption – shopping malls, museums, video arcades, food courts – that increase spectacle and ballpark profitability. Postmodern ballparks simulate some early modern features, like downtown locations or monuments to former players. Time and space are confused to play on nostalgia, giving the park 'an aura of the old'. Some parks possess old-fashioned facades, or operate stylized old technology (like beer pumps or mini-trains), to play with notions of authenticity. Spatial specificity is emphasized by linking stadium experiences to local cultural symbols, either through special backdrops or themed products (e.g. crab cake sandwiches in Maryland). Yet this simulated re-enchantment disguises continuing McDonaldization. Retail outlets are craftily situated and are highly rationalized in operation. Human activity is reduced further by, for example, digital scoreboards to communicate information. Like Disneyworld, these ballparks allude spatially to the past, but avoid the irrational, inefficient, pre-McDonaldized features of early modernity that fans find irritating and park owners find unprofitable (Bryman 1998: 124–5).

Ritzer and Stillman provide an empirically persuasive periodization of ballpark design. The model recognizes the cultural significance of stadiums' topophilic or enchanting qualities. Nevertheless, it overplays Weberian as opposed to political economic factors, since stadium rationalization, and subsequent 'surface de-McDonaldization', still pursue profitable ends. Postmodern ballparks attract more corporations and wealthy middle-class fans. Rows of 'bleacher seats' have been rationally replaced by corporate boxes or more luxurious seating, to house richer families that spend liberally on merchandise, food and auxiliary entertainment.

The model has limited cross-cultural applicability. Some sports resist environmental homogenization. All golf courses, for example, have unique features, determined primarily by peculiarities in the environmental setting (Adams 1995: 254). Outside North America, issues of crowd control and safety have been pivotal to stadium standardization and modernization. (Understandably, Ritzer and Stillman do not discuss security issues, although such matters have acquired obvious importance in the post-9/11 context.) Football has a lengthy international chronology of stadium disasters, caused by various decrepit or inhuman stadium facilities, and ineffectual or deadly policing techniques (Murray 1996: 189–91). The Heysel[3] and Hillsborough disasters transformed European thinking about crowd safety and control. Major UK stadiums are now all-seated, while football's international governing bodies have insisted on similar measures at grounds hosting major fixtures. In tandem, sports crowds across Europe, Latin America and Africa are subject to an increasingly sophisticated economy of discipline, surveillance and social control, as illuminated through application of Foucault's theories.

Social regulation and spatial control: the sporting panopticon

Foucault (1977) advances the concept of 'panopticism' to explain the modern, spatial disciplining of bodies and populations. The concept derives from Jeremy Bentham's (1791) model of the panopticon, intended as the purest architectural arrangement to enable human surveillance. In prison, the model envisages a watch-tower at the centre of a perimeter ring of cells, each containing one prisoner. All cells are entirely visible from the guard's watch-tower, hence prisoners must assume that every action is under surveillance. Panopticism is the organizing principle of all social relations, so that prisoners monitor each other (Dreyfus and Rabinow 1983: 192). Although Bentham's model was never implemented precisely, its logic is incorporated within standard modern buildings. As Foucault (1977: 228) himself asks, 'Is it surprising that prisons resemble factories, schools, barracks, hospitals, which all resemble prisons?' In recent times, the CCTV systems that span work-places, shopping centres and sports grounds constitute panopticism's most sophisticated manifestations.

Eichberg's (1995) notion of the 'pyramid', or *panoptical* sport stadium, develops Foucault's thesis. Here, the 'hegemony of the view' prevails, the most powerful gaze being held by those in the highest seats. Space is organized uniformly and functionally, producing distinctive lines of vision: the 1936 Berlin Olympics, the 'ornamental mass games', exemplify this spatial logic. While spectators 'gaze' upon play in the centre, they remain highly visible and so become part of the spectacle, such that 'the crowd impresses itself'.

Fiske (1993: 84–5) argues that modern sport stadiums are 'inverted panopticons', since they permit the masses in the perimeter stands to gaze upon the few in the centre. Spectators are further empowered by access to (often discrediting) information about events in the centre, as facilitated by television monitors that replay sports action. Fiske's model is in effect a sport-specific application of the 'synopticon' or 'viewer society', wherein television, theatre, religious and festival audiences gaze upon the few (Boyne 2000: 301).

However, the 'inverted panopticon' thesis fails to consider the reproduction of the hierarchical stadium gaze. The wealthiest possess higher, central viewing positions, putting themselves (and their conspicuous wealth) up for Veblenesque display. Private facilities, like executive boxes, can be panoptical shields that prevent the masses from gazing upon this elite. While the synopticon may apply in part to North American stadiums, it cannot explain the overriding surveillance of European spectators. In the UK during the 1980s, football stadiums were social laboratories for testing CCTV systems' efficacy in controlling public gatherings; subsequently, these devices were installed in most town and city centres (Armstrong and Giulianotti 1998). Panopticism's 'disciplinary procedures of partitioning and verticality' are

realized through the rows of individual seats in stadium stands, atom-
izing amorphous sports crowds into single units of action and conduct,
assisting their surveillance by stewards, police officers and cameras.
Seats are physical impediments to expressive, even aggressive spectator
actions, restricting rapid fan movements. Individuals who rise from
seats to express themselves are instructed *by fellow spectators*, in acts
of self-policing, to sit down so that all can spectate in orderly fashion
(Giulianotti 2001).

As Foucault (1977: 95) notes somewhat loosely, resistance always
arises to challenge power. Panoptical disciplinary mechanisms inside
sporting spaces can be challenged. For example, the redevelopment
and social regulation of the 'Hill' at the Sydney Cricket Ground
met with transgressive behaviour (Lynch 1992). Until the late 1980s,
the Hill was a large, undeveloped grassy area, occupied mainly by
working-class fans, whose spectator folk culture was 'one of loose,
rowdy, raucous, collective action . . . humour, wit and playfulness were
present next to coarse vulgarity and profanity' (Lynch 1992: 25). These
cultural practices helped define the Hill's topophilic meaning to its reg-
ulars. Crowd disorder, brawling and drunkenness were not unknown,
but became more serious from the late 1970s onwards. Subsequently,
the Hill was redeveloped into a more expensive, seated area. Such
'rational control of recreational space' has been mirrored elsewhere in
Sydney, notably at Darling Harbour. However, continuing incidents of
disorder around the Hill pointed to a kind of resistance to restrictive
socio-spatial control:

> Part of the unruly behaviour at this site, as ugly as it may have become,
> is arguably a reaction by collections of people against the sanitisation
> of leisure, against the corporatisation of sport, against control, against
> encroachment onto the turf of 'the mob', against being placed in a
> plastic seat and enclosed. (Lynch 1992: 44)

A longer struggle over spatial control has involved police forces and
football hooligans in the UK. During the 1960s and 1970s, the football ground was the major venue for hooligan confrontations, as each
group sought to invade and claim the 'end' that 'belonged' to the other.
Various anti-hooliganism measures were introduced, like the enforced
segregation of rival supporters via high fencing or 'thin blue lines' of
police officers. In turn, hooligan incidents became more prominent
outside grounds, in city centres, at public houses or transport termini.
More concentrated policing techniques – like employing plain-clothes
officers, electronic surveillance and 'dataveillance'[4] – forced hooligans

to adopt new tactics. Some hooligans turned to pre-arranging violent incidents against opponents, to take place in 'non-place' locations often far removed from the football match and carrying little topophilic or symbolic meaning for the combatants (Giulianotti and Armstrong 2002).

These Australian and UK cases are more disorderly examples of a wider, popular cultural relationship to sporting spaces. Eichberg (1995) associates such 'folk culture' with a *labyrinthine* view of sport stadiums, enabling dance, entanglement and other carnivalesque practices among spectators. The labyrinthine view encompasses the stadium's hidden aspects, and so is diametrically opposed to panoptical control of public space. While some military dictators have exploited invisibility inside stadiums to 'disappear' their imagined opponents, Eichberg argues that the labyrinthine stadium view is primarily experienced through a sense of place, with the stadium offering warmth and togetherness. Across the terraces, the stadium's noises (banging of drums, singing and shouting), alongside the freedom and uncertainty of crowd movements, contest the panopticon. The labyrinthine model discloses the vibrancy of public spaces and, in my view, is an important referent in constructing topophilia.

Trends towards post-panoptical thinking are highlighted through risk- management models that simulate bomb alerts or terrorist attacks (Boyne 2000; Bogard 1996). Simulation models typically assume that panopticism can fail to control public spaces. More routinely, Latour's (1993) notion of the 'oligopticon' provides a 'middle-range' vision of panopticism. Here, the span of surveillance is restricted to local settings and small social groups; examples include traffic lights or street cameras, work-place databases or criminal records. Diffuse oligoptical systems might combine into a geographically broader surveillance super-system. Nevertheless, Latour's more modest model is certainly applicable to individual sports events, where different oligopticons are deployed: CCTV inside and outside stadiums, various teams of stewards and police officers watching crowds, combined with access to criminal records and databases regarding potentially unruly fans. All of these might be networked to a centralized, directing police agency. However, Latour's model recognizes that, on the ground, oligopticons are relatively autonomous of each other. Information flows between surveillance units are inevitably imperfect, unlike the totally integrated, omniscient, surveillance network that panopticism implies.[5]

Foucauldian thinking facilitates critical sociological readings of the construction of public geographies. Modern urban architecture is designed in part to control deviant or potentially rebellious bodies: for example, compared to the old alleys and back streets, Paris's boulevards are far less suitable for mounting barricades against repressive state forces. Modern public geographies also facilitate the socio-spatial practices of dominant social groups, particularly those of the urban *flâneur*, or stroller. A typically male, adult, European and bourgeois individual, the *flâneur* emerged during the late nineteenth century to gaze upon and momentarily engage with the city's new malls, parks and buildings, and their constituent kaleidoscope of life-styles and identities (Featherstone 1995: 149–50; Benjamin 1999). A good reflective bourgeois, the *flâneur* was drawn to avant-garde, counter-cultural impulses in early consumer culture. The contemporary sporting *flâneur* likes to glide, in semi-detached fashion, through a cornucopia of experiences. During sporting mega-events, *flâneurs* can float among different spectator groups outside stadiums or in city centres, absorbing the international interplay of different national dresses, colours, tongues and intoxicating substances within a single public space.

The *flâneur* identity is masculine, so thrives in public spaces that are objectified, hostile to women, unsuitable for social interaction, and replete with anonymous fellow strollers (Wearing 1998: 131–7; E. Wilson 1995; Grosz 1995). Grosz suggests the *chora* as a feminine alternative to the *flâneur*, whereby public space is not 'gazed' upon, but fully engaged with and occupied by 'chorasters'. Wearing (1998: 134–5) illustrates the categorical differences by discussing the saltwater swimming pool at Manly in Sydney. Today, the *flâneur*-friendly pool is a scenic spot, gazed upon by snack-eaters and rarely used for swimming; in the past, as a *chora*, local families had regularly and informally met there to paddle around and socialize.

Contra the *flâneur*'s habitus, Wearing notes, children prefer to interact with the immediate environment. I would add that socialization into *chora*-focused practices has serious effects into adulthood. For example, Argentinians understand that, among the 'popular classes', young boys (*pibes*) play football in undeveloped urban wastelands (*potreros*) (Archetti 1998: 180). The dribbling skills learnt there help to reproduce the national *criollo* football style, associated with the 'freshness, spontaneity and freedom' of *pibes*. Hence, as Archetti (1998: 181) explains, sporting landscapes and personal/national identities are intertwined, their meanings becoming interchangeable: '*Pibes* are liminal figures and *potreros* are territories where freedom and creativity are experienced.'

Chora spaces like *potreros* contain topophilic meanings, but are threatened by commodification and rationalization. Urban planners typically prioritize the transformation of spaces into pacified sites of consumption, rather than leaving environments for fuller, more open-ended engagement by non-*flâneurs*. Across the UK's suburban and inner-city domains, we find the intensive 'redevelopment' of open spaces, the ubiquitous 'no ball games' signs across public thorough-fares, registering another triumph for the gazing *flâneur* over the *chora's* playful participants. Such spatial denials impose an adult, bourgeois, symbolic violence upon the ludic energies and imaginations of children. As partial and more profitable alternatives, we simulate the pleasures of *choras* through virtual, fantastic, postmodern land-scapes built more for consumption than playful engagement.

Towards the postmodern: fantasy, consumption, entertainment

Here, I seek to elaborate the earlier discussion of postmodern sporting spaces. The spatial dimensions of the postmodern sporting experience fall into two general categories, centring on actual and virtual sport settings.

Hannigan (1998) indicates that in North America, the ideal type 'Fantasy City' is gaining prominence. Key elements of Fantasy City are found in most contemporary shopping malls, tourism resorts and sports stadiums. Fantasy City fulfils the twin American middle-class desires to enjoy new experiences while minimizing interaction with lower classes. Fantasy City possesses six key characteristics, and each can help us to imagine the 'Fantasy Sport Stadium'. Fantasy City is:

- *theme-o-centric*, linking all spatial matter to a theme or themes that usually ignore the socio-historical characteristics of local neigh-bourhoods. In sport, the fantasy stadium has a definitive theme (the sports discipline itself), but some parts may facilitate multi-theme experiences: food outlets may be product-themed (Hispanic signifiers at Tex-Mex counters, or English pub décor at the beer outlet), while specific stand entrances may be named after former players and themed architecturally to fit their playing era.
- *aggressively branded*, often involving 'synergy' partnerships with transnational corporations; for example, corporate investment in building sports venues, resulting in specific stands or entire stadiums being named after sponsors.
- *a 24/7 enterprise*, running day and night, offering flexible consump-tion outlets to fit with new, varied employment routines. The fan-tasy stadium might be part of a wider multiplex facility comprising restaurants, shops, cinema halls, pubs, bowling, hotels and car parks.

- *modular*, mixing many standardized consumer outlets: for example, units of restaurants (Burger King, KFC, a Tex-Mex outlet), fashion stores (Nike, GAP, Levis), music stores (Virgin, HMV) and cinema halls. Again, this applies to larger multiplex sport facilities.
- *solipsistic*, emphasizing illusion and disregarding social problems and injustices in local neighbourhoods. The fantasy stadium might be located beside a declining housing project, but its internal themes will ignore outside civic issues and public problems.
- *postmodern* as a cultural form, via virtual reality, architectural pastiche and an emphasis on pure entertainment. For some analysts, the spatial 'Disneyization' of American culture means that urban architecture is increasingly influenced by Disney theme parks (Rojek 1993; Baudrillard 1996b). Contemporary sport spaces are encountered as theme parks, where categorical differences between fantasy and reality, past and present, local and global, are increasingly blurred. Inside the fantasy stadium, spectators encounter life-size cartoon characters, play at interactive museum displays, spend more time watching giant screens than the field of play, have an international cuisine tour in the food court, and exit the ground through art-deco gates.

For Hannigan, Fantasy City has created three hybrid consumer activities: 'shopertainment', 'eatertainment' and 'edutainment'. Specific public–private partnerships between civic authorities, sports club owners and real estate companies have been especially prominent in developing themed sports environments. In line with the arguments of Ritzer and Stillman and the political economy of sports geography, these partnerships are beneficially skewed towards club owners, producing a heavily themed environment rationally organized to maximize consumption.

More extreme visions of postmodern sport spaces focus on a *virtual*, mediated form of culture that spawns a new spatial consciousness. For Baudrillard, the world's virtual, themed aspects are our 'fourth dimension' (*la quatrième dimension*), our postmodern reality. Thus, 'It is more and more difficult for us to imagine the real, History, the depth of time, or three-dimensional space, just as before it was difficult, from our real world perspective, to imagine a virtual universe' (*Liberation*, 4 March 1996). In sport, Baudrillard anticipates the triumph of the virtual over the real; spectators at football matches are replaced by television cameras, such that the '"real" event occurs in a vacuum, stripped of its context and visible only from afar, televisually' (1993: 79).

Eichberg's *zapping* model of society is close to this postmodern vision, and is associated with the market and its impact upon stadiums. Zapping functions through television sport's hyper-visuality, and is instanced through giant stadium screens playing slo-mo replays of 'live' events. Zapping produces an 'everything goes', 'chaotic multiplicity' of scenes and images in regard to television channel hopping; in the stadium spectators switch attention distractedly 'from the grass to the screen, from picture to picture' (1995: 340).

More mundane, spatial forms of the postmodern occur when mediated representations eclipse 'realist' experiences of sport. For many, the sporting landscape is a digital screen across which computerized games are played, rather than a field of grass for physically striking a ball and/or opponents. Even for those who still play or watch sport in the real outdoors and on real turf, the logic of virtual space may still prevail. The golf course, ballpark and athletics stadium are increasingly designed according to virtual standards – using digital planning, or with television viewers in mind – rather than as public venues that allow folk-emotional attachments to evolve at everyday level.

Concluding comments: dodging topophilia

In this chapter, I have sought to provide a critical sociological analysis of sport space. 'Topophilia' and 'patina' conceptually denote sporting publics' emotional engagements with sport places. Topophilia is evident in the 'early modern' ballparks discussed by Ritzer and Stillman; in the folk culture that adopts, in Eichberg's terms, labyrinthine views of the stadium alongside carnivalesque movements of bodies; and in readings of the material environment as *chora*.

This empowering, expressive socio-spatial model is not culturally hegemonic, but squeezed by three kinds of modernization. First, 'semi-public spaces' allow public engagement with sport, but at a price. In North America, clubs may forsake local fans in pursuit of greater earnings, or collude with political elites to finance new stadiums at the expense of essential services. Sporting mega-events like the Olympics usually cost far more than their trumpeted spin-off benefits. Second, rationalized stadiums (notably 'late modern' ballparks) can be highly disenchanting for sport audiences; postmodern design helps alleviate alienation while heightening sports consumerism. Third, Foucault's model of spatial control fits the all-seated stands and CCTV systems geared to spectator pacification. Admittedly, 'middle-range', oligopticon surveillance techniques are more prevalent than models of omniscient observation. However, the cultural logic of the 'gaze' is realized at everyday level through the creation of leisure spaces which suit that veritable micro-panopticon himself, the bourgeois 'stroller'. These three modernization impulses are all rooted in organizing principles that are either independent of, or directly antithetical to, the everyday generation of topophilia within sport. Each is identified by a different philosophical standpoint: namely, neo-Marxism, neo-Weberianism and post-structuralism (Foucauldian social theory). But it is important to combine these theoretical frameworks to explain the social construction of sporting landscapes – to consider, for example, how contemporary sport stadiums constrain spectator behaviour, to increase wealthier family audiences and optimize service efficiency.

Consumption, social exclusion and virtual surveillance permeate the postmodernization of sporting spaces, notably in the fantasy sport stadium. Within postmodern culture, as noted in chapter 11, the triumph of virtual culture seems to imply that sport's folk elements may survive only in simulated form, as artificial crowd noises in an empty stadium, as literal echoes of the past. Yet there is resilience in sport's folk culture that sustains the importance of topophilia, the *chora*, and the carnivalesque.

As Bale (1998) notes, virtual sports may be watched quietly in homes, or in far more informal gatherings within larger public spaces that house giant screens. In these latter circumstances, I would argue, we find a postmodern occasion in process, not just in the virtual relaying of the event to an outside audience, but also through the collapsing of categorical boundaries between folk, rationalist, panoptical, consumerist and virtual kinds of cultural logic. Watching the giant screen highlights the *virtual* elements of the occasion. The spectators may engage in *folk* pastimes such as heavy drinking and partisan support for a specific team, within a pre-modern public space (such as a park or piazza) that has long-standing topophilic meanings. The setting may be *rationally* organized with alcohol outlets, portable toilets and public transport all catering to basic needs. CCTV cameras and security figures may be scattered around, undertaking *surveillance* and ensuring some degree of corporeal discipline. Special product promotions may add to the money-making *consumerism* taking place.

The extent to which any of these categorical features comes to dominate in sporting spaces will vary across space (between cultures and subcultures) and across time (as the occasion unfolds). But my sociological sense is that, in market democracies, the cultural politics of sports geography ultimately boils down to an uneven contest: between dominant political economic forces of consumerism, panopticism and rationalization, on one side, and sport's subordinate grass roots folk cultures of carnival, topophilia and self-expression on the other. Don't forget the Brooklyn Dodgers.

9

Elias on Sport: The Interplay of Figurations

Since the early 1980s, the figurational or 'process sociology' perspective of Norbert Elias has acquired a prominent position in sociology. Elias's magnum opus, *The Civilizing Process* (1978/1939, 1982/1939), was written before the Second World War, but only published in English in the late 1970s, when Elias was an octogenarian. From the early 1970s, Elias and his followers sought to validate their standpoint within the sociology of sport, notably in England and the Netherlands. While at Leicester University, Elias co-authored his major statement on leisure, *Quest for Excitement* (1986), with Eric Dunning, and exerted influence over later sociologists like Chris Rojek, Grant Jarvie, Kevin Young, Joseph Maguire and Patrick Murphy.

Here, I examine the figurational standpoint in four main parts. First, I assess Elias's theorization of social life in terms of human figurations, enabling discussion of sport's location within the 'spare-time spectrum'. Second, I address the civilizing process and its applicability to explaining the 'sportization' of games. Third, I examine how process sociologists explained modern football hooliganism according to the civilizing process. Finally, I argue for critical, selective deployment of figurational sociology regarding sport.

Human figurations and the spare-time spectrum

Elias's process sociology views societies as comprised of associative lattices or webs of interdependent people. Figuration is a 'generic concept for the pattern which interdependent human beings, as groups or as individuals, form with each other' (Elias 1987: 85). Figurations like families, leisure associations or working environments possess different power balances and tensions. Elias's position on figurations thus opposes both the compartmentalization of social structures into, for example, 'the economic sphere' or 'the cultural sphere', and the dichotomy between structuralist and interactionist theories of society (Dunning, in Elias and Dunning 1986: 11–12). He further rejects *homo clausus* interpretations of people which understand humans as distinct from, or in analytical opposition to, the wider society. Instead, Elias insists on the *homines aperti* conception of humans, as 'open beings' (1978: 115–25). Thus, people are figurational processes in themselves.

Sport arises frequently when Elias illustrates figurations. Methodologically, we sociologists, in Elias's view, should 'perceive ourselves as people among other people, and involved in games with others' (Elias 1978: 121). Like Bourdieu, Elias employs 'game models', like card-games or football matches, to explain his key concept. Games highlight player interdependencies through the constant flux of play and the 'progressive interweaving of moves' (Elias 1978: 97):

> If one watches the players standing and moving on the field in constant interdependence, one can actually see them forming a continuously changing figuration. In groups or societies at large, one usually cannot see the figurations their individual members form with one another. Nevertheless, in these cases too people form figurations with each other – a city, a church, a political party, a state – which are no less real than the one formed by players on a football field, even though one cannot take them in at a glance. (Elias and Dunning 1986: 199)

Figurations of sports groups extend well beyond players, to include referees and umpires, spectators, administrators and officials of clubs and governing bodies, and other relevant groups like local and national government personnel, business sponsors and media workers (Dunning, in Elias and Dunning 1986: 207). Social interdependencies ensure that games and sports cannot be conceptually detached from the wider social domain. For Elias, power relations are dependent on continuing figurational relations between people. Even in gladiatorial combat, when opponents seek to kill each other, interdependencies exist between the two. Power is also seen as a relatively fluid, if usually asymmetrical, phenomenon, reflecting the dancing flux of social relations within the figuration.

Figurational sociology advocates the explanatory interdependencies between hitherto partitioned academic disciplines like biology, psychology and sociology, to produce more 'reality-congruent' readings

of human beings (Elias 1978: 96). This necessitates the greater prominence of *homines aperti* within the sociological imagination, enabling
positive dialogue across different theoretical frameworks. Unfortunately, Elias and his followers have not been particularly adept at
observing these principles in practice. Elias rarely acknowledged his
intellectual debts and influences, leaving the comparative impression
of a theoretical *homo clausus* who had 'done it all by himself'. Moreover, there is a significant culture of 'with us or against us' among
his most ardent sociological followers, which rather contradicts their
insistence on human interdependence.

More positively, Elias places sport and leisure activities within mainstream sociology in three particular ways. First, as indicated, he employs sport metaphors to illustrate human figurations. Second, his
focus on social interdependence encourages us to view sport as en-
meshed with other realms of sociological inquiry. Third, substantively,
Elias locates sport and leisure within a 'spare-time spectrum' that spans
human activity outside paid work.

The three defining categories of the spare-time spectrum highlight
tensions between routinization and de-routinization. First, 'spare-time
routines' are the most routinized, and include care for biological needs
and household chores. Second, 'intermediary spare-time activities'
combine duties with some self-fulfilment – for example, in voluntary
or private work, religious activities and voluntary self-improvement
(ranging from reading newspapers to adult education). Third, leisure
activities are the spectrum's most de-routinized aspect, and include primarily sociable pastimes, mimetic or play activities, and less specialized relaxation (such as 'long-lies' or sunbathing) (Elias and Dunning
1986: 96–8).

The categories of sociability and mimetic activity are particularly
germane here. Almost all recreation is sociable. Drawing implicitly
upon Tönnies (1955), Elias points to the 'leisure-gemeinschaften'
within industrial societies, wherein loosened affective controls enable
people to enter more stimulating, exhilarating environments. Social
drinking illustrates how life's routinization is escaped, at least temporarily, through suspended social inhibitions. The 'mimetic' sphere
provides emotional arousals that 'are closely related to, yet in a
specific way different from, those which people experience in the
ordinary course of their non-leisure life' (Elias and Dunning 1986:
124). Mimetic activities allow enjoyment 'with the approval of one's
fellows and of one's own conscience as long as it does not overstep
certain limits' (1986: 125). Many specialized institutions, including
sporting ones, have grown to induce and reproduce mimetic pleasures.

Mimetic and sociability categories typically combine within everyday experience: sports institutions promote the construction of a 'leisure-gemeinschaften', forging senses of common identity between individuals, encouraging sociability among spectators, and providing spaces for mimetic enjoyment. Through the 'civilizing process', Elias theorizes the social history of the emotions, sociability and the mimetic in regard to sports.

The civilizing process

Despite being written prior to Nazism and the Holocaust, *The Civilizing Process* is Elias's major sociological statement and the seminal text for figurational sociologists. The book consists of two volumes: the first addresses the 'history of manners' regarding bodily control and social etiquette; the second examines state formation and more macro-sociological issues regarding societal changes, social institutions and structures. The empirical focus is England, Germany and France since the Middle Ages.

On manners, Elias traces the European sociogenesis of ideas regarding civilization. He examines the historical change from relatively unrestrained behavioural codes and conventions towards greater concern with bodily control and comportment from the Renaissance onwards. The civilizing process includes increasingly constrictive table manners, growing shame and repugnance towards bodily functions, and more constrictive codes of conduct within the bedroom, notably hiding the naked body and establishing private sleeping spaces. Embarrassment and shame necessitate greater self-control in sexual behaviour. Emotional expressiveness and volatility during the Middle Ages gave way to greater self-restraint and increasing revulsion towards public violence or aggression. Nevertheless, public excitement and emotional engagement were not abolished. Tensions arose between the codes of self-control and underlying desires for emotional fulfilment. Elias's observations derived from civility and etiquette books published after the Middle Ages, and aimed initially at the courtly circles of Europe and then the upper bourgeoisie. These pedagogical texts both influenced and reflected changes in social manners.

The key elements of court society and subsequent state formation are closely tied to constrictive corporeal controls. For these psychological and interpersonal changes to occur required that people inhabit reasonably stable political environments, where authority was exercised consistently and predictably. Within English court society, warriors underwent a civilizing 'courtization', in part for political reasons. Various aristocrats, military figures and religious leaders established growing courts in which control of information was crucial alongside gaining knowledge of political changes inside each court figuration. However, cycles of violence erupted between rival social formations. In England, the Civil War prompted the 'parliamentarization' of politics; military conflicts were replaced by debate and persuasion, personal restraint, and more orderly, predictable, non-violent conduct.

Parliamentary state formation, in tandem with other societal processes, produced a 'civilizing spurt'. When the State establishes monopolies on taxation and violence, violent conflict is less likely (Elias 1982/1939: 235–6). The rise of monetary relationships and economic growth also promote civilizing spurts. Rationalization goes hand in hand with civilizing processes; increased self-control forces individuals to jockey for influence within social figurations through calculation and argument rather than force. More complex divisions of labour and functional democratization characterize the civilizing process too, as complex chains of interdependence at work and in other social spheres bind people into numerous reciprocal relationships (Elias 1987: 76–7). As the civilizing process advances, power differences are reduced. 'Established', powerful groups must use increasing constraint, as weaker, 'outsider' groups exercise greater influence and adopt many of the superiors' social mores and outlooks. Struggles between established and outsider groups can arise, as modern conflicts between classes, genders and ethnic groups testify. Nevertheless, urban, industrialized, modern parliamentary democracies have given rise to more civilized, complex human figurations in which 'people become more sensitive to what inspires others' and 'the mutual urge of people to take each other into account grows' (Elias 1982/1939: 114).

The broad, long-term Western trend has been towards increasingly restrained social conduct; but the civilizing process is not unidirectional. 'Decivilizing spurts' occur, when people's enjoyment of violence or expressive emotions increase, and extreme disturbances arise in state formation. Elias (1996) attributed the extreme decivilizing spurt of Nazism in Germany to the long-term German perceptions of national threat and isolation, the failure to pacify Germany's warrior nobility, the inculcation of violent mores among the urban bourgeoisie, and German citizens' child-like dependence upon authority figures.

The civilizing process illuminates sport's rising socio-cultural importance. Modern societies must resolve the dilemma of sustaining pleasurable emotional excitement while observing bodily and social control. Modern sport provides one resolution, by offering 'the liberating excitement of a struggle involving physical exertion and skill while limiting to a minimum the chance that anyone will get seriously hurt in its course' (Elias, in Elias and Dunning 1986: 165).

Games and pastimes took more civilized forms when the civilizing process was advancing in England from the seventeenth century. The 'sportization' of games involved establishing rules and conventions within play that necessitated self-discipline and reflected growing repugnance towards public violence.

> In the form of 'sports', in other words, game-contests involving muscular exertion attained a level of orderliness and of self-discipline on the part of participants not attained before. In the form of 'sports', moreover, game-contests came to embody a rule-set that ensures a balance between the possible attainment of a high combat-tension and a reasonable protection against physical injury. 'Sportization', in short, had the character of a civilizing spurt comparable in its overall direction to the 'courtization' of the warriors where the tightening rules of etiquette played a significant part. (Elias, in Elias and Dunning 1986: 151)

Elias draws direct connections between the social ethos behind the parliamentarization of English politics and the advanced 'sportization' of English game-contests.

> The 'parliamentarization' of the landed classes of England had its counterpart in the 'sportization' of their pastimes . . . One could see there that rules for non-violent combat between rival factions in Parliament and for peaceful handing over of governmental power to a victorious faction or party emerged more or less at the same time as the stricter constraint on violence, the greater demands on personal self-control and on sublimatory skill which gave leisure-contests involving muscle power and agility the characteristics of sports. (Elias, in Elias and Dunning 1986: 34, 48)

During the eighteenth and nineteenth centuries, fox-hunting, for example, was transformed by the more civilized, landed classes. The huntsman's enjoyment of killing the fox was replaced by his more civilized appreciation of the pleasures of the chase. The huntsman's hands were no longer bloodied, as the actual kill was delegated to the hounds. In pugilism, sportization occurred through the introduction of particular rules of combat, notably the Queensberry Rules, the use of gloves to reduce bloodshed, and the rise of an aesthetic code centred on self-defence rather than violence.[1]

Figurational sociologists explain football's transformation, from folk pastime to modern sporting discipline, according to the civilizing process (Elias and Dunning 1986: 175–90). They emphasize the perceived wildness of medieval 'folk football' games and the 'relative powerlessness' of authorities to control or eradicate these pastimes. Non-literate communities played football according to local customs, not written rules, but the games' disorderly aspects were uniform: 'The character of the game as a struggle between different groups, the open and spontaneous battle-enjoyment, the riotousness and the relatively high level of socially tolerated physical violence, as far as one can see, were always the same' (Elias and Dunning 1986: 184). During games, old scores were settled violently, bones were regularly broken, deaths not unknown. Other 'uncivilized' aspects were apparent: no equality of numbers arose between rival sides, little separation existed between spectators and players, and ideas of 'fairness' or competitive balance were absent (Dunning and Sheard 1979). Meanwhile, pre-industrial British 'state formation' had a long way to go. Only the ruling aristocracy and gentry perceived themselves as a national force, and possessed senses of that 'other-directedness' which competitive sport requires (Dunning, in Elias and Dunning 1986: 217–18).

Football games underwent 'sportization' during the nineteenth century, when they were adapted by certain English public schools to exercise boys. The schools established rules and principles of fairness for games, though violence was still higher than it is today. At this time, functional democratization arose, as the bourgeoisie and aristocracy entered longer interdependent chains within the industrializing society. The bourgeoisie sought to emulate and influence the aristocracy's norms and practices. Differences were still manifested through playing of alternative football codes. Among the most established, aristocratic classes, a 'higher order of self-restraint' was found in the soccer-style code of football that prohibited ball handling. Among the middle class and upper-middle class, the more violent game of rugby was established (Dunning and Sheard 1979: 128–9). Overall, games fulfilled civilizing functions within schools, promoting self-restraint and social order in locations marked previously by riotous behaviour (Dunning 1977).

Figurational sociology and football hooliganism

The most substantial, contested application of the civilizing process to sport concerns English football hooliganism. In *The Roots of*

Football Hooliganism, a team of Leicester researchers examine the civilizing and decivilizing spurts in English crowd behaviour since football's transformation into a mass spectator sport in the late nineteenth century. Drawing on English Football Association records and *Leicester Mercury* newspaper reports, the researchers argue that, until the First World War, violence within crowds was part and parcel of attending football. Much violence was expressive, and a consequence of events on the field of play, germinating attacks or threats aimed at football officials and players. Such incidents reflected the comparatively low emotional restraint of largely working-class crowds, and their relative toleration of open aggression and violence. After 1945, until the early 1960s, football crowds were markedly more peaceful and civilized. Violent or disorderly incidents declined, greater self-restraint was apparent, and higher thresholds of repugnance towards disturbances took hold within football's massive crowds. The researchers attribute this relative peacefulness to the growing representation, within football crowds, of 'respectable' working-class people who had been 'incorporated' into adopting the more civil norms and values of their social betters, and who were party to greater functional democratization within work and politics (Dunning, Murphy and Williams 1988: 126–8). Greater numbers of women, and middle- and upper-class males were also attracted to football, thereby feminizing and further civilizing the dominant behavioural codes within spectator crowds.

When the 'respectable' working classes became less prominent within football crowds, and turned instead to alternative, more domesticated forms of leisure, notably from the late 1950s onwards, crowd disorder increased at matches. Working-class youth began to be seen as an increasingly serious problem by 'established' political and social forces. Football authorities became concerned about declining crowds, a problem exacerbated when reports of violence among young working-class people further dissuaded 'respectable' fans from attending games (Dunning, Murphy and Williams 1988: 235–6). All of this provided fertile ground for the sociogenesis of modern football hooliganism.

For the Leicester researchers, contemporary football hooligan groups have been established since the 1960s and hail overwhelmingly from 'rough', lower-working-class locales. Hooligans are most unlikely to have been incorporated into 'respectable', civilized standards of conduct; instead, they have been socialized on the streets from a young age, coming to view violent and aggressive behaviour among peers as normal. Hooligans have a narrow, 'experiential homogeneity', marking their restricted contact with other locales and cultures, and re-inforcing strong identification with kin, neighbourhood and the 'home turf' (Dunning, Murphy and Williams 1988: 205–6). Single-parent families, petty crime and delinquency, and high unemployment and dependence on state benefits are common to the hooligan's social habitat. Evidence for the Leicester thesis hails from police arrests at English football, a television survey of self-reported 'hooligans' at the London club West Ham United, some interviews with young people from a lower-working-class housing estate in Leicester, and Gerald Suttles's (1968, 1972) studies of a multi-ethnic slum area in Chicago.

Hooligan groups are formed through the 'ordered segmentation' of young males from different neighbourhoods, who combine to fight as followers of a specific club against equivalent groups that support rival clubs. Their violence is more instrumental than expressive: it is less connected to events on the field, and more premeditated in targeting opposing supporters (Dunning, Murphy and Williams 1988: 236–8). As violent incidents have increased at football matches, more and more 'rough' young men have been attracted to fixtures.

Nevertheless, significant qualification arises regarding the socio-economic and cultural genus of hooligan groups. The researchers describe relations between 'respectable' and 'rough' fans as a 'continuum', whereby they overlap and shade into each other. More-over, noteworthy 'rough' elements within the middle and upper classes are prone to violent behaviour, including football hooligan-ism (Dunning, Murphy and Williams 1988: 215; Dunning, Murphy and Waddington 1991: 474).

More macro-social aspects of the civilizing process are employed to explain hooliganism. Hooligans, it is claimed, play relatively passive roles within the growing chains of interdependence across complex industrial societies (Dunning, Murphy and Williams 1988: 228–9). Hooligans' occupations do not soften 'macho tendencies'. Hooligans experience prejudicial treatment from more 'established' social groups, notably through the 'law and order' political credo that prevailed in Britain during the 1970s and 1980s. Football hooliganism is one manifestation of a serious 'decivilizing spurt' across British society, as otherwise instanced by inner-city riots, escalating Troubles in Northern Ireland, and confrontational industrial disputes. The Leicester researchers conclude that hooliganism, and the 'decivilizing upsurge', is rooted in widening social inequalities and divisions. While the majority are 'incorporated' into civilized society, sizeable minorities are excluded – notably working-class people, women, ethnic minorities, young people – within a climate of 'acquisitive individualism' and 'hard line' social policies. Hooliganism will only be tackled effectively by reducing these inequalities (Dunning, Murphy and Williams 1988: 243–5). These comparative structural observations and critical recommendations show the politically radical potential of figurational sociology. However, the Leicester researchers suggest more practical strategies for tackling hooliganism, such as increased participation of women and families, which can reduce 'aggressive masculinity' and 'feminize' the crowd (Murphy, Dunning and Williams 1990: 78, 224–5).

Critical evaluation: towards the selective, imaginative application of Elias

Figurational sociology provides cogent, accessible and apparently comprehensive explanations of sport's social history. Sport is located agreeably near the heart of figurational sociology's analytical framework. The concept of social interdependency helps illuminate the basic elements of human relations. However, the figurational paradigm succumbs to major theoretical, methodological, empirical and dialogical weaknesses that dissuade me from its adoption within the sociology of sport. I shall deal with these in turn.

First, the key hypotheses of figurational thinking erect defective social theories: they are not framed for rigorous testing because, in the terms of Karl Popper (1963: 33–9), they defy falsification. For example, when faced with counter-evidence to the theory of the 'civilizing process', the Eliasians trundle out the idea of 'decivilizing trends' as their saving, sociological *deus ex machina*. Similarly, on football hooliganism, the Leicester sociologists unveil the notion of middle- or upper-class 'roughs', to explain away evidence that many hooligan groups have few lower-working-class members. Explanatory discrimination is a prerequisite for any operating theory; yet the Eliasians imply, rather absurdly, that their theory can explain any social eventuality. Tomorrow, if the IOC's headquarters were to be the focus of major public rioting, or the forum for the signature of international peace treaties, the Eliasians would still insist that either or indeed both events confirm their core hypothesis. Such defence mechanisms add to the suspicion that the 'civilizing process' is not a social theory *per se*, but an elaborate piece of sociological description.

Figurational sociologists have tended to view sport as an arena for demonstrating, not testing, proposed theories. Elias hoped that sport would afford a 'comparatively manageable field' to 'explore' figurational sociology and 'to show how I think it should be used' (Elias, in Elias and Dunning 1986: 154). The rectitude of figurational sociology was clearly not in question (R. W. Lewis 1996: 335). This weak, affirmative methodology extended into the Leicester researchers' fieldwork on football hooligans. To 'test' the lower-working-class hypothesis, they undertook research in a particularly poor locality, rather than within a city-wide hooligan group. They prioritized employment data gathered (in questionable circumstances, by television documentary makers) from fans of England's most famously working-class side, West Ham United. A more legitimate methodological approach would favour testing the theory at clubs like Chelsea, where a large hooligan reputation arises within a more affluent 'home' location.

Second, conceptually, the civilizing process appears evolutionist and Eurocentric. Certainly, critics and even his supporters have recognized, to varying degrees, Elias's Eurocentrism (Goudsblom 1995; Blake 1995: 48–50; Robertson 1992: 120). Eliasians do not account adequately for the development of manners and state formation in non-Western contexts, notably the Far East. Moreover, the 'civilizing process' cannot provide a sufficiently critical analysis of imperialist expansion and neo-colonialism beyond Europe. In South America, for example, the 'civilization process' show-cased extraordinary European capacities for violent invasion, mass enslavement, genocide and ecological disaster (Ribeiro 2000). Given their experience of modern globalization, non-Europeans might justifiably adopt a rather more sceptical stance towards questions of modern 'civility'. As Mahatma Gandhi once famously remarked, when asked what he thought of Western civilization, 'It would be a good idea.'

The charge regarding Elias's evolutionism may seem at first to be problematic, given his introduction of 'decivilizing spurts' to describe apparent trends towards social breakdown. The figurationalists insist that their preferred terms 'civilized' and 'uncivilized' do not constitute 'ethnocentric value judgements' (Elias and Dunning 1986: 133). His strongest followers, notably Dunning and Mennell, constantly cite passages in which Elias denies evolutionism. However, other passages by Elias suggest otherwise. He uses value-laden terms – such as 'fossilization', 'semi-petrified' and 'drag effect' – to describe the condition of so-called simpler societies relative to industrial societies. Maguire (1999: 43) seems to sustain this evolutionist thinking when describing relations between the West and non-Western societies as 'equivalent' to those between court society and lower social classes during Renaissance times. Elias dismisses cultural relativism, insisting that 'knowledge systems' are like a staircase with different levels that *must be* passed to reach the top floor. Presumably, the civilized West has climbed rather higher than 'simpler societies'. In this way, Elias's civilizing process comes to resemble 'a highly sophisticated variant of the theory of modernization' (Gruneau and Whitson 1993: 179–80), with its emphasis on evolutionary development according to the Western model of modernity. While working in Ghana in the early 1960s, Elias showed little sophisticated interest in local culture, thereby ignoring a comparative approach to cultural diversity regarding paths of 'civilization' (Goody 2002: 402, 410). These failings are apparent, more modestly, in figurational analyses of football hooliganism. The Eliasian model is essentially 'Anglocentric', and is comparatively weak if applied within other European nations (including Scotland) (see Dunning 1994: 154). Notably, researchers outside England employ figurational theory at most partially, or more commonly not at all, when explaining spectator disorder within their own societies.

Third, the civilizing process's theoretical and empirical case remains highly dubious. Late modernity is crammed with instances of unprecedented barbarism, as modern technology has facilitated the annihilation of entire populations. As Armstrong (1998: 305) reports, 'the latter half of the twentieth century has seen 130 wars with 27 million dead, whilst the first eight decades of the century saw 99 million die in warfare – a figure twelve times greater than that for the previous century and twenty-two times that of the eighteenth century.' Surely such figures cannot be explained adequately by 'decivilizing spurts' or anomalies in 'state formation'.

Political economic models of international history explain these human tragedies more plausibly. The theory of the civilizing process says too little on structured power relations and the reproduction of social inequalities. Even inside the 'civilized' West, forms of *symbolic* violence within education and other social institutions retard the realization of human potential among the lower social classes (Bourdieu and Passeron 1977). Equally, parliamentarization could be argued to have 'disempowered' people, rather than to have improved public influence by suppressing expressive behaviour. Elias's lack of concern with gendered violence also points to his comparative 'conservatism' (Blake 1995: 48–50). Foucault, by contrast, provides a far more incisive analysis of power when examining bodily discipline and surveillance.

These weaknesses permeate Eliasian analyses of football hooliganism. Historians have argued that the Leicester researchers seriously exaggerate the 'civility' of public school football games compared to 'violent' 'folk football' and working-class games; in fact, folk and especially working-class football games included high levels of rule-following behaviour (Goulstone 1974; 2000: 135–6; A. Harvey 1999: 114). Other historians have examined newspaper archives far beyond the parochial confines of the *Leicester Mercury* to conclude, *pace* the Leicester researchers, that crowd disorders before 1914 were extremely unusual (Mason 1980: 166–7; Lewis 1996; Tranter 1998: 47–8). Substantial research in England and Scotland indicates that contemporary football hooliganism has tended to involve relatively 'incorporated' young men, with an upper-working-class or lower-middle-class *habitus*, and not the essentially lower-working-class *habitus* claimed by the Leicester researchers (Armstrong 1998; Giulianotti 1999: 46–52; Giulianotti and Armstrong 2002: 215–17). The Leicester case was not assisted when the chief researcher, John Williams (1991), pronounced his dissatisfaction with Eliasian theories of football hooliganism. Williams sought more critical proposals for confronting hooliganism, rather than following the Leicester researchers' earlier pragmatism that had centred on 'policing and criminalization' (see Smith 1997: 119–20). The other Leicester proposal, to 'feminize' disorderly fans by attracting more female supporters, has a dubious ethical base in terms of exploiting women to pacify another domain of male disorder (A. Clarke 1992: 217). As noted in chapter 7, Foucault's theories of panopticism and governmentality provide more critical insights into the political dimensions of bodily control and conduct within sport. On the other hand, not all sports practices can be seen simply in terms of civilizing or decivilizing spurts. For example, the use of comparatively violent playing styles in team sports may have no connection to a 'decivilizing spurt', but may simply reflect how some coaches think they can best obtain good results with the available players.[2]

Fourth, the intellectual culture of Elias's strongest supporters can damage the sociological community. Rojek (1995: 56) makes the remarkable claim that there is 'an underlying humility' and 'modesty' within figurational sociology, reflected in its proponents' acceptance that they do not have all the answers, in comparison to the 'hubris found in many functionalist, neo-Marxist and feminist contributions to the study of leisure and sport'. Frankly, I am not persuaded. Among senior figurationalists, as well as Elias, there has been precious little clarification of where exactly they consider their weaknesses to lie, whether in conceptual or empirical terms. Indeed, leading figurational sociologists, particularly within sport studies, are renowned for their acute sensitivity to criticism and their reluctance to engage in open, self-critical debate.[3]

If we imagine the sociology of sport in religious terms, as an interdenominational totality, then we might begin to see the Eliasians as a curious, religious sect. Their devotion to Elias's work (to the general exclusion of other master sociologists) can appear liturgical, and there is no doubting their sense of personal mission to promote Elias's global standing and to proselytize. In terms of professional practice, the Eliasians are generally 'world-accommodating': they work on a mainly internal, self-reliant basis while maintaining some formal relations with other sociological schools, such as through professional organizations or within edited collections. However, in terms of intellectual dialogue, the Eliasians can appear as a 'world-rejecting' sect, by directing trenchant criticism at other sociological 'faiths' while distrusting or denouncing those who work with rival scholars.

Elias will join the pantheon of great sociologists when his work is selectively, consistently utilized to build new theoretical models. That will not occur if his followers 'wall him up in a temple to be tended only by the faithful'; this deification will merely frighten off the curious through the suggestion that 'they are not "good enough" to be true Eliasians' (D. Smith 2001: 14). In terms of master theories, 'no key turns all locks'; the craft of sociology necessitates working imaginatively with different theoretical constructs and empirical data to explain social phenomena (Guttmann 1992: 158). A sense of intellectual security might be provided by always returning to 'the Word', to discern some hidden sociological insight, but such reversion is both intellectually stultifying and certain to under-explain the phenomenon in question.

In this light, Eliasian explanations of football hooliganism appear somewhat crude. They take the simplest possible figurational position by insisting on the 'rough', comparatively uncivilized lower-working-class *habitus* of hooligans, to show how the civilizing process 'works' as a theory. It would have been far more innovative, and probably more 'reality-congruent', to develop other elements of Eliasian theory to explain contemporary fan violence. For example, the theories of 'informalization', initiated by Elias and further outlined by Wouters (1977, 1986, 1990), might have been introduced. Informalization refers to apparent relaxation of standards of self-control and bodily discipline – for example, in liberal parenting techniques or more public forms of sexuality. Informalization, for Wouters, actually reflects new levels of self-control marked by greater self-consciousness and reflection. The interdependency between formalization and informalization is complex; for example, some trends towards informality may become formalized (e.g. 'smart but casual' leisure wear for dinner parties). 'Informalization' does not occur among social groups that have not properly experienced the formalization of the civilizing process, although it does reflect the greater convergence of working- and middle-class traditions of conduct (Wouters 1977: 449). It is within this class convergence that we find football hooligans, rather than within the lower working classes, as the Leicester researchers have claimed.

To outside critics like this one, the formalization/informalization argument has some inimitable figurational weaknesses, not least its untestability and descriptivism. Yet, for an Eliasian of some invention and with basic empirical knowledge of football hooliganism, the general informalization argument should appear better suited to explaining contemporary hooligans. Informalization offers some openings for explaining how those of incorporated social status can slip into relatively instrumental violence within quite strictly defined time periods (match-days) against strictly defined opponents (rival hooligans, and not just any opposing supporter). Tensions between informalization and formalization may also be identified within the 'soccer casual' style prominent among football hooligans, with its rather constrictive emphasis on the consumption of designer leisure wear. Instead, the Leicester researchers insisted instinctively on the lower-working-class 'roughness' of hooligans. This assertion was founded on very partial evidence and a closed form of theoretical elaboration and invention. It would be a great disappointment to the discipline of sociology if such a research exercise were to become paradigmatic of future process sociology.

10

Bourdieu on Sport: Distinction, *Symbolic Violence and Struggle*

The late Pierre Bourdieu, who died in January 2002, was one of the world's leading post-war sociologists. His work has been most influential in France, but several of his books, in particular his masterpiece *Distinction*, have gained global renown. A prominent intellectual and critic in the public sphere, Bourdieu increasingly condemned contemporary systems of domination, particularly Western neo-liberal policies that bring job insecurity, crime, social stress and disregard for the developing world. For Bourdieu, sociologists have a crucial role to play in challenging social domination (Wacquant 2002b: 556).

Unlike most *maîtres à penser*, Bourdieu wrote several papers on sport. In *Distinction*, Bourdieu intends to provide a sociology of cultural tastes; sport and physical culture are elements of an overarching analysis that discloses the geneses of, and practices within, deep social and cultural struggles (Defrance 1995: 124; Bourdieu 1990a: 159). Bourdieu was concerned not with sport *per se*, but with behind-the-scenes factors of socialization and social differentiation that instil different sporting tastes. The research questions for Bourdieu are:

> How is the demand for 'sports products' produced, how do people acquire the 'taste' for sport, and for one sport rather than another, whether as an activity or as a spectacle? . . . More precisely, according to what principles do agents choose between the different sports activities or entertainments which, at a given moment in time, are offered to them as being possible? (1978: 819–20)

This focus has many conventional sociological and political strengths, but can over-simplify sport's complexities.

I consider Bourdieu's relevance to the sociology of sport in three main parts. First, I address the philosophical and categorical roots of Bourdieu's sociological perspective, with reference to the subject–object dualism, and his concepts of 'habitus', 'capital' and 'field', and his understanding of symbolic violence. Second, I consider the sports-related research findings of Bourdieu and his followers; I focus principally on *Distinction* and its contribution to sociological analysis of social stratification in sport. Third, I assess Bourdieu's more explicitly political writings and their relevance to sport sociology. I conclude by proposing critical amendments to Bourdieu's approach within sport.

Bourdieu's theoretical framework

Dissolving dichotomies

Like many influential sociologists ranging from Parsons to Giddens, Bourdieu claimed that his social theory dissolved sociology's traditional binary oppositions of 'subjectivism' and 'objectivism', action and structure. 'Objectivism' is, in effect, structuralist social theory. For structuralists, all societies contain underlying logical structures or patterns which exist beyond the consciousnesses of the society's members, but which are open to identification by social scientists. Conversely, 'subjectivism' is nearer 'interpretivism', producing social theories founded on subjective understandings and explanations of the social world. Both objectivism and subjectivism struggle to rebut fundamental criticisms: like functionalism, structuralism fails to account for social actors' critical and creative faculties; subjectivism ignores how social structures shape and constrain individual actions. Bourdieu, by contrast, sought to evade both extremes while retaining ideas of 'action' and 'structure' within his conceptual framework (Bourdieu and Wacquant 1992: 121–2).

Unlike Giddens, whose structuration theory is rather interpretivist, Bourdieu's dissolution of the subject–object dichotomy precipitates a significantly structuralist result (1990a: 125–6). Bourdieu advocates a 'genetic structuralism': an approach that adopts a more personal, action-focused version of structuralism, examining how structures are constituted and reconstituted through everyday 'practices'.[1] For Bourdieu, 'practice' discloses both people's practical understanding of the social world and how social reality is made. Through social practice, people seek to master (rather than consciously theorize) their everyday activities. Practical comprehension of the world is embedded in subjectivity, because the world 'comprises me' and 'has produced me'. The world generates the subject's categories of thought, and so its 'self-evident' appearance produces a stronger concern with practical mastery rather than withdrawn, objectifying reflection (Bourdieu and Wacquant 1992: 127–8).

The body is central to practical mastery of the world. Sport is 'perhaps the terrain *par excellence*' in which such practice is most apparent:

> There are heaps of things that we understand only with our bodies, out-side conscious awareness, without being able to put our understanding into words. The silence of sportspeople... stems partly from the fact that, when you are not a professional analyst, there are certain things you can't say, and sporting practices are practices in which understand-ing is bodily. (Bourdieu 1990a: 166)

Sport illustrates how this pre-objective, 'practical sense' functions for individuals:

> It constitutes the world as meaningful by spontaneously anticipating its immanent tendencies in the manner of the ball player endowed with great 'field vision' who, caught in the heat of the action, instantaneously intuits the moves of his opponents and teammates, acts and reacts in an 'inspired' manner without the benefit of hindsight and calculative reason. (Wacquant, in Bourdieu and Wacquant 1992: 20–1)

For Bourdieu, social reality is intrinsically 'relational', created from re-lations between social groups, rather than from the substance qualities of individuals in themselves.

Bourdieu seeks to dissolve the theory–evidence binary, insisting that the 'logic of research' is 'inseparably empirical and theoretical' (Bour-dieu and Wacquant 1992: 160). His own sociological researches mixed social data (both detailed surveys and sophisticated ethnography) and theoretical reflection – for example, when examining Berber house-holds or French academia. Moreover, sociological practice must be intensely reflexive. Sociologists seek to formulate scientific 'objectifi-cations' about the social world, but they must reflect upon the socio-historical conditions behind their knowledge production, to objectify their objectifications.[2] By turning their disciplinary tools back onto themselves, sociologists can extricate biases from their work (Bourdieu 2000: 121). Such reflexivity is not confined to 'post-research' periods. When doing fieldwork, sociologists must show a 'reflex reflexivity' in terms of sociological 'feel', making connections between what happens 'on the spot' and the wider social structures (Bourdieu, in Bourdieu et al. 1999: 608).

Bourdieu recommends that sociologists practise 'participant objectivation' during research. This necessitates a full understanding of the everyday, taken-for-granted world of the research subjects, and exacting self-criticism regarding the researcher's personal biases (Bourdieu and Wacquant, in Bourdieu and Wacquant 1992: 67–8). He identifies three levels of bias that undermine the sociological perspective (Wacquant, in Bourdieu and Wacquant 1992: 39):

- the researcher's specific social background;
- the researcher's relative position within the specific academic field, and the general position of social scientists within wider social relations of domination;
- the researcher's superior intellectual status, encouraging him or her to perceive social practices not as practical activities involving social actors, but as spectacles for an objective, withdrawn kind of interpretation.

These biases may certainly operate within sport sociology. The sport sociologist's privileged economic and cultural background may produce ambivalence or disdain towards working-class sport subcultures. The researcher may 'play the academic game' to secure a successful career, avoiding explicit criticism of powerful sociologists and their work, to ensure publication in good journals and research grant income, while producing modest critiques of those dominant groups that are generically antagonistic to sport sociologists *per se* (for example, the elite business class, state officials, sports governing body figures). The researcher may produce a detached, speculative, even dismissive interpretation of the social practices of the research group, rather than seeing these practices for what they are to social actors.

To elaborate Bourdieu's positions regarding practice and sociological work, I turn now to his reading of the concepts of *habitus*, capital and field.

Habitus, *capital and field*

Habitus describes the 'socialized subjectivity' of people, and represents the system of classification that shapes people's practices, beliefs, habits, 'tastes' and bodily techniques (see Fowler 1997: 17). The *habitus* tends to operate outside individual self-awareness, and is 'always orientated towards practical functions'. It possesses 'an infinite capacity for generating products – thoughts, perceptions, expressions and actions – whose limits are set by the historically and socially situated conditions of its production' (Bourdieu 1990b: 52–5). Elsewhere, for Bourdieu, the *habitus* 'expresses first the *result of an organizing action*, with a meaning close to that of words such as structure; it also designates a way of being, a habitual state (especially of the body) and, in particular, a *predisposition, tendency, propensity* or *inclination*' (1984: 562, cited in Tomlinson 2004: 166).

In regard to capital, individuals have different volumes and kinds. Economic capital relates to material wealth; cultural capital to cultural resources like educational and artistic knowledge; social capital to social networks across friends, families, workmates and wider circles; symbolic capital to honours, prestige and other valorized accreditation. *Field* is more concerned with objective social reality, and is comprised of 'a set of objective, historical relations between positions anchored in certain forms of power (or capital)' (Wacquant, in Bourdieu and Wacquant 1992: 16). As we shall see, Bourdieu understands each field to be a kind of game.

These terms are interdependent. A person's *habitus*, combined with her capital and added to her field position, will determine her cultural practices. This interplay is captured through the 'generative' formula: (habitus × capital) + field = practice. Although there is an 'ontological complicity' between the terms, 'habitus' and 'field' carry different respective weightings of the 'subjective' and 'objective' (Bourdieu and Wacquant 1992: 127–8). The *habitus* is a form of subjectivity, but a socialized one; the field is an objective construct constituted by contested relations between social actors.

The field possesses a specific *doxa*, constituting common sense or tacitly accepted ideals, or 'everything that goes without saying' (Bourdieu 1993: 51). The *doxa* is internalized unquestioningly by dominant and dominated groups; for the latter it can constitute 'the most absolute form of conservatism' whereby the conditions of oppression are simply part of the taken-for-granted world (Bourdieu and Wacquant 1992: 73–4). Social analysts must go beyond *doxa* to produce 'para-doxal modes of thought' that destabilize this practical sense, unsettling the habits of the conservative bourgeoisie, and forcing Left liberals to dissect power relationships more clinically.

Bourdieu (2000: 151–3; Bourdieu and Wacquant 1992: 98–100) understood the 'field' as a 'game'. Social agents take game positions according to their different kinds of *habitus* (which define their different kinds of 'feel' for the game) and their different capital endowments relative to game requirements. 'Position-takings' within the game are never entirely predictable. Endorsing Elias, Bourdieu recognizes that even the absolutist king must play inside the game to obtain the benefits of domination:

> There would be no game without players' (visceral, corporeal) commitment to the game, without the interest taken in the game as such which is the source of the different, even opposite, interests of the various players, the wills and ambitions which drive them and which, being produced by the game, depend on the positions they occupy within it. (2000: 153)

New players must acquire practical understandings of the game and its history. Interpretative workers – biographers, historians and archivists – play a crucial role in conserving the game, thus protecting their own positions within it (Bourdieu 1993: 73–4). Players' prior investments in learning and gaining distinction within the game ensure that its destruction is 'unthinkable'. Each game has its own definitive interests and stakes that mark differences between players; attempts by some players to transfer across fields (into other games) are typically resisted by those seeking to protect pre-established positions within the other game.[3] Indeed, as a game, sport is 'relatively autonomous' *vis-à-vis* other games, as its history, 'even when marked by the major events of economic and social history, has its own tempo, its own evolutionary laws, its own crises, in short, its specific chronology' (Bourdieu 1993: 118).

Game players have different mixtures of capital whereby to secure or improve their positions. Bourdieu pictures capital in terms of game tokens with different colours to designate each player's varied capabilities. To understand player strategies, one needs to examine the actual volume of tokens/capital that she possesses, and how that capital has evolved over time. Players adopt different tactics to protect and augment their capital. They may play 'trump' or master cards whose capital values vary according to the game. They may play more radically, to 'transform, partially or completely, the immanent rules of the game', such as by changing token colours or devaluing the particular colour of tokens held by opponents (Bourdieu and Wacquant 1992: 99).

Bourdieu's game/field model has notable sports applicability, particularly during moments of tension. Olympic sport is one sporting field that includes diverse groups of competing players (athletes, coaches, officials, media workers and producers, sponsors, and so on) that possess different capital mixtures. Olympic sport has much taken-for-granted *doxa*, such as the IOC's ultimate authority; Olymp-ism's continuation of virtuous, ancient Greek athleticism; and the specific ethical balance between amateurism and professionalism/commodification. Critical social scientists seek to provide 'para-doxal' research that challenges these *doxa*. To influence the game, new Olympic players must 'serve their time', increasing their capital lev-els through training, networking and effective performances. The Olympics' revolutionary transformation is almost universally resisted, to protect the various players' sizeable capital holdings. Interpretative workers like journalists sustain the Olympic field by constructing its history, debating its traditions, elaborating and reforming its *doxa*. The most powerful athletes, coaches and officials display their large capital holdings in the game, to play 'master cards'.

All of these processes arose in the struggle over the switch of many Olympic sports from official 'amateur' to 'professional' status during the 1980s. The move reflected the growing influence of those who held large amounts of economic capital within Olympism, notably televi-sion corporations, sponsors and full-time elite sports workers (coaches and athletes). Leading IOC officials retained their powers by increas-ing their holdings in new token colours: as their aristocratic social and symbolic powers waned, they reasserted control over economic capital entering the game. Long-term players within Olympic sport present personal 'trump cards' to protect their status and influence the game's direction: for example, the greatest Olympic athletes may argue that economic 'modernization' should become a new Olympic *doxa*; or they may criticize the strong position of television execu-tives and sponsors, arguing that these groups are unwanted interlop-ers from 'other games' (like product marketing). Para-doxal players like investigative journalists expose IOC authoritarianism, corruption and betrayal of Olympian ideals. Yet no player argues for the game's complete abolition; the most radical argue for reinventing the system that produces the game's rules, procedures and distribution of capital.

Cultural divisions and symbolic violence

While appreciating that capital has diverse colours, social class un-derpins Bourdieu's understanding of social stratification. He defines class more in cultural than neo-Marxist terms, as a group of agents that 'share the same interests, social experiences, traditions, and value system, and who tend to act as a class and define themselves in relation to other groups of agents' (Clément 1995: 149). Each class struggles to impose itself on the collective *habituses* of other social classes, to secure and exercise domination across a specific field (Urry 1990: 88). The *habitus* of each social class is revealed through sport and other cultural pursuits (Bourdieu 1993: 129–30).

Oppositions between sexes, classes and class fractions are expressed through the 'system' of sports practices that confront social agents. In respect of class, sports are 'classified and classifying, rank-ordered and rank-ordering' (Bourdieu 1984: 223). In 'selecting' certain sports, so-cial agents 'follow the leanings of their habitus' to find sports 'just right' for them. Class distinctions carry socio-spatial dimensions; ex-clusive social spaces possess a 'club effect', in longevity, differences to other spaces, and the exclusion of those lacking certain attributes (Bourdieu 1993: 129). Thus exclusive sports clubs restrict membership to those with high capital levels: economic (annual fees), social (mem-ber contacts), cultural (particular dress, language, ethnicity, general demeanour) or symbolic (sport title-winners). Physical or symbolic distance separates people without capital from rare social goods, for-cing them to inhabit a specific locale. 'The lack of capital intensifies the experience of finitude: it chains one to a place' (1993: 127).

'Symbolic violence' maintains field disadvantages among low-capital social groups. Echoing Gramsci's theory of hegemony, Bourdieu defines 'symbolic violence' as a form of social harm 'exercised upon a social agent with his or her complicity' (Bourdieu and Wacquant 1992: 167). More fully explained:

> Symbolic violence is the coercion which is set up only through the con-sent that the dominated cannot fail to give to the dominator (and there-fore to the domination) when their understanding of the situation and relation can only use instruments of knowledge that they have in com-mon with the dominator. (Bourdieu 2000: 170)

Educational institutions perform intensive symbolic violence. Schools inculcate the dominant groups' codes, values and predispositions, thus reducing dominated groups to *collaboration* in their symbolic coercion (Bourdieu and Passeron 1977). Symbolic violence marks the social ex-clusion of specific populations (notably women and ethnic minorities) from sports participation.[4] Symbolic violence ensures that women or people of Asian descent believe that they do not 'belong' in sport, that they are not 'natural' athletes or capable of intense exertion.

Overall, the roots of Bourdieu's sociological approach are primarily structuralist, concerned with social practices, and committed to reflex-ive research that blends empirical content and theoretical strength. Through more nuanced readings of capital than neo-Marxists had proffered previously, Bourdieu reveals the different means through which human inequalities are reproduced. He accounts for subjectivity through the concept of *habitus*, although interpretative sociologists would argue that Bourdieu reads the term as over-socialized and pre-determining of action and meaning.

Four aspects of Bourdieu's imaginary are particularly appealing. First, despite contradicting his claim to have transcended the subject–object opposition, Bourdieu's more structuralist reading of social action, embedded in the term 'practice', is satisfyingly sociological, and captures power relations within human agency. Second, the concept of 'field' enables useful game models of social struggles. Third, Bourdieu advocates the critical reflexivity of sociologists in confronting underlying biases and producing critical, 'para-doxal' research. Fourth, use of the term 'violence' to explain symbolic oppression strikingly captures the injurious nature of the dominant groups' powers. The execution of material violence is both inefficient and redundant when more potent psychological and cultural resources may be mustered to violate the human potential of dominated groups.

Distinction: the stratification of sporting tastes

Basic principles

In *Distinction*, Bourdieu posits that dominant groups use their greater capital to claim 'taste' or cultural legitimacy for their cultural preferences; this 'distinction' separates dominant from dominated culturally. Thus, 'In the struggle between groups, each group expresses disgust for the taste of other groups' (Defrance 1995: 126).[5]

Bourdieu maps links between social stratification and cultural taste across three dimensions. The *vertical* dimension measures differences in capital volume (economic and cultural), from the richest to the most impoverished. The *horizontal* dimension differentiates kinds of capital, specifically economic and cultural. The *temporal* dimension traces the general historical trajectory (rising or falling) of each specific group. In the UK, for example, the old-money upper classes are markedly high in their (vertical) volumes of capital, claim slightly more (horizontal) cultural than economic capital (mixing education, etiquette and landed wealth), and have long-standing (temporal) capital strengths. Hence, the old-money elite prefer traditional sports like equestrianism that require significant capital outlays for early training and maintenance of equipment, and necessitate access to old sources of economic wealth, notably land and domestic animals. Thus, sports are not innocent pastimes with only 'intrinsic profits' (like health or fitness), but produce 'social profits' from the 'distributional significance' between different classes (Bourdieu 1984: 35). Golf may have healthy 'intrinsic profits' regarding exercise, but its superior, social profits derive from French bourgeois social capital. Conversely, weight-lifting may have 'intrinsic profits' regarding strength for working-class supporters, but its weak 'social profits' ensured that it lacked recognition among aristocratic Olympic authorities.

Sport and class habitus

The dominant classes' *habitus* favours 'aesthetic', 'contemplative' and 'healthy' sports: for example, 'golf, tennis, sailing, riding (or show-jumping), skiing (especially its most distinctive forms, such as cross-country) or fencing' (Bourdieu 1984: 215). The dominant classes stand aloof from impassioned, vulgar crowds at popular sports. 'Legitimate' sport is less intense, often acquiring the ambience of a social encounter, and less likely to involve strong bodily contact between players.

Sport differentiates groups *within* the dominant class. Sport's glorification by aristocratic, managerial and business elites 'implies a certain anti-intellectualism'; their support for rugby symbolizes overt opposition to dominated elements within the dominant class, like university teachers and artists who prioritize intellectual cultural capital. Rugby is defined as manly, virile, character-building and practised through will-power, in contrast to the passive, effeminate and self-critical attributes associated with cerebral pastimes (Bourdieu 1993: 122).[6]

Middle-class fractions possess different sporting tastes (Bourdieu 1984: 219). Teachers display 'aristocratic asceticism' through mountaineering, cycling and rambling, fitting their claims to post-materialist, high cultural capital alongside low economic costs. Doctors and modern executives pursue 'health-oriented hedonism', escaping the masses financially and spatially through exotic, expensive pastimes like yachting or skiing. Similarly, business employers favour consumerist life-styles and sports with social 'profits'.[7]

Conversely, the working classes understand the body 'instrumentally'. Male tastes in boxing or weight-lifting are culturally akin to manual work, 'building' the body-object via painful exertion and subjugation. 'Gambling with the body' arises in boxing, motor-cycling and violent play in football or rugby league. While working-class females in sport are ignored, Bourdieu does imply their corporeal instrumentality in dieting or beauty care. For the 'privileged classes', the body is an end in itself, connecting sports practices with physical health. Characteristically, the lower middle classes take this corporeal philosophy to literal extremes. Gymnastics embody their 'ascetic exaltation of sobriety and dietetic rigour' and the embracing of scientific theories that orientate practical actions towards predetermined ends (Bourdieu 1993: 130).

Different sporting tastes are not caused simply by material divisions (Bourdieu 1984: 217). Skiing, golf and cricket require relatively expensive equipment, yet 'more hidden entry requirements' ensure social closure for potential working-class practitioners. Family habits, childhood sports experiences, initiation into the correct bodily *habitus*, and socializing techniques: such cultural and social factors secure bourgeois domination, and reaffirm these sports' socio-cultural and corporeal meanings.

Individuals with high sports proficiency can be endowed with specialist cultural capital (such as coaching certificates) and economic (salary) and social (contacts, elite circles) capital; symbolic (national and international titles, positive media representation) capital may also follow. For dominated groups, however, sport is an insecure, capricious career path dependent on physical fitness. Bourdieu and Balazs (1993: 361–9) recount the case of a Portuguese family that appeared to integrate successfully within a small French town, partly through the father's football skills. After being injured, the father's social and symbolic capital evaporated overnight; old friends disappeared, and the French state offered no welfare security.

Generational differences connect to class *habitus* within sports (Bourdieu 1984: 212). 'Popular', energetic sports correlate strongly with youth. Rugby league, football and boxing are usually abandoned by working-class males entering adulthood, since 'excess' libidinal or playful energies are channelled into marriage and domestic provision (Bourdieu 1993: 129). Bourgeois sports like golf or tennis require less physical exertion, enabling longer life-course participation, healthy exercise and the local club's social benefits. Among Japanese business executives, golf involves bodily mastery and a subtle 'embodiment of organizational seniorship' that includes belonging to the right group and understanding relevant information (Ben-Ari 1998: 154–6). Sports like golf nourish the bourgeois *habitus*, notably through receiving (upon payment) a technical pedagogy, a one-on-one tuition, enskilling the body and cultivating the mind into more artful yet strategic insights into the game's potentialities.

For Bourdieu, the sporting field is not static. Any sport's dominant meanings may be transformed through social struggle, just as musical

works like Beethoven's Ninth Symphony acquire different social definitions over time (see Buch 2003).

> A sport, at a given moment, is rather like a musical work; it is both the
> musical score (the rules of the game, etc.), and also the various com-
> peting interpretations (and a whole set of sedimented interpretations
> from the past); and each new interpreter is confronted by this, more
> unconsciously than consciously, when he proposes 'his' interpretation.
> (Bourdieu 1990a: 163)

From his research in the 1960s and early 1970s, Bourdieu identified the rise of 'Californian', 'counter-cultural' sports that favour
'authentic' natural products or crafted attire, and evince a social
and somatic weightlessness, as in hang-gliding, trekking and wind-
surfing. They are favoured by the 'new petite bourgeoisie', notably
employed in 'cultural intermediary' professions of commercial seduction, such as in fashion, advertising, photography, journalism and
design (Featherstone 1991b). Whereas the old petite bourgeoisie advocates duty, self-restraint, modesty and self-control, the new petite
bourgeoisie regards pursuit of pleasure as a personal and ethical im-
perative (Bourdieu 1984: 367).

Bourdieu's arguments have strengths and limitations, as indicated
when applied to surfing, a prime counter-cultural sport. Surfing did become associated with a vaguely bohemian culture and the pursuit of
oceanic 'peak experiences'. Yet surfing's meaning has been subject to
struggles between different strata *within* the pastime, including more
orthodox life-saving groups, hedonistic surfers, consumer-focused
surfers, triathletes, and those promoting surfing's general professionalization (Booth 2001). Surfing's social history thus accords with
Bourdieu's insistence that social struggles define the meanings of sporting pastimes. However, the direct correspondences between surfing
subcultures and specific social classes cannot be assumed. I return
later to this problem in Bourdieu's thesis.

Applications in sport sociology

Bourdieu's work has been hugely influential within French sport sociology, producing research that connects sport's meanings and practices
to social identities and divisions (see Vigarello 1995: 225). His regular
collaborator, Loïc Wacquant (1995a, 1995b), has drawn particularly
on the concept of capital to produce several studies of Chicago's boxing culture. Defrance (1976, 1987) has traced the social history of
French gymnastics and other sports from the late eighteenth century

onwards. In combat sports, class *habituses* are reflected through different tastes: the established bourgeoisie appreciate aesthetic body-shape and economic movement (notably in aikido), while the lower classes favour bodily contact, physical exchanges and strength (notably in wrestling) (Clément 1981, 1985).

Others have engaged Bourdieu to examine the class, gender and ethnic distribution of sports participation. One study in Memphis found that youth football club membership demarcated the white, suburban culture from the 'urban depravity and difference' of non-white, lower-class locales (Andrews et al. 1997: 271–2). In Canada, sociologists reinterpreted Bourdieu's classifications to examine physical activity and general leisure among 180 local Francophone women from the middle class (such as nurses and librarians), the working class (such as cleaners and factory workers), the intellectual bourgeoisie (compared here to Bourdieu's 'new middle classes') and the upper class (partners of wealthy and highly-paid professionals). The results confirmed the correlation between physical activity and class *habitus*. Middle-class women favoured work-outs, aerobics and swimming, reflecting both 'self-imposed rules of behaviour' to stay slim and healthy-looking, and their labour market subordination to the dominant norms surrounding female body-shape. Working-class women were least active, because exercise had few instrumental benefits: slimness has no impact on a machine operator's working life. The intellectual bourgeoisie preferred relatively 'liberating', new (but not 'popular') physical activities, like orienteering or 'body awareness through movement' programmes requiring educational and cultural capital. Finally, upper-class women enjoyed luxurious consumption, accumulating social capital and transmitting cultural capital (allowing the husband to act as role model) – for example, membership of exclusive golf or skiing clubs, with substantial 'après-sport' opportunities (Laberge and Sankoff 1988).

More recent testing of Bourdieu's theories confirms the presence of class and regional imbalances in sport spectatorship in Canada (White and Wilson 1999; T. C. Wilson 2002). Elsewhere, in adventure racing, the *habitus* of management-level corporate participants led them to rationalize their activities in terms of transferable skills regarding risk taking, team building and self-development (Kay and Laberge 2002). T. C. Wilson (2002) also found that while 'cultural omnivores' in sport possessed higher economic and cultural capital, they still had no taste for 'prole sports' like cycle racing.

Overall, Bourdieu debunks sport's 'sacred aura'. Instead, sport is one of many cultural means through which the different social classes distinguish themselves from one another (Clément 1995: 149). There is nothing particularly counter-intuitive in his thesis, although Bourdieu is extremely sharp in relating the minutiae of a social class's *habitus* to its interpretations of specific sports. One problem concerns the very sense of over-determination with which class and sporting preferences hang together. There is little scope for any sport to evolve aesthetic principles, techniques and practitioner subcultures that are not determined by class *habitus* and struggle.

The politics of research

For Bourdieu, sociology is not politically disengaged but is, instead, a 'combat sport' (Müller 2002). From the mid-1990s Bourdieu became increasingly outspoken on public issues, thereby cementing his status as an *intellectuel engagé* in the French tradition of Sartre, Zola and Voltaire.

In *Acts of Resistance*, Bourdieu attacks the aura of inevitability surrounding neo-liberal economic and social policies. Western conservatism has produced greater inequalities and social insecurity (especially among the young) through unemployment, low wages and criminalization; thus, in the United States, lower-class African-American males inhabit 'the first genuine prison society in history' (Wacquant 2002a: 60). Culture is infected by 'the reign of commerce' that undermines social-scientific critical inquiry and artistic creativity. Bourdieu advocates instead an 'economics of happiness' that recognizes non-material, symbolic profits and losses. Such an economics would enable us to reckon with the 'law of the conservation of violence', which would show that, for example, company 'retrenchments' have wide-reaching, pernicious consequences:

> All violence is paid for, and, for example, the structural violence exerted by the financial markets, in the form of layoffs, loss of security, etc., is matched sooner or later in the form of suicides, crime and delinquency, drug addiction, alcoholism, a whole host of minor and major everyday acts of violence. (Bourdieu 1998a: 40)

Dominant groups routinely represent the dispossessed as immoral, degenerate, stupid and unworthy of political influence. The educational system inculcates these false perceptions of fated, self-evident worthlessness among the dominated. Bourdieu (1998a: 52–9) advocates a more reflexive battle against conservatism, while forging a 'transnational struggle' across Europe. New social movements (like environmental groups) effect social resistance, but cannot match the symbolic power of conservative forces in communicating their messages. Social researchers should help through dialogue with activists and advancing 'para-doxal' critiques of conservative media. Bourdieu berates his intellectual colleagues for their political 'ambiguity', their constant 'surrenders' and 'collaborations' in dealings with neo-liberalism. Intellectuals are a dominated element within the dominant group, but their 'uncommitted' politics, disguised as 'professional competence', are unacceptable to Bourdieu.

Bourdieu's politics have direct consequences for sport sociology. Researchers should engage with new social movements within sport, publicizing scientific studies that critique transnational corporations and governing bodies. Lenskyj's (2000, 2002, 2004) participation in social movements critical of the IOC, and her sociological work on the Olympics, exemplify the publicly engaged (in Gramsci's terms, 'organic') intellectual work that Bourdieu advocates. As noted in earlier chapters, some of sport's new social movements (in Europe, North America and Australasia) argue that commodification and rationalization in major sports have alienated or disenfranchised many of these pastimes' old custodians. In English football these 'modernization' processes have been assisted, in part, by the negative portrayal of long-standing football supporters by 'competent' intellectuals. Such 'collaboration' between intellectuals and corporate interests continues, by other means, the symbolic violence that is waged against dominated groups in favour of dominant elites.

In terms of sports policy, Bourdieu advocates a 'realistic utopia' that would restore 'those values which the world of sport proclaims and which are very like the values of art and science (non-commercial, ends in themselves, disinterested, valuing fair play and the 'way the game is played' as opposed to sacrificing everything for results)' (Bourdieu 1998b: 21). He recommends a 'coherent and universal model' with several policy features, to promote:

- sport's educational dimension
- state support for unpaid sports officials
- anti-corruption initiatives
- more coaching and development of young players
- tightened links between grass roots and elite level sport
- realistic forms of identification among young people towards elite professionals
- integrating immigrants socially through sport
- establishing a Sports Charter governing all athletes, officials and media analysts
- enabling sport journalists to act as the 'critical conscience for the sporting world'.

These laudable recommendations signify a switch in discursive emphasis. The earlier Bourdieu adopted a comparatively objectivist stance to explain how cultural preferences and practices functioned to distinguish social groups within specific cultural fields. The later, engaged Bourdieu adopted a more subjectivist position that inclined towards viewing cultural preferences and practices as good *in themselves* within the specific cultural field. In this way, Bourdieu came to counterbalance his often dense sociological theorizing with the pragmatic, critical politics required of a public intellectual.

Critical considerations: towards cultural comparisons through Bourdieu

To conclude, Bourdieu's work has many sociological virtues. He essays a solution to the structure–agency division, while (in my view, correctly) evading pure voluntarism by favouring a more structuralist focus on power inequalities. His sociological keywords – *habitus*, field, capital, practice and distinction – are highly beneficial conceptual tools for social researchers. His sociological blend of theory and evidence is 'good to think with', and invites elucidation in research fields like sport (Jenkins 1992: 61, 98). The resultant research findings, notably in *Distinction*, may somewhat predictably trace class taste and disclose patterns of cultural snobbery, but this work is a model of systematic analysis, with a satisfying reach into cultural totality. Bourdieu's concern with the potential biases and critical responsibilities of sociologists is an important, underrated contribution to research methodology that must be read alongside his critique of education. His concept of 'symbolic violence', to expose the patterns and experiences of symbolic subjugation, is extremely important, and enables more sophisticated understanding of violence *per se*. Bourdieu's argument that social scientists should actively expose and challenge systems of domination is hard to contest, and fits with his wider sociological theories. His political legacy compares favourably with that of his English contemporary, Anthony Giddens, whose social theory is too closely aligned with Tony Blair's vacuous 'third way'.

Bourdieu's theoretical framework, however, does contain an unwarranted determinism when explaining cultural aesthetics, the positions people adopt inside a field, and how different fields relate to each other. For Bourdieu, a sociological examination of sport's aesthetic codes and meanings is a somewhat superfluous exercise, unless we view these as mere means towards the goal of securing distinction. This argument means that social scientists would overlook, wrongly in my view, the capacity of sport and culture generally to 'manifest autonomous non-utilitarian forms of beauty' (Canclini 1995: 20–1).

Though he trumpets sport's 'relative autonomy' *vis-à-vis* other fields, Bourdieu reduces sporting tastes and practices to competing *habituses* that are shaped in other social fields. For example, the content of working-class, male body culture is pretty much read off from this category's industrial condition: manual work begets highly physical sporting preferences. Similarly, playing golf becomes a sign that the golfer wants to 'look like' an old bourgeois (Bourdieu 1990a: 132). However, I would argue that sporting tastes and practices are not so conveniently class-connected, suggesting that we need to increase categorical flexibility to deploy Bourdieu's thinking within sport.

Bourdieu's empirical claims linking class and cultural practice have been challenged. Gans (1999: 19) insists that those in American elite occupations have used cultural practices as mere 'status indicators', and not as forms of capital that are 'virtual job requirements', as Bourdieu implies. In Finland, sports interests cross class boundaries, although some pastimes (like golf and surfing) carry distinction between and within classes. Heinilä (1998: 194–5) concludes that 'Few sports are still interwoven with the different lifestyles and with the habitus and dispositions people afford in the particular social field in which they live.' Later research across Scandinavia argues that socio-economic capital, but not cultural capital, influences patterns of sport spectatorship (Thrane 2001). More problematically, social surveys suggest that, while an upper-class high culture exists, a cross-class 'mass culture' of 'taste' for consumer items like food and furniture is predominant (Gartman 1991).

Bourdieu's current framework struggles to explain international differences or local cross-class continuities in aesthetic preferences and sporting habits. First, for example, Scandinavian ice hockey players are often described as better 'stick-handlers' than their North American counterparts. While this provides Scandinavian players with an aesthetic/identity difference, and an alternative playing system for defeating North American teams, how this constitutes a badge of distinction within wider social struggles is hard to say. Second, for example, in Brazil, there are different styles of play in football, but these are popularly differentiated by region rather than by the vast class inequalities that pertain across the nation. In Rio, for example, the fluid and free-floating *carioca* style has cross-class support. In São Paulo or especially Porto Alegre, the aesthetic is traditionally more pragmatic and combative. The point here is that Bourdieu's analytical framework is notably weak when we examine the cultural conflicts and symbolic differences that arise *within* specific sporting fields.

A pro-Bourdieu solution to this problem lies only in the founding of a research programme that can produce a more culturally flexible, global and sports-focused version of *Distinction*. Such a programme would require cross-cultural, international survey research into sporting practices and tastes. The project would need to allow for geo-cultural variations in how each sporting field is constituted and contested, recognizing the 'relative autonomy' of every 'game'. Sociologists examining contemporary subcultures have hinted inadvertently at this need to soften Bourdieu's framework, to concentrate on struggles for distinction *within* specific cultural practices. Thornton (1995: 11–14), for example, argues that young people in subcultures pursue distinction that is measured in terms of their 'subcultural capital'. J. B. Thompson (1995: 223) argues that contemporary fan cultures have their own power hierarchies and sets of conventions whereby amateurs and the *cognoscenti* are differentiated. In both instances, distinction is gained through possessing mixtures of capital that are meaningful specifically within the relevant subcultural field. A similar point comes into play regarding sport. Sport fans employ numerous interactive strategies to identify and evaluate the cultural capital of one another. Do other fans recall key moments in major sports events? Can they identify specific techniques or individual players? To what extent did they grow up with the sport? Answers to these questions are often found in the distinctive social and historical relations within each sporting field, rather than in the external influences of wider social stratification.

11

The Postmodern: Premonitions of Virtual, Post-Industrial Sport

During the 1980s and 1990s, postmodernism provided a strongly contested, highly prominent debate within social science. Sympathizers argued that postmodern theory expanded sociological grasp of the post-industrial, consumerist, sign-saturated, globalizing world. Sceptics countered that postmodernism was a sociological fad lacking rational principles or critical foundations, whilst over-dramatizing changes within advanced modern societies. Certainly, the first criticism appears increasingly germane: by the late 1990s, the 'postmodern debate' had largely disappeared, to be replaced by questions of 'globalization' or, less importantly, 'risk'. That decline was accelerated by postmodernism's notoriously elusive meaning and the tendency of 'postmodern prophets' (notably Baudrillard) to distance themselves from the term.

This discussion of postmodern issues develops two key terms. I take 'postmodernity' to designate the particular forms of social relation and reflexivity that arise in post-industrial societies. I take 'postmodernism' to designate the aesthetic codes and material products of particular cultural schools and *genres*, notably among the artistic avant-garde. In sport, debates regarding postmodernity may focus, for example, on specific kinds of gender or family relations in stadium attendance, or new forms of self-consciousness regarding sports-related consumption. Alternatively, debates over postmodernism may focus on stadiums' architectural design, or on techniques of film production in adverts for sports merchandise.

Here, I discuss sport and the postmodern in six parts. The opening three parts discuss the postmodern's theoretical and categorical foundations, and refer specifically to critiques of modern philosophy,

the 'dedifferentiation' of modern taxonomies, and the postmodernization of identity. Parts four and five discuss the more conventional
sociological approach towards explaining postmodernity, focusing on
changes in class and cultural practices and the genesis of post-Fordist,
'disorganized capitalism'. Part six develops earlier points on dedifferentiation to examine postmodernism's cultural eclecticism and Jean
Baudrillard's provocative premonition of postmodernity. I conclude
by evaluating the postmodern's political dimensions.

Deconstructing modern 'metanarratives': postmodern and post-structuralist social theory

Much postmodern social theory rejects our modern faith in scientific, rational knowledge. According to Lyotard (1984), 'modern'
knowledge ('science') seeks to establish universal 'truths' that
legitimize themselves by appealing to modern norms and principles, specifically 'emancipation' and 'speculation'. Each science claims
to transcend local customs and belief systems to produce distinctive, universal 'metanarratives'. Each metanarrative builds cultural
legitimacy through speculative, universal truth-claims and advocates
human emancipation.

For Lyotard, the postmodern condition germinates 'incredulity' towards these metanarratives. The grand narratives of modernist emancipation (rationalism, socialism, parliamentary liberalism, *laissez-faire*
capitalism and Keynesian economics) are invalidated historically by
seminal events like Auschwitz, Budapest in 1956, Paris in May 1968,
the Wall Street crash of 1929, and the mid-1970s recessions (Lyotard
1993: 29). Thus, knowledge is not universally 'true', but culturally
relative and organized into different 'language games' with their own
communicative standards and principles. *Pace* Habermas *inter alia*,
there is no modern metalanguage or universal ethic that can underpin
all language games. Instead, postmodern knowledge involves 'paralogy' – that is, the undermining of the foundations and framework
within which science has been constructed (1984: 66–7).

The modernist promise in sport is that physical exercise produces
stronger, healthier, happier, 'better' bodies as forms of personal and
collective emancipation. However, postmodern incredulity towards
these discourses is reflected through rising public consciousness concerning sport's hidden costs, ranging from injury and pain to systematic sexual harassment, social control and exploitation. Alternative
knowledge systems and 'language games' are explored to challenge the

rationalization, competition, bureaucratization and secularization of modern sporting disciplines. These alternative, anti-modernist trends combine pre-modern and postmodern impulses.[1] In physical culture, non-competitive practices arise alongside a 'return' to the countryside through hill-walking and mountaineering. Western countercultures, notably New Age movements, have engaged in postmodern, cross-cultural syncretism by blending Eastern spiritual knowledge and religiosity with Western organization and commercialism. Books like *The Zen of Muhammad Ali and Other Obsessions* by Davis Miller and *The Tao of Golf* by Leland T. Lewis suggest that a sports-related paralogy is gaining hold, utilizing non-scientific, Eastern knowledge systems to pursue transcendence within sports performance. The popularity of Eastern martial arts also suggests a more concerted rejection of modern sports, although these 'other' disciplines typically undergo substantial Western 'sportification' (Guttmann 1988: 179–81).

'Post-structuralist' social theories, notably produced by Derrida and Foucault, constitute an important strain of postmodernist theorizing. Structuralist social theorists like Lévi-Strauss have argued that each culture is underpinned by its 'deep structures' of linguistic rules and classificatory systems. As objective social phenomena, these structures typically exist beyond the social actors' consciousness.[2] In contrast, French post-structuralists advance more critical theories of rationality and power. Whereas structuralism provides snapshots of a society's social categories, Foucault's post-structuralism, as noted earlier, highlights the radical historical breaks between categorical systems, and discloses the role of power relations in reproducing these taxonomies. Post-structuralism exposes the interdependencies of power and knowledge and the role of scientific discourses in disciplining and governing populations.[3]

In Derrida's literary post-structuralism, the 'death of the author' is proclaimed, since authorial control over a text's meaning is impossible. Writing, for example, is highly contextual, unstable and eternally exposed to critical 'deconstructions'. Chiming in with Lyotard, Derrida (1978) deconstructs the narrow, universalist 'logocentrism' of Western rationality, attacking its claim to contain a 'transcendental signified' – that is, its objective, eternal, scientific foundations. As his concept of *différance* suggests, any text's fixed meaning is always 'deferred' before its next reinterpretation.

Derridean theory has had little impact upon sport sociology, but it does suggest fruitful application within sport's artistic and constitutional dimensions. First, the 'decentring' of authorial control enables athletes to evade the iron laws of coaches, to establish more creative,

experimental, autonomous play roles. The performing arts should facilitate performer creativity and the playful interaction of difference
(Derrida 1978: 235–48). Derridean theory engenders fresh ideas for
the fruitful, practical and humane restructuring of sport's social relations and practices.

Second, to legitimize their universal power, many sporting rule-
books and governing bodies appeal to 'logocentric' values like
'gentlemanly behaviour', 'fair play' and (most tautologically) 'sporting conduct'. Deconstruction of these 'transcendental signifieds' can
destabilize the political might of sport institutions.[4] Deconstruction-
ism embraces the inherent, popular suspicion that all sporting rules
are always up for reinterpretation, that sport's 'judges' (referees or
umpires) do not author the sole truthful interpretation of laws.

Sports events always generate argument, but any contest involving
committed Derrideans would degenerate into a ceaseless farce wherein
every play action or decision underwent endless reinterpretation. A
softer, more cultural Derridean perspective would assist the recognition that cultures do interpret sport's rules and aesthetics differently.
International sport fixtures facilitate the commingling of these different cultural language games wherein a shared interpretation is always
deferred. When teams from different nations enter competition, sporting bodies usually appoint 'neutral' referees from a third nation to ensure that this third language game is dominant. However, this should
lead us to consider whether the third (referee) perspective is significantly closer to that held by one team rather than its opponents.[5]

Three problems arise in the postmodern relativism of Lyotard,
Foucault and Derrida. First, their attack on Western rationalism pivots
on an illogical, Ishmael effect: the denial of universal 'truth' is itself
advanced as a universal truth-claim. Likewise, postmodernists actually appeal to rational reflection in critiquing the nefarious sporting
effects of science (e.g. doping) or Western sports corporations. Second,
postmodernist theories provide no firm foundations for establishing
authoritative arguments. Postmodernists talk themselves out of work
by undermining sociology's privileged position for explaining social
affairs. These anti-authorial theories also misrepresent sociological
methodology. Following fieldwork, the postmodernist does not claim
to write a coherent narrative, but instead juxtaposes various fragments
of human voices to create a pastiche text (see T. Bruce 1998: 12). However, this procedure still displays an authorial, critical intervention in
initially selecting or omitting specific textual slices. Thus, the postmodernist researcher remains a 'modernist' author, albeit a reluctant
one.

Third, via Habermas, postmodernists produce a 'cultural relativism' that abandons political hope and moral critique. Postmodernism should not relativize fundamental points on our moral compass. We cannot avoid responding to, on the haughty grounds of 'cultural difference', the pleas of desperate, oppressed peoples living under harsh, 'other' regimes. In sport, one morally indefensible practice involves the sale or abduction of young Pakistani children to work illegally in the Gulf States as camel-racing jockeys. Many suffer serious or fatal injuries; the vast majority endure physical or sexual abuse. Adopting a postmodern stance of respect for cultural difference, a position of 'tolerant open-mindedness' towards such abuse, ensures only that our brains, and our moral scruples, will fall out of our heads (Morgan 1998: 362–3, via Rorty 1991).

A softer postmodern social theory is more plausible. Modern 'universal ethics' must undergo constant critical interrogation, but core universal ethics, concerning fundamental citizen rights, are inalienable. To communicate across sport's language games, we must strive to deconstruct the incumbent meanings of sporting ethics. For example, 'fair play' in sport is in itself a morally defensible ideal, although we must always strive to deconstruct how its dominant meaning connects to power inequalities. Moreover, postmodernists and post-structuralists correctly sense a relativistic, playful mood within postmodernity. Sports cultures show-case rising public interest in cultural diversity and alternative knowledge systems. Finally, international sport promises the playful, postmodern commingling of difference, affording psycho-cultural space for creativity, corporeal transcendence, and possible escape from the routines of rationalized instruction.

Dedifferentiation and the postmodern: collapsing modern boundaries

For Lash (1990: 11–15, 173–4), whereas modernity was characterized by an increasing differentiation of categorical boundaries, institutions and identities, postmodernity is marked by the 'dedifferentiation' (breaking down) of these distinctions. Dedifferentiation involves culture's penetration of social and economic spheres. For example, cultural icons like Michael Jordan generate vast incomes and consumer revenue streams (an estimated $10 billion by 1998) to accelerate 'the implosion of business, entertainment, and sports' (Andrews 2001: 44). Mediated sport is at the cutting edge of the 'culturalization of economics' (Rowe 1999: 70). Sports media productions (like chat shows and newspaper stories) connect different audiences to specific consumer markets (for example, wealthy male football fans and prestige car brands that sponsor televised fixtures).

Dedifferentiation is commonly associated with the alleged collapse of high/low cultural divisions. Modernity had divided the corporeality and expressivity of low-culture, working-class sports like greyhound racing, rugby league and (in the UK) football, from more cerebral, aesthetically valid, middle-class high culture like the performing arts and literature. Sports like English cricket were deemed to have high cultural characteristics, facilitating the audience's critical detachment from play. Cultural postmodernism, it is argued, dedifferentiates these boundaries: hence, poets write on rugby league, prize-winning authors effuse about 'bad-boy' football players, and football operas are composed (Rowe 1995: 165).[6] Mass media outlets juxtapose and interconnect high/low cultural signifiers. English football's transformation, from 'slum sport' to European sophistication, was envisioned in 1990 by British television's postmodern mixing of operatic arias (plus the 'three tenors') with images from the Italian World Cup finals. Films like *When We Were Kings* and books such as *Fever Pitch* suggest that sport-related media are more critical in detail, and more aesthetically framed, than before the 1990s.

Boundaries between audience and author (or performer) have undergone dedifferentiation (Lash 1990: 173). Sport's modernization included the categorical spatial differentiation of audience and athlete. Postmodern dedifferentiation arises through marketing discourses that make spectators 'part of the show': team mascots mix with crowds, individual spectators enter the field during breaks to participate in shoot-out competitions. Sport's mediation collapses these differences further: the on-car camera in motor racing, or cricket's stump-camera, place viewers visually inside the action.

Postmodern culture compresses time–space boundaries. Contemporary technology and institutional globalization allow images, people and capital to move around globally with increasing rapidity and frequency. An evening's televised sport can cover all continents through recorded, live or digitally accessed content (see Gottdiener 1995: 50–1). Nostalgic shows compress time by flitting across decades, or integrating images of athletes from yesteryear and today in a single film (see Rail 1998: 154). Sports clubs in specific 'home' cities can employ elite athletes from across the globe; new athletic talents are purchased globally and instantaneously via international finance houses, sports agents, media and flight companies. Sports mega-events 'bring the world to one city' as athletes and spectators from many nations meet in one urban environment.

Virilio (1986) advances an intriguing elaboration of the time–space compression thesis. His concept of 'dromology' assumes that 'speed is power', whereby the social strata that possess the fastest velocities (as in human travel or weaponry) must dominate. The recent, digital acceleration of information transmission has eclipsed transport velocity as the main source of global power. Virilio examines how military-industrial complexes in post-industrial societies have utilized speed-wealth to create a world of 'total', ongoing warfare. Driven in part by his Christian convictions and wartime resistance in occupied France, Virilio attacks technological dangers, disparaging the nuclear age as 'a pure parody of religion' (Gane 2000: 97).

Compared to warfare, sport inhabits a secondary, albeit symbolic and strategic position in Virilio's framework. Non-white or developing-world athletes may dominate many sporting disciplines via the old velocity in physical movement. However, the instantaneous digital mediation of sports symbolizes the high-tech potency of the white-dominated West's military-industrial complexes. Commodification of televised sport advances the material-speed divisions between the haves (who buy instant televised rights) and the have-nots (who receive old, inferior highlights packages). Strategically, the surveillance and social control of sport spectators, using advanced gadgetry, allows the military-industrial complex to test its latest techniques in case of more overt political resistance (see chapter 8 on CCTV systems). Thus, Virilio promotes our general understanding of how time–space compression connects to technological exercises of power.[7]

Postmodern identities: sociality, post-nationality and consumption

Reflecting the move towards dedifferentiation, postmodernity has also been associated with shifting identities. Three particular aspects of this process require discussion.

First, for some analysts, postmodernity transforms social relations; Baudrillard (1983: 82) even suggests that the social itself is dead. For Maffesoli (1996), the social now comprises postmodern, transitory, emotional communions between individuals. Like pre-modern tribalism, postmodern 'sociality' shares a quest for community, but its '*neo*-tribalism' is confirmed by urban locations and the constant identity flux of tribe members (Bauman 1992: 137). Sociality possesses a vitality and distinctive *puissance* (or 'will to live'); in the piazza-like cultures of postmodernity, sociality constructs a playful public theatre of temporary styles and human expression (see Hughson 1999: 13).

Second, geo-politically, the 'nation' is an increasingly problematic concept. The idea of a modern, homogeneous nation is outmoded by polyethnicity and multi-culturalism. Postmodern political science dismisses the nation's modern claims to political and social determination. National identity is read instead as a medley of dissimilar cultural constructs and signs (A. D. Smith 1999: 170). Postmodern societies harbour more dual and multiple identities, as well as sharpened senses of intra-national difference. Alternative cultural and political nationalisms challenge modern, official national identities, most successfully in the former Communist East. This postmodernist account of post-nationalism can be Eurocentric, however. Nations in the developing world have undergone different kinds of national definition during colonial and early post-colonial times. Latin America, for example, has long contained 'hybrid' nations that mix and socially stratify black people (descendants of African slaves), the indigenous ('Indian') population, and white people (descendants of colonial conquerors).

Third, fluid postmodern identities arise in consumer and popular culture. Modern subcultures, notably youth styles, tend to possess homologous identity signs that connote permeable membership: consider the skinhead style with its short hair, heavy-duty boots, rolled-up jeans, distinct musical genre, even the life-style pet (a fighting dog, such as a pit-bull). Postmodern identities are more neo-tribal (à la Maffesoli) or 'mix and match', often involving a hybridity of signs and styles from earlier, competing subcultures. Postmodern identity signs are more aesthetic and transitory, less tied to territorial communities. Consider tattoos: previously, these 'branded' the lifelong ties of males to loved ones, community and nation; today, Chinese calligraphy and laser surgery permit a more aesthetic, personalized and reversible use of tattoos as postmodern body design (Turner 1999).

Postmodern identities feature in sport. Several researchers have disclosed the neo-tribal social relations that link football club supporters in the UK, Australia and South America (Armstrong 1998: 306; Giulianotti 1999: 51; Hughson 1999; Alabarces 1999: 82). My own research into football hooligan groups in Scotland and England suggests that a theoretical balance must be struck between modern subculture and postmodern neo-tribe. Hard-core hooligans are evidently subcultural: they meet regularly to attend matches, pursue opposing hooligans, discuss hooligan-related issues with friends, and visit and contribute to hooligan websites. Subcultural hooligans open up neo-tribal, expressive spaces for others to explore irregularly or temporarily.[8] The idea of a subculture still helps to explain the reproduction of cultural identities over time (for some hooligan groups, this extends to over 20 years). It also explains how neo-tribes can emerge and cluster round existent styles and core identities, albeit temporarily, rather than flit across such styles in an entirely unpredictable and peripatetic fashion.

Sport can play a key role in constructing postmodern, polyethnic or 'post-nationalist' identities. Specific 'national' teams may be polyethnic in composition, ensuring that sports commentators struggle to 'narrate the nation' according to old assumptions regarding national identity. For symbolic interactionists, postmodernity's sign culture destabilizes identities and meanings. Product advertisements illustrate this process; consider Benetton's juxtaposition of brandname with images of human suffering. In sport, constant contradictory media signifiers often fail to produce a dominant public identity for superstar athletes. For example, UK media presented the leading English football player Paul Gascoigne variously as a wife-beater, philanthropist, joker, hero, alcoholic, reformed character, vulnerable child, loyal friend, local boy, jet-setter, athlete, slob, victim and offender (Giulianotti and Gerrard 2001: 131).

Postmodern culture is marked by eclecticism and pastiche: barriers between cultural styles and artistic movements, or systems of identity difference, break down. In theory, consumers may play with contradictory cultural signs and practices: enjoying punk and operatic music, for example, or ballet and American football. Under postmodernism the individual's *habitus* becomes far more fluid, fragmented, expressive and ultimately unpredictable than sociologists like Bourdieu could envisage. Aestheticization of everyday life encourages consumption of multifarious sports-related merchandise that connects (ever-more loosely) with numerous global sports and teams.[9] Contemporary media promote this eclecticism through pastiche production techniques. For example, Australian cricket's television coverage utilizes youth and pop culture styles, combined with commentary techniques borrowed from tabloid journalism and Australian Rules football (Cashman 1995: 199).

Postmodernity is marked too by more fluid sports consumption (Giulianotti 2002). We may identify four ideal types of spectator identity within sport: supporters, followers, fans and *flâneurs*. Modernity produced 'supporters' with relatively fixed forms of team identification towards local clubs. Sports professionalization, marketing and mediation germinated 'follower' and 'fan' identities. Followers identify with other clubs for particular biographical (not market) reasons: for example, if a favoured local player moves to that club. Fans connect to clubs by consuming team paraphernalia and through media-dependent identification with star players. The most postmodern spectator category is the *flâneur* who, like the urban bourgeois stroller of the late nineteenth century, shifts sporting allegiances with little regard for spectator solidarity. The true sport *flâneur* buys into sport's global commodity signifiers, such as the New York Yankees' baseball hat, the Chicago Bulls' holiday T-shirt, the Brazilian football jersey, or the tracksuit with 'Italia' emblazoned across the chest. *Flâneur* identities embody a fluid, transnational consumerism that implies the potential breakdown of national sports identification. However, just as subcultural identities are not abolished *in toto*, so more modern spectator identities also remain. For example, leading football clubs build community relations with local 'supporters', sell shares and merchandise to 'fans', attract 'follower' audiences by signing popular players, and appeal to international *flâneurs* by winning Continental trophies or designing the club's logo and image as a global commodity sign. Thus, just as postmodern neo-tribes require modern subcultures to preserve expressive spaces, so cosmopolitan *flâneurs* require modern spectator types to sustain the sports institutions around which they oscillate.

The sociology of postmodernity, 1: social class and cultural practices

Conventional sociological approaches examine social stratification and societal changes within postmodernity. Post-industrial production, the rising service sector, growing higher education, and the dissolution of European Left–Right political divisions all suggest postmodernity's arrival. The modern class structure fragments: the old working class decomposes, and the swollen middle classes take variegated forms. The 'service class' or 'new middle class' is engaged in advanced production, mediation and consumption of symbolic goods (Lash and Urry 1994a: 164). Unlike the traditional bourgeoisie, this class embraces popular culture, and is trained to engage critically (not passively) with consumer products. It enjoys the 'aestheticization of everyday life', notably in consumerism, and its numbers include 'cultural intermediaries': the taste-makers and life-style educators in advertising, fashion, media and therapeutic professions (Featherstone 1991b: 35, 44–5).

These class changes impact upon sport. The service classes popularize sport's physical and cerebral pleasures without bourgeois intellectualist guilt. Sports advertising, marketing and fashion are important constituents of aestheticized consumer life-styles. The new middle classes' more cosmopolitan, critical *habitus* corresponds with postmodern, *flâneur* sport spectator identities. This class fills many sport-related media posts in publishing and electronic media. In UK football, 'fanzines' (fan magazines) were typically founded at individual clubs by the new middle classes. Using cheap, contemporary desktop publishing technology, fanzine contributors advanced critical, humorous, playful analyses of the football scene, challenging the political passivity of most official supporters' organizations in dealings with football clubs (Giulianotti 1997; Haynes 1992).

Some analysts refer to tourism to demonstrate the relationship of class to new leisure identities. For Feifer (1985), 'post-tourists' abandon mass tourism in three particular ways. First, using electronic media, post-tourists 'visit' new destinations or gain fresh experiences while still at home. Second, post-tourism emphasizes choice, easy mobility and playful engagement with high and low culture. Third, post-tourists are highly reflexive regarding the invention of tourist experiences and landscapes. In postmodern style, post-tourists are playful, coolly detached, ironic, and enjoy simulated cultural practices (Featherstone 1995: 120).

'Cultural intermediary' and 'post-tourist' are useful sociological generalizations, but I would argue for caution in reducing either to new middle-class identity. 'Cultural intermediary' appears to abolish conceptually the relevance of youth subcultures, but such a negation may be premature. Youth subcultures may fill the cultural intermediary role in some sport contexts. In UK football, for example, the decline in male supporters wearing team paraphernalia and the rise of designer menswear were largely inspired by the 1980s 'soccer casual' subculture (Giulianotti 1993). Similarly, we may transfer the post-tourist's characteristics into sport to create the 'post-fan', a spectator category adopting a playful, ironic, detached attitude towards the social construction of sports events. At international sports tournaments, post-fans may be post-tourists by playfully enjoying public events stage-managed by the organizing authorities. The post-fan identity is not necessarily tied to a specific class fraction. It is more associated with a particular sports *habitus* that reflects in large part the length of sporting engagement, and resulting critical reflexivity, of the specific social actor (Giulianotti 1999: 148–50).

My point here is that a reasonable sociology of postmodernity must look beyond the rearranged chairs of middle-class identity. Critical reflexivity on sport requires lengthy 'stocks of knowledge' and bio-graphical engagement within that sport. Moreover, postmodernity still generates new forms of social inequality. Gottdiener (1995: 134–5), for example, notes that postmodern architecture does not dissolve difference or destitution. Alongside a cornucopia of pleasure centres and consumption palaces we have rising crime levels, new patterns of immigration, homelessness and the 'hyper-ghettoization' of black people. Similarly, for most of the developing world, and large sections within the developed world, a fundamental lack of resources under-mines entry to commodified, postmodern sport.

Sociology of postmodernity, 2: post-industrial relations and disorganized capitalism

According to some analysts, postmodernity is marked by 'post-Fordist' and 'disorganized' relations of production. Modern, organized cap-italism piloted 'Fordist' systems of production, as witnessed at the Ford motor company: large, complex divisions of labour entailed employee specialization and restricted craft autonomy in return for higher wages and job security. Cost-effective mass production (and consumption) of identical units was implemented, 'just in case' any surplus was sold. Strong rationalization and bureaucratic procedures smoothed the organization of vertically integrated firms, connecting manufacturing, marketing and sales wings (Gramsci 1971: 310–13; Grint 1991: 294–7). By contrast, 'post-Fordism' is marked by flexi-bility in manufacturing, product content and design. Diverse, niche (not mass) markets are pursued. Firms disintegrate vertically to cre-ate smaller, loosely connected production units with short-contract workers. New products are rapidly introduced, 'just in time' with market demands. In culture industries like popular music or sport, post-Fordism is knowledge-intensive and reflexively productive (Lash and Urry 1994a: 121–3). For example, sports media programming requires computing software specialists and sharp media analysts to upgrade regularly production techniques and product design.

Switches from Fordism to post-Fordism arose in sports merchan-dising. Until the 1970s, sports merchandise was more functional than aesthetic, and was restricted in design range; playing kit de-signs, for example, varied only in colour over the years. Sports equipment production involved lengthy divisions of labour and 'just in case' marketing. Post-Fordist production involves constant redesign of equipment. In football, new boot styles, scientifically tested and endorsed by the latest celebrity players, keep entering the market. Each club constantly changes its kit design and leisure wear to target different markets (children, adolescents, adults, males, females, various social classes).

The neo-Marxists Fredric Jameson and David Harvey connect postmodernity to changes in organized capitalism. Jameson (1991: 400) defines postmodernism as the 'cultural logic of late capitalism', or as the post-war, 'third stage' of capitalism. It is characterized by the commodification of media and cultural content, from art to television entertainment (Jameson 1991: 276–8). David Harvey (1989) traces postmodernity's origins to the early 1970s, when flexible accumulation arose alongside cultural fragmentation and unpredictable change. For Harvey, postmodern social theory correctly prioritizes difference, social complexity and the disorientation of 'time–space compression' (most notably in the global flows of information and human travel). Harvey criticizes postmodern theories for dismissing modernity's 'metanarratives' (notably Marxism), and prioritizing aesthetics over the ethics and economic base of postmodernity. While we might follow Featherstone (1995: 78–9) in arguing that their own 'metanarratives' should be deconstructed, Jameson and Harvey are right to consider how postmodern cultural trends connect to structured inequalities. Thus, for Jameson (1991: 406–7), the 'ethos' and 'life-styles' of the new middle classes, or 'yuppies', constitute a dominant ideological and cultural project within postmodern capitalism. In sport, this class, in one 'cultural intermediary' role, normalizes commodification and tutors markets into product consumption.

For Lash and Urry (1987, 1994a), globalization drives the rise of 'disorganized capitalism', wherein 'the flows of subjects and objects are progressively less synchronized within national boundaries' (1994a: 10). Disorganized capitalism connects to specific social processes, such as international capital and technological flows, the emergence of global cities and financial structures, global 'risks' and intensified reflexivity, transnational communication networks (notably mass media), the exponential growth of human mobility, the dissolution of hierarchical class structures, the rise of 'cosmopolitan' postmodern individuals, and the decline of the nation-state (Lash and Urry 1994a: 323).

The global flow of images, capital, people (whether spectators or athletes) and commodities appears to have changed elite sport. International media networks facilitate heightened knowledge and reflexivity regarding the sport world. Management of sport *qua* business is increasingly disorganized. Athletes, agents, lawyers, sports administrators, media moguls, sport reporters, team owners, union leaders, corporate sponsors, pressure groups and spectators all have political and economic interests to defend (not to mention their cultural differences or internal contradictions), according to their various positions within the global sports 'field'. Disorganized capitalism in sport is thus registered by struggles between each group's diverging, shifting interests.

Nevertheless, Lash and Urry overplay the sociological changes within postmodernity: notably, the dramatic structural changes within their own social strata. Long-term fieldwork in the provinces of Britain or Belgium, in housing estates or shop-floors (factory or office), would find that labour, identity, social hierarchy and cultural preference are markedly less mobile, unpredictable or global than the authors presume. Post-Fordism does not abolish Fordist (or indeed pre-Fordist) modes of production: instead, the three systems operate interdependently. Capitalism may be more complex, global and (in some elite sports) somewhat disorganized, but its constituent industries order their global business interests. Rupert Murdoch's major media corporations possess a global platform for sports-related broadcasting and do not thrive on disorganization.

Postmodern culture: seduction, pastiche and Baudrillard's hyperreality

Jean Baudrillard has been the most provocative commentator in debates surrounding postmodernity. For Baudrillard, postmodern culture features the rise of 'seduction' over modern 'production'. Seductive cultures prioritize image over reality, and exchange- over use-value; thus, a commodity's cultural wrapping supersedes its actual utility. Seductive cultures like Brazil's are predicated on anti-productivist themes of enchantment, chance, symbolic exchange and gift giving, and so cannot be modernized along Western lines (Kellner 1989: 187; Baudrillard 1996a: 74-6).

Sport is often caught in dilemmas between production and seduction. Sports competitors must produce good results and seduce audiences by playing with style. Through gambling (notably in sport), modern peoples return playfully to the seductive, wasteful principles of chance and destiny. Through Baudrillard, we can see sports audiences in the Northern (productivist) hemisphere as enchanted by

Southern, non-Western sporting cultures, such as African running, Brazilian football or Asian cricket. However, this account rather romanticizes the non-Western other, as 'exotic', in nostalgic, aristocratic and unsociological style.

Baudrillard explains postmodern culture through the concepts of 'simulacrum' and 'hyperreality'. Strictly defined, a simulacrum is a particular copy of something that does not actually exist (Jameson 1991: 18). For Baudrillard, our fake, postmodern culture is full of simulacra (Baudrillard 1994b: 6). 'Hyperreality' refers to a media-saturated world that is both simulated and 'realer than real', engendering vertiginous, real-yet-simulated experiences. For example, television presents a 'quadrophonics' of sport: all offensive background noise is removed, while surround-sound audio systems amplify and simulate crowd 'atmosphere' to levels that do not arise in real stadiums. Visually, television provides a 'pornography' of sport: 'interactive' television packages allow viewers multiple camera angles and highlights packages at any time during play. Key moments during play are viewed from numerous angles, producing a visual excess of reality that no stadium spectator enjoys (see Baudrillard 1995: 104; 1996c: 29; 1990: 31–6). Sport is now organized to fit with these simulated, hyperreal models: the sport stadium *qua* home-entertainment lounge pipes in artificial crowd noise and, on giant screens, displays reruns of real events just witnessed by spectators. In extreme cases, sports events are simulacra: for example, 'virtual' horse-racing – a sport created by computers and decided by random calculations – is devoid of everyday problems, like steward inquiries into results or gamblers' suspicions regarding the efforts of losing jockeys.

In sport, 'real' identities seem to arise after their virtual invention: star athletes seem to conform to earlier, fictitious celebrity identities; and media constructions of hooligans seem to prefigure actual hooligan practices (Baudrillard 1998: 47–8; Redhead 1991). Baudrillard's (1994a) provocative suggestion that 'The Gulf War did not take place' indicated that the conflict was hyperreal, a television moment, a virtual war (Gane 1993: 185), its fatal realities supplanted by the powers of simulation.[10] Similarly, for most people, sports are televised events rather than actual experiences (Baudrillard 1993: 79–80). Major sports events are organized to 'take place' in the 'real time' of television as media events (Baudrillard 1995: 98). Commercials or television deadlines determine event times. Television units emerge from special media complexes to cruise the passive stands, invoking the masses to sing, chant and celebrate, to simulate a social occasion. Hyperreal spectator cultures simulate 'atmosphere' or the social

cultures of past sports crowds, their favoured songs lifted from media commercials. Banners and flags are constructed, not to influence
sports events, but to attract television cameras.

For Baudrillard, the United States is paradigmatically hyperreal,
particularly California's theme parks and *faux* Greco-Roman architecture. Whereas Eco (1984) identifies profit-seeking motives
behind theme parks, Baudrillard ruminates on America's historical and cultural shallowness: America is 'the primitive society of
modernity' due to its limited history relative to Europe (1989: 73). In
Americanized sport, hyperreality annihilates history: Los Angeles is
envisioned as the final resting-place for a postmodern Olympics that
is 'totally sponsored, totally euphoric, totally clean, a 100 per cent
advertising event' (1989: 57). Hence, after the United States hosted
football's 1994 World Cup finals, Redhead (1998: 231–3) reasonably
inquired whether the tournament, like the Gulf War, had actually
occurred.

Hyperreality is the 'catastrophe of modernity', in which social action is dead. Only the masses remain – the 'silent majorities', that
'black hole' of energy, absorbing endless streams of mediated images.
Sociology is doomed, because its essential categories – of power, class,
social relations and so on – are outmoded (Baudrillard 1983: 4–5).
Baudrillard (1983: 12–13) dismisses crude Marxist claims that sport
dupes the masses out of political emancipation. Instead, the masses'
political inertia and weary consumerism disguise their 'cunning', their
'fatal strategies' (1998: 40). Various 'subjects' – such as opinion poll-
sters and media pundits – seek to 'know' the masses, to contain and
reshape their desires and values. Seductively, the masses play along,
letting each 'subject' believe (falsely) that they do have such desires
and wishes (Poster 1988: 216–17; Baudrillard 1993: 169). Thus, 'The
political scenario is reversed: it's no longer power that pulls the masses
in its wake, it's the masses that drag power down to its fall' (1983: 95).
In sport, as in any other branch of postmodern culture, the masses'
playful pleasures arise in seducing the sport reporter or the marketing
executive into believing that they really care.

For Baudrillard, postmodern culture is highly paradoxical. Hyperreality is founded upon advanced technology like digital media, whereas
the masses embrace pre-modern ruses and spectacles that deceive
the seemingly powerful. For example, Formula One motor racing is
founded upon immense technological research and development, producing a 'living prosthesis of the driver', as Schumacher and the rest
merge into their automotive projectiles. However, Formula One still

stirs the masses' passion for spectacle, and for the 'absolutely vital' risk of death that it carries (and can never eliminate). The masses ensure that the 'monster' of Formula One is not 'domesticated' but survives instead as 'pure event', in contrast to our 'era of daily insignificance' (Baudrillard 2002: 166–70).

Politics and problematics: evaluating the postmodern

I have sought to provide here a detailed, empathetic but critical reading of postmodernity and postmodernism. Critics like Giddens (1991: 27) prefer to talk about 'high', 'advanced' or 'late' modernity, not 'postmodernity'. By contrast, I contend that postmodernity (as post-industrial social order) and postmodernism (as form of cultural logic) validly describe structural transformations and cultural changes in the post-war era. Postmodern theorizing helps to explain the interplay of cultural difference, the emergence of new social class categories and relations, and the nexus between media simulation and fresh patterns of social consciousness and identity. We must theorize these trends with reference to models of production and accumulation, and patterns of social division and exclusion. Overall, it is important to advocate a critical standpoint regarding postmodernity, reading social change according to more modern sociological themes such as rationalization, commodification, military-political subjugation, and the resultant frameworks of social inequality and division.

Sport illustrates the analytical and empirical relevance of modernity to the postmodern. In identity terms, as noted for sport spectators, modern subcultures enable 'neo-tribal' forms of fluid sociality. Sports corporations and media platforms show how capitalism has become relatively more complex and global, combined (via Harvey and Jameson) with new strategies of organization and commodification. Postmodern sport is influenced significantly by the new middle classes, as commodification sustains the social exclusion of other social groups. 'Dedifferentiation' in sport compresses divisions between high and low culture, although these collapses affect some classes more than others. An aestheticized culture of pastiche and eclecticism arises in sport-related media and consumer culture. Baudrillard advances some fascinating insights regarding simulation cultures and new forms of cultural consciousness: the hyperreal dreamscapes of sport theme parks or video consoles become 'real' spaces in which sport is experienced; identikit, xeroxed sport celebrities emerge; and North America sustains its role in advancing hyperreal sport. His arguments regarding the death of the social and the arrival of 'mass society' have greater heuristic than strictly empirical value.

Postmodern social theorists abhor universalizing reason and meta-narrative truth-claims, hence they contribute few serious political visions or strategies. Instead, their political and ethical positions are primarily localized, cautious and concerned with spaces for action. Some arguments are more persuasive than others. Derrida and Lyotard envisage a future featuring the powerful interplay of differential identities, opening spaces for new interpretative frameworks and language games to mingle and interact with necessarily uncertain consequences. For Lyotard particularly, formulating a fixed political strategy is pointless; rather, we may only 'make experimental moves within the language games that situate us' (Barron 1992: 39). This, I would argue, is the weakest position, not least because it asks social theorists to have more 'respect' for language games than we usually find among the everyday speakers. Indeed, speakers are critical agents who like to fuse or redefine language games to suit local needs – a point I make in the next chapter, in regard to concepts of 'glocalization' and 'creolization'. Practical social scientists should forsake postmodernism's *angst* and do the same: critically interpret language games, according to the rational, universalist principles that sustain their academic disciplines.

Alternatively, Foucault's strategy focuses on micro-political struggles at the everyday level. For women in relation to leisure, this means protecting and cultivating private recreational spaces (Wearing 1998: 156–7). In sport, micro-political strategies are constantly operative. For every continent-wide anti-racism movement, there are thousands of daily attempts to free specific sporting niches and spaces from intolerance and discrimination. The body becomes a site of struggle as marginalized populations seek to legitimize and sustain their own physical cultures at everyday level in defiance of dominant Western disciplines.

Baudrillard has been criticized for failing to leave any space to envision human emancipation in a simulated world (Kellner 1989: 50–1). Modern social critics pursue humanity's improvement by operating as 'surgeons', identifying and advocating the excision of social cancers. By contrast, Baudrillard is like a homeopath, encouraging malignant social viruses to show themselves and run their course (Hebdige 1988: 209). His writings point to at least three different, fatal strategies for subverting power. First, the masses may stay a 'step ahead' by giving the false impression that they want the products of a hyperconformist consumer market. Second, gambling and other wasteful pleasures serve to replace momentarily the principles of production and value with those of chance and destiny. Third, most dramatically, the socially excommunicated may seize control by creating their own spectacles – for example, through spectators staging dramas of protest, or (more likely) violent disturbances that eclipse the on-field attraction.

For most of the 'masses', the first strategy – that of ecstatic consumption and hyper-conformity – seems initially to have the greatest prominence. It seems we must all become fans of the richest sports institutions, and rush to consume the most 'fashionable', transparently useless commodities. Marketing and media people seem to assume that our expressions and choices are genuine. But so what if these 'market choices' really are Baudrillardian ruses? What of the human damage caused by the enactment of these fatal strategies? For example, consider the continuing public expressions of racism or sexism by sports crowds. Are we to explain these phenomena as the ruses of a 'fatal strategy', such that 'real' sexism or racism does not exist? Racism and sexism, just like deaths in the Gulf and living in poverty under postmodernity, are surely real human experiences that carry genuinely harmful consequences. As such, these realities, even if they occur in the era of postmodernity, must remain central to critical sociological investigation.

12

Globalization: The Politics of 'Glocal' Sport

Globalization has become sociology's most prominent research theme, and the subject of major public debate. Globalization is marked by numerous social processes: rising global interdependencies between individuals, groups and societies; growing global circulations of people, commodities, images and ideas; increasing transnational links between states, corporations and non-governmental organizations; and intensification of the public's subjective awareness of global connectivity, of the shared interests, tastes, values and futures across humanity's different branches. The founder of globalization studies, Roland Robertson, captures these objective and subjective processes through his understanding of globalization as 'the compression of the world and the intensification of consciousness of the world as a whole' (1992: 8).

In my view, globalization points to the full maturation of the sociological imagination, enabling the theoretical location of social actions and structures within the fullest (global) context. We can be neither 'for' nor 'against' globalization. Rather, globalization has become an ontological dimension of social life, a kind of multi-faceted social fact. Thus, the 'anti-globalization' movement of recent years is misleadingly named, since its diverse followers typically oppose one *particular* dimension of globalization associated with neo-liberal capitalism. Anti-globalization movements are themselves consequences of globalization through their members' global consciousnesses, international travel, communication networks and organizational frameworks (Robertson and White 2003: 10–11).

Globalization has very basic historical, economic, cultural, political and social dimensions. Modern sporting events like the Olympics illustrate these aspects. Historically, the Olympics have become a 'world' event, from 14 participating nations in 1896 to 199 in 2000. Economically, the Olympics generate global revenues from world-wide television deals, corporate sponsorships and ticket sales. Culturally, the Olympics enable the global interplay of different sporting styles and techniques, modes of dress and self-expression. Politically, particular international elites run the IOC, while the tournaments enable host nations or social movements to communicate with global audiences. Socially, the Olympics draw spectators and athletes from across the world, providing global television audiences with common conversational topics.

Here, I explore the relations between sport and globalization in five sections. First, I employ Robertson's five-phase model to examine sport's historical globalization. Second, I address political economy arguments regarding globalization, notably by Wallerstein and Sklair, within sport. Third, I assess the Americanization and Orientalism arguments that point towards cultural homogenization. Fourth, I examine arguments regarding the rise of cultural heterogeneity within globalization through the particular interplay of the local and the global. Fifth, I conclude by examining issues surrounding political reform and globalization. I argue that while all cultures engage creatively with global cultural phenomena, major reforms inside world sport should enhance democracy and protect cultural agency.

Historical elements of globalization: Robertson's five phases

Modern sports like cricket, football, rugby, baseball and hockey have been globalized since their foundation in particular nations. To trace this global diffusion, I employ Robertson's (1992: 58–9) general model of globalization, divided into five historical phases:

- Globalization's first, or *germinal*, phase (early fifteenth to mid-eighteenth century) witnessed Catholicism's expansion as a global religious system, the early emergence of national communities, heliocentrism and early world mapping, and 'accentuation' of ideas regarding the individual and humanity.
- The second, or *incipient*, phase (mid-eighteenth century to 1870s) involved the rise of unitary nation-states, international relations, legal frameworks, communication systems, fuller conceptions of citizenship and humanity, the question of non-European involvement in 'international society', and early international exhibitions.

- The third, or *take-off*, phase (1870s to mid-1920s) involved increasingly global, standardized expectations regarding national societies. National and personal (male-dominated) 'identities' predominated, and formal ideas concerning humanity were advanced. Global communication grew exponentially, and immigration was restricted, although non-European societies entered international society. Global sport competitions began, while military conflicts acquired global proportions. 'Wilful nostalgia' arose among Western elites, alongside the 'invention of traditions' (Robertson 1992: 147–9).
- The fourth, or *struggle-for-hegemony*, phase (1920s to late 1960s) witnessed warfare and military tensions in resource distribution and execution of global power. The United Nations formalized global governance and principles of national self-determination. The Third World was so designated. Threats to humankind were contained in the Holocaust and rising nuclear capabilities.
- The fifth, or *uncertainty*, phase (late 1960s to the present era) displayed greater levels of global consciousness, post-materialist values, civil and human rights, environmentalism, notions of world citizenship, and ideas of identity difference. The Cold War ended, the international system became more 'fluid', ethnicity became more prominent, and Islam became a 'de-globalizing' force. Global media systems, often in rivalry, became more established, as did increasing numbers of global institutions.

Since the 1870s, globalization has been underpinned increasingly by interrelations and tensions between 'four elemental reference points': the individual, the nation, the international (or world) society and humanity (Robertson 1992: 26–7). Consider, for example, the nation-state's relationship to the other reference points: each nation-state grants citizenship rights to individuals, which may weaken its military or labour bases; engages in binding agreements with other nations, which may weaken its international autonomy; and is pressured to respond unilaterally, without aid ties, to the humanitarian needs of citizens in other nations.

Robertson provides a potentially valuable, under-utilized model for explaining sport's globalization. Maguire (1999: 77–89) has reformulated Robertson's last three stages (1870s to the present) largely to prop up a pro-Eliasian vision of sport's globalization. Bale and Sang (1996: 134–5) apply the model more briefly, but consistently, to explain the history of Kenyan movement culture.

Robertson and I have sought to apply his model to explain football's globalization (Giulianotti and Robertson 2002). We modify the model's time frame when assessing football's earliest two phases, but otherwise the phases synchronize with the sport's history.

- Football's *germinal* phase spans the game's prehistory, up to the early nineteenth century, before its formal codification in 1863. Urbanization, industrialization, and British colonial and trade expansion provided the socio-cultural and administrative infrastructures for football's future diffusion. Localized 'folk' football games were played in the British Isles and on the Continent, thereby establishing wide cultural receptivity for a future, codified sport.

- The *incipient* phase covers the early nineteenth century up to the 1870s, as English public schools and working-class clubs played games according to various rules. A common legal framework emerged, and the first international fixture was contested in 1872. Stronger unitary nation-states and a growing international society allowed the British to exhibit football abroad, and diffusion began.

- Football's *take-off* phase spans the 1870s to the 1920s, establishing a massively popular sport across Europe and South America, African colonies, and parts of Asia and North America. The four elemental reference points gained prominence: *individuals* (males) practised the game, the best becoming local and national heroes; *nations* were ritually sustained through national tournaments or international fixtures; FIFA's foundation in 1904 institutionalized football's *international system*; and *humankind* questions arose over the right of disadvantaged groups (women, non-whites, working-class players) to participate. Football was contested at the Olympics and played by soldiers during military conflicts (including Christmas fixtures in no man's land). Particular playing styles were invented, reflecting national identity constructions.

- During the *struggle-for-hegemony* phase, football's international system acquired complexity, with large continental governing bodies and tournaments established. European and South American forces struggled to prevail during matches and inside FIFA. Many international fixtures reflected political tensions before the Second World War and through the Cold War. Brazil reflected the continuing relativization of the four elemental reference points: its players were brilliant *individualists*; the national team served to unify a vast, highly stratified *nation*; the team's *international* successes mirrored Brazilian officials' global influence; and Brazil's playing style provided *humankind* with a common aesthetic standard.

- Football's *uncertainty* phase involves greater political struggles through ever more complex relations between rising numbers of collective actors such as FIFA, continental bodies, national associations, clubs and sponsors. Football institutions highlight human rights issues by building partnerships with charitable NGOs and the United Nations, and initiating anti-racism and anti-sexism campaigns. Global media systems battle to control image rights. New football nations emerge in the post-Cold War era, highlighting the rising complexity of cultural difference.

Robertson recognizes that it is too early to tell if, following 9/11, we have entered a sixth phase of globalization that carries significant continuities with the 'uncertainty' phase. Sport's role in this phase would be open to conjecture, although security issues would certainly be more prominent.

Critical political economy arguments

Some analysts focus on the structural consequences of inequality in shaping global relations. Dependency theories address globalization's colonial and neo-colonial dimensions. From at least the sixteenth century, Western nations systematically colonized and enslaved the indigenous peoples of other societies, while exploiting local natural resources. As noted in chapter 5, the British and other colonial powers institutionalized highly racialized sporting systems in Africa, the Asian subcontinent and the Caribbean. In the post-colonial era, the colonized societies became constitutionally independent nation-states that remain dependent on the West in neo-colonial fashion. Powerful Western transnational corporations strongly influence Third World commodity production, while the IMF and the World Bank effectively control the economic policies of heavily indebted national governments. 'Underdevelopment' can occur, whereby dependent nations must produce cash crops like bananas or sugar for Western markets rather than meet their own development needs.

Klein (1989; 1994: 193–4) has deployed theories of neo-colonialism and dependency to explain Latin American baseball. This American game's predominance reflects US historical hegemony within Latin America. In Dominica, baseball academies operate like local sugar plantations. Both are established by American institutions, gather the best local resources (whether it be sugar-cane or ball-players), undertake some basic refining, and despatch the best products to North

America, where final refining takes place before consumption by rich local consumers. Dominicans are left to consume the inferior residue. This neo-colonial arrangement is highly wasteful: just as American consumers waste much hard-produced sugar, so many Latino baseball players disappear into lower-level American leagues. Finally, most academies 'underdevelop' their human resources: young people are trained simply to become baseball players rather than to gain wider skills (see also Marcano and Fidler 1999). Similar neo-colonial projects may be discerned in the NBA's pursuit of new consumer markets, while opening a 'new international division of cultural labour' through recruiting players from a wider pool of countries (Miller et al. 2003).

However, as Klein (2003) indicates, neo-colonialism or dependency arguments should not ignore the empirical complexities and cultural agency found within specific social circumstances. Rewards available to Latinos entering American leagues enable them to remit monies to dependants. Similarly, we should condemn European agents and clubs that abandon young African footballers who have failed to become full professionals in Western leagues. But we should recognize that entering Europe often provides these young men with job and educational opportunities that are not available at home.

Wallerstein (1974) advances the most established, systematic critique of globalization from a neo-Marxist standpoint. The modern world system, he argues, comprises three kinds of state:

- *core*, rich, strongly governed and dominant states like the USA or Western European nations;
- *semi-peripheral*, financially expanding societies with modest governmental powers and limited technological development or commodity diversity, such as Asian 'tiger' nations, or Eastern European nations;
- *peripheral* locations with weak government, contested borders and structural dependencies on Western nations – for example, African and Latin American societies.

Wallerstein's model fails to account sufficiently for internal class divisions within nations, common class interests across nations, and the contemporary relevance of 'transnational corporations' (TNCs) like GE, Microsoft, Shell, Matsui and Unilever.

According to Sklair (1995: 61), the global system is dominated economically by the 'transnational capitalist class' (TCC), which constitutes a form of 'international managerial bourgeoisie'. The TCC has a global outlook and self-identification, and diverse national origins and consumption patterns (notably in luxury goods and services). It comprises TNC decision-makers and local partners, 'globalizing state bureaucrats', 'capitalist-inspired politicians and professionals', and 'consumerist groups' (for example, in business and media). For Sklair, the TCC advances a 'culture-ideology of consumerism', generating a 'buying mood' and 'consumerist world-view' across national boundaries that collapse distinctions between information, entertainment and advertisement. In my view, Sklair's model too readily assumes that functional friendships exist between different types of TCC member.

Sklair's model invites exploration of how the TCC controls national and international sport. Even in the 'peripheral' nation of Zimbabwe during the 1990s, local professionals and business elites controlled the elite game of cricket, and worked most effectively among TNC executives (working for finance houses or satellite broadcasters) to expand the sport's revenue streams (state bureaucrats and politicians also approve of foreign currency entering the nation). In turn, Zimbabwean cricket stadiums and cricket merchandise became wrapped in the 'culture-ideology of consumerism'. However, Sklair's model does not explain effectively the real political and economic tensions within elite groups, such as between cricket's white controllers and the Mugabe-led regime, or between the controllers of different sports, merchandise companies and television stations, that result in middle-class consumers being pulled in different sporting directions.

Since the late 1980s, critical political economy perspectives have focused particularly on neo-liberalism. Neo-liberalists advocate global tariff-free trade, minimizing state social programmes, and enabling wealth creation in the expectation that it will trickle down to the poor. To gain World Bank and IMF aid, governments in developing nations have been forced to introduce neo-liberal 'structural adjustment programmes' (SAPs). While curtailing some local corruption and market inefficiencies, SAPs and economic globalization have exacerbated severe social inequalities and shown little evidence of wealth trickling down to the dispossessed (Scholte 1998: 287). State-owned assets were privatized, and welfare programmes curtailed, with disastrous impacts on education, health, employment and poverty. Meanwhile, Western nations still rig world 'free trade', subsidizing local producers to distort competitiveness and imposing tariffs and other trade barriers to prevent foreign competitors from penetrating domestic markets.

Neo-liberal policies have ravaged developing nations' sports infrastructures. In Zambia's copper belt, privatization of state mining interests resulted in large drops in football crowds (due to unemployment), while mining corporations put a stop to expenditure on sports and recreation for workers. The Asian economic downturn also affected sport badly; Korea's 'IMF crisis' produced major cut-backs in public and private sector funding of sports programmes and development projects (J. K. Park 1999).

Evidently, neo-liberalism is most harmful to the 'Fourth World', that is, the Western underclass and the great majorities in the developing world (cf. Castells 1998). Growing inequalities give rise to some highly pessimistic predictions for the global social order. Beck's (2000: 161–3) nightmare envisions the neo-liberal 'Brazilianization' of Europe, whereby the wealthy live and work in fortresses, travel in super-limousines, and hire private armies to ward off the disenfranchised. Beck's model is highly unlikely to occur but it has critical heuristic value.

Neo-liberalism *disconnects* rather than interconnects some communities. Deindustrialization and demodernization curtail participation in global markets and the communications revolution. In developing world 'mega-cities' like São Paulo and Buenos Aires, social 'dualization' occurs: sophisticated global products and industries sustain wealthier, educated communities, while urban violence and unemployment intensify in slum neighbourhoods. Sport is implicated in dualization, as communities are excluded from sports-related exercise and markets (in terms of buying commodities or engaging with mediated sports culture). Spiralling violence among Latin American football supporters may be explained in terms of dualization processes.

Neo-liberalism raises questions about the possible emasculation of the nation-state, notably in failing to control the national economy (TNCs invest where they like), international crime and immigration (Castells 1998; Habermas 1999; Strange 1994). However, economic history suggests that the nation-state remains a powerful player, and that we still inhabit an 'under-globalized' world (Hirst and Thompson 1999). Most industrial production is still for domestic consumption. Trade is more regional than global, and is actively *promoted* by nation-states through international trade agreements, investment, and employee recruitment and training (L. Weiss 1998). The nation-state delegates powers to international and more local bodies, while seeking to build regional influence (García 2002: 61–2). Typically, TNCs rely heavily on the nation for their headquarters, corporate identity and labour force. Thus, in reality, there are few 'truly transnational corporations' (P. Smith 1997: 39).

Likewise, in sport's 'under-globalized' economy, most consumers still buy tickets, pay-TV packages, merchandise and even company shares for *national* sports institutions. Income from international competitions tends to be regional, such as from Continental football and rugby tournaments. The circulation of elite athletic labour follows particular international rather than global routes – for example, with Spanish football clubs recruiting from South America (Lanfranchi and Taylor 2001). Nation-states back football authorities in recruiting foreign coaches and training athletes, bidding to host international tournaments, and attracting foreign direct investment (FDI). In South Korea, for example, the hosting of the 1988 Olympic games and football's 2002 World Cup finals served to boost FDI within Korea *and* strengthen the state's domestic hegemony (Min-Seok 2002: 168–9).

Critical political economy arguments encourage us to consider world sport's major governing bodies and sports clubs as corporations rather than as profit-free NGOs. Admittedly, bodies like FIFA and the IOC are not market-listed institutions owned by rapacious shareholders. However, they do maximize their products' commodity values, and are run by elite, right-wing business cliques with minimal transparency (Hoberman 1995: 36). The IOC's 'sporting' status allows it to evade proper public scrutiny and OECD anti-corruption conventions (Lenskyj 2000: 192–3). However, it is perhaps better to consider the world's largest sporting clubs, rather than governing bodies, as corporations, or indeed TNCs. In the United States, the New York Yankees, the Chicago Bulls and the San Francisco 49ers have international labour and consumer bases, and retain a 'home' identity (although flitting is always possible). The world's richest football club, Manchester United, has a fixed home city and stadium, but its 50 million global fan base means that, in theory, it could play 'home' games anywhere in England, or even East Asia.

Overall, critical political economy arguments on globalization accurately theorize how neo-liberalism intensifies the structural global inequalities between different peoples. In sport, theories of neo-colonialism and underdevelopment capture the continuing political economic dependency, and the artificial retardation of human potential, in the 'developing' world. Wallerstein and Sklair provide useful models of the world's political economic system, but these require major amendments when applied to specific circumstances. Actual economic globalization is still not particularly advanced, as reflected in the continuation of culturally specific or internationally defined forms of market production, consumption and exchange. These issues become more apparent when evaluating arguments regarding cultural imperialism.

Cultural imperialism, Americanization and Orientalism

An important offshoot of critical political economy arguments concerns the perceived homogenization of cultures according to the norms and practices of dominant states. Thus, sport constitutes an important domain for analysing the realization of cultural imperialism. Undoubtedly, the global diffusion of games was connected inextricably with British imperialism (Mangan 1986). The more prominent cultural imperialism argument, however, has long revolved around the perceived 'Americanization' of world culture.[1]

Sport offers the Americanization thesis some initial corroboration. American television corporations appear to constitute a 'global media-industrial complex' that is empowered to transmit American sports globally. The NBA and NFL subsidize teams, tournaments and huge numbers of television hours of programming outside the USA. American sports practices, like pre-event razzmatazz and employment of cheer-leaders, have penetrated numerous sporting cultures. American sport icons and the products they endorse dominate world sport headlines and retail markets. Reflecting that international power, American sports appear remarkably ethnocentric in competitive logic: for example, only American teams compete to win baseball's 'World Series' (Gannon 2000: 225). Meanwhile, for non-American sports, the perception lingers that, to become genuinely global, they must crack the world's richest market.

Yet all of this is more than negated by counter-evidence. While American media content is internationally available, just as non-American television audiences favour local (not American output), so most continents favour local and national sports. Football remains the world's most popular sport, and now enjoys mass participation across America, despite poor interest in the professional American soccer leagues. Nike's engagement with football and other non-American sports reflects their relative failure to convert overseas consumers to American sports like basketball (Katz 1994). Non-American sports produce national and global icons, like Wayne Carey in Australia, Sachin Tendulkar in India, Brian Lara in the Caribbean, David Beckham in the UK, or Alberto Tomba in Italy, all with associated endorsement deals and high media exposure. America's economic and political power impedes global cultural dialogue, thereby *undermining* (not promoting) the international popularization of American sports (Martin and Reeves 2001). Football's World Cup beats the NFL's Superbowl in television audience figures, partly because the former reflects the cultural heterogeneity of the 'global game', whereas

American sport remains locked into traditional, national sporting imagery, such as masculinity, US military power and whiteness.

In Australia, the Americanization thesis has been critically exposed. The thesis does recognize Australia's semi-peripheral status, deep dependence upon international trade, and post-war absorption of US popular culture (Guttmann 1994: 95–6). Most Australians encounter regular broadcasts of American sports, but the reverse is not true. However, historically, relations between the two nations are rather more complex (Cashman and Hughes 1998a). Australian media remain doggedly committed to national (not American) sports. In 2002, Australian Rules football gained the richest ever (free-to-air and subscription) television contract, worth AU$100 million annually. Rugby league gained $400 million over six years, rugby union earned over $30 million annually, and football drew only $2.5 million annually for live relays of national team fixtures. Several sports contracts were brokered with the 'Foxtel' pay-TV network, controlled by global media magnate Rupert Murdoch. Thus, Australian television stations (Foxtel included) are clearly *not* seeking to remould national sporting preferences in favour of imported North American sports. Some Australian sports are media-packaged in 'American' ways, but commentators still differentiate themselves explicitly from American individuals, institutions and symbols (McKay and Miller 1991).

One significant strain of the Americanization thesis emerges from Ritzer's McDonaldization argument, according to which the standardized production and marketing of American fast foods has spread globally into all domains of everyday life. Yet, research in East Asia suggests that local practices and cultural tastes still influence production and product ranges within McDonald's outlets (Robertson and White 2003: 15–16).

The cultural politics surrounding Americanization can reflect an intuitive unease or explicit opposition to the pro-American consequences of international neo-liberalism. Through sport, some Canadians express cultural resentment towards the United States. 'Free trade' in North American sports has led to Canadian sport stars and franchises enduring intensive pressure to move south to richer pastures (Jackson 2001). More stridently, Bourdieu (1992, 1998b) identified the United States and France as proffering two opposing world visions: American individualistic neo-liberalism versus French state-supported collectivism and solidarism.[2] Most Western nations privilege the market, letting private corporations soak up profits, before the State enters to pay off the largest costs. Australian sport, for example, commodifies its stadiums and mediation, but public authorities must fund essential (and unprofitable) capital projects, grass roots sports coaching, and elite athlete development at the Australian Institute of Sport.

While the cultural Americanization thesis contains empirical and theoretical flaws, Edward Said's (1995; see also 1994) theory of 'Orientalism' affords a more intriguing, innovative, post-structuralist explanation of pan-national cultural power. Said focuses on Western cultural inventions of the 'Orient'. Between 1800 and 1950, Westerners wrote some 60,000 texts on 'the Orient' in a one-way circuit of knowledge production. The powerful Occident came to 'invent the tradition' of the East as an object of knowledge, and 'Orientals' themselves subsequently internalized these discourses as self-knowledge (Said 1995: 325). In Foucauldian terms, Orientalist knowledge constitutes a 'discursive formation' imbued with Western ideological, racial and imperial 'truths'. Substantively, the 'principal dogmas' of Orientalism differentiate the 'rational, developed, humane and superior' West from the 'aberrant, undeveloped, inferior' Orient. The Oriental other is 'eternal, uniform, and incapable of defining itself', enchanting and erotic, but potentially fearful and requiring Occidental control (Said 1995: 300–1).

In discussing Middle Eastern culture, Said advances a variant of the Americanization thesis. Arabs, he notes, consume 'a vast range of United States products, material and ideological'. The 'vast standardization of taste' is 'symbolized not only by transistors, jeans and Coca-Cola but also by cultural images of the Orient supplied by American mass media and consumed unthinkingly by the mass television audience' (Said 1995: 354). While Said focuses on the Middle East and North Africa, notably Egypt, his arguments are extendable to other post-colonial contexts in Asia, Latin America, the Caribbean and Africa.

Orientalism is itself an underdeveloped theory within sport sociology. One rare, substantive study reveals how Australian sport and media discourses Orientalized Pakistani cricket and society around themes of fear, enchantment and contempt. Pakistanis were portrayed as endemically corrupt, evasive towards direct questions of fact, impossible to understand rationally, and stuck in the punishing physical realities of dirt, dust and dysentry (Jaireth 1995).

The theory of Orientalism may be deployed to explain the historical, cultural construction of Brazilian football. According to the Brazilian sociologist Gilberto Freyre (1963: 287–8), Western modernizers pursued 'the complete triumph of Occident over Orient in Brazilian life, so the country would become a Western or sub-European cultural area'. Westerners sought to enlighten the Oriental 'culture of shadow' in Brazil, in the small alleys, the veiled dresses, the shawls, the beards, and the manners and habits of the people (1963: 278). European football culture has long presented Brazilian players as natural, flamboyant, expressive, rhythmic and carefree, in contrast to the scientific, methodical, watchful, well-drilled and predictable character of European professionals. Discourses surrounding Brazilian play continually refer to its 'natural' state, notably beach football, and to some spectacular highlights from past matches, rather than to modern, contemporary Brazilian football tactics, techniques and images. Watching Brazil play generates immense Occidental fascination; for a male audience, the 'enchantment' of this other's different playing style blends with the eroticism of its female supporters. European football club coaches who recruit Brazilians endeavour to control these players, to curb excesses, to contain risk taking during matches. Finally, Orientalism in Brazilian football and society is such that its core tropes are internalized as self-knowledge within Brazil itself. Through their football, then, Brazilians are complicit in their own Orientalizing.

While containing important insights, the Orientalism thesis possesses some inherent weaknesses. Its discursive determinism ensnares any claim to critical reflexivity or creative agency. From the Occidental viewpoint, Orientalism has a boomerang effect in sport that Said could not anticipate: non-Western cultures acquire Orientalist self-understandings that actually assist in defeating Western rationalism. Brazil, for example, is the world's most successful football nation, while English cricketers struggle to contain the 'sorcery' of Asian spin bowlers. Finally, both Orientalism and the Americanization thesis exaggerate the extent to which local cultures passively absorb powerful cultural images, beliefs and traditions. We need to put forward an alternative model that can explain the heterogeneous consequences of cultural communication.

Cultural heterogeneity and local–global relations

Through concepts like 'glocalization', 'creolization', 'hybridization' and 'indigenization', several theories of globalization emphasize the socio-cultural complexity of local–global relations, and the heterogeneity of cultural forms and practices that result.

Appadurai (1990) differentiates local–global cultural flows according to their specific fields or 'scapes'. These 'scapes' are the technoscapes (diffusion of technology), ethnoscapes (movement of people), financescapes (capital flows), mediascapes (movement of signs and information) and ideoscapes (flows of ideas and ideals). We can apply these classifications to sport to explain, for example, the globalization of a football club like Glasgow's Celtic. In terms of 'ethnoscape', the club was founded in Scotland by Irish-Catholic immigrants, thus enabling Celtic to appeal to people of similar ethnic background across the world. In terms of 'financescape', Celtic purchase players from across Europe and other continents while gaining international television revenues and sponsorship from TNCs. Through the 'technoscape', Celtic use specialist training equipment that is tested and manufactured overseas. Through the 'mediascape', Celtic fixtures are beamed out on satellite television across the world, while Internet communications facilitate other kinds of information diffusion. Through the 'ideoscape', Celtic have sought to work alongside similar European clubs to improve their income and competitiveness. As Appadurai allows, some serious disjunctures can arise: for example, while Celtic's 'ethnoscape' may emphasize their primordial Irish Catholicism, the 'financescape' and 'mediascape' favour investment, recruitment and audiences from beyond this community.

Robertson (1990a, 1990b, 1992, 1995) rejects the simple 'local versus global' argument by noting two parallel processes of globalization. First, the 'particularization of universalism' involves the world becoming 'more concrete socio-politically' – for example, through creation of world time zones or global calendars. Second, the 'universalization of particularism' describes the greater relativization of cultural identity and difference (Robertson 1992: 102–3). At world sports events, each nation asserts its relative particularity through differences in dress, anthem, social demeanour and sporting style.[3]

The concept of 'glocalization', which originated in Japanese business practice, is the 'constitutive feature of contemporary globalization' (Robertson 1995: 28–9; 1995: 41). 'Glocalization' describes how local social actors interpret global processes or phenomena to suit their particular needs or cultural contexts. Thus, global (standardized) sports events are framed or interpreted by local television stations or newspapers in accord with particular interests and tastes. Sport's historical diffusion has reflected glocalization as particular cultures amend and adapt the playing techniques, rules and organization of sport to suit local needs. Football's diverse cultural meanings – as rugby league, rugby union, soccer, American 'gridiron', Gaelic or 'Aussie Rules' – ensure that local sports programming usually lacks a smooth, universal, homogenous appeal (Rowe 1999: 80). Yet, given the 'universalization of particularism', the local's distinctiveness is explored in globally meaningful ways. Thus, in Ireland, football's rise at the relative expense of 'Gaelic football' is connected to the international success of the Irish national football team, and to the cultural space opened up for a small nation to become the focus of global attention through playing the 'global game'. Gaelic football cannot provide Ireland with an equivalent 'universal' platform for expressing its national particularity (Giulianotti 1996; Holmes 1994).

'Creolization' and 'hybridization' are terms similar to glocalization, and show how cross-cultural contacts and transmissions produce dynamic new cultural forms. Trobriand cricket provides probably the most spectacular illustration of sports creolization (Kildea and Leach 1975). Cricket was invented by the English and intended by colonial elites to dramatize the conservative values of discipline, obedience and rigid hierarchy. In the Trobriand Islands, cricket was radically refashioned to fit tribal beliefs: the home side always wins, dozens of players play for either side, specific cricket rules are amended to fit local custom, and tribal dances are part of the game. As Guttmann (1994: 186), in agreement with Cashman (1988) explains, 'Trobriand *cricket* has become *Trobriand* cricket.'

Rather problematically, the creolization thesis assumes that the 'creole' cultural product emerges from the fusion of two pure, authentic cultural entities. But, we should consider these 'pure' cultural forms as the product of earlier creolization processes. For example, while some cultures change baseball's rules to suit local circumstances, the game itself is a 'creole', American version of the English game of 'rounders'. Thus, a historically informed development of the creolization thesis would encourage critical analyses of how specific cultural 'traditions' are socially invented.

The New World provides particularly succinct demonstrations of the hybridity of modern cultural traditions. Archetti (1998) applies the concept of hybridization to Argentinian sports like polo and football. He defines hybridity in terms of cultural creativity, strength and vigour, involving extensive networks. In Argentina, influences from different immigrant groups (notably Italian, Spanish and British) were amalgamated to create a distinctive, *criollo* cultural style in polo and football. Through sport, Argentinians understood their hybridity as culturally stable, while remaining keen to absorb new influences (1998: 102–4).

The concepts of glocalization, creolization and hybridization capture the vitality of specific local cultures in relation to globalization processes. These concepts problematize the meaning of the 'local' in appropriating the global, giving rise to constant reinvention of particularity. They underline the need to undertake more fieldwork, particularly in developing cultures, to explore the real local impact of global sport (Kobayashi 2001). I would argue that contemporary globalization is transforming the local in four specific ways: with regard to self-identity, territory, collective nostalgia and social cleavage.

At the affective level, globalization is reshaping social relationships and the individual self. The rise in globally mediated sports intensifies celebrity-focused fandom, as defined by 'non-reciprocal relations of intimacy with a distant other' (J. B. Thompson 1995: 220). For such fans, community occurs within a 'virtual locality', such as Internet chat rooms or specialist websites.

Second, globalization moulds fresh geo-political and cultural identities alongside new, post-national institutions. In golf, the biennial Ryder Cup fixture between the United States and Europe has grown into the single most important sporting event, whereby strong senses of shared European identity and solidarity are constructed around partisan support for a single representative team. Moreover, the 'PGA European Tour' highlights globalization's deterritorializing impulses by including tournaments outside Europe (such as in Australia, Africa and Asia) on its official itinerary.

Third, globalization germinates postmodern forms of mediated nostalgia (Robertson 1990a: 53–5). Previously, during globalization's take-off stage (1870s to 1920s), a 'wilful nostalgia' was focused on 'lost golden ages'. Maguire (1994) suggests that the UK Conservative government reactivated such discourses in the early 1990s through an anti-European, wilful British nostalgia. But if so, it failed to last: the Labour Party won subsequent landslide elections in 1997 and 2001. Instead, postmodern nostalgia is more media-centred and schizophrenic in confusing the past and present, such as through retro television production techniques. Contemporary nostalgia also mixes the global-cultural with the national-societal in appeal and content. In sports media, while nostalgic programmes may recall past national successes and failures, they also appeal to the 'global-popular' by recalling the glories of global celebrities, such as Ali, Jordan or the great Brazilian football teams.

Fourth, while recognizing cultural glocalization, I would argue that political economy issues should not be forgotten. Thus, glocalization projects are inevitably skewed towards the more powerful social forces. Africans and Latin Americans develop their own cultural understandings of football, but their cultural contact with this and other 'global sports' is rooted in colonial and post-colonial relations. Meanwhile, the developing world cannot throw cultural flows into reverse: Malawi cannot transfer its pre-colonial movement culture into the global arena, for it to undergo glocalization by developed nations.

One offshoot of this 'political economy of glocalization' argument concerns the distinction between 'cosmopolitan' and 'local'. The concept of cosmopolitanism has a diversity of historical usages and anthropological meanings. In its more enlightened sense, the cosmopolitan adopts an ethically mature, reflexive relationship towards different cultural practices (see Robertson and White 2003: 24–5). However, sport's commodification is inducing a growing trend towards *flâneur* styles of cosmopolitanism rooted more in economic than cultural capital, to use Bourdieu's terms. As the political philosopher Michael Walzer (in Carleheden and Gabriels 1997: 120) indicates, cosmopolitans are somewhat 'parasitic' upon non-cosmopolitans: locals provide cosmopolitans with places to visit, and sports settings and community traditions to experience. Without locals, cosmopolitans have no diversity to consume or enjoy. For example, it is fascinating to witness how local peoples 'glocalize' world sports tournaments that are hosted in their home city. But, if tickets are so highly priced and scarce that only wealthy cosmopolitans gain access, locals are literally squeezed from the event, thereby negating the glocalization cultures that cosmopolitans find so interesting. The paradox of a self-interested cosmopolitanism opens further political debates within globalization.

Politics, cosmopolitanism and globalization

In pondering globalization's future, Robertson (1992: 183) asks whether humankind can ever become 'for-itself', whereby our heightened global consciousness might work primarily towards genuinely resolving world problems. Many theorists are not optimistic. Most disturbingly, Virilio's concept of 'globalitarianism' envisions the world as a totalitarian monoculture dominated by military technology, surveillance and population control (Armitage 2000). More empirically informed perspectives point critically to the global damage wrought by economic neo-liberalism and the post-9/11 imperialism of the new American military-industrial complex. In this light, the future source of positive global reform is difficult to discern.

In sport, as in other cultural domains, radical new social movements have emerged to combat neo-liberalism and TNCs. For example, in North America, the Workers' Rights Consortium seeks to improve industrial conditions in sports merchandise factories across the developing world. Its virulent anti-Nike campaign across American campuses provoked the company into withdrawing millions of dollars in university grants (*The Guardian*, 6 May 2000). Perhaps more significantly, through anti-racism and anti-sexism campaigns, post-war sport has long demonstrated how the globalization of new social movements can advance social equality and justice (Harvey and Houle 1994).

Appadurai (2000: 15) favours analysis of 'globalization from below', that is, of the global networks produced through local NGO practices and strategies. In sport, this 'grass roots globalization' can connect local sports associations to international donor institutions and other NGOs. Many sports governing bodies run development programmes via commercial sponsors, and help to finance local building projects and distribution of equipment through regional or national NGOs. Corruption often reduces project efficacy. However, by concentrating on NGOs, Appadurai too often considers what I would term a 'landscaped' variant of grass roots globalization. Analysis of real 'globalization from below' in the developing world must look beyond organized and institutionalized responses, to explore the real grass roots, the 'actual below'. We need to examine how, every day, people in slums, shantytowns or 'high density areas' live through the structural and cultural realities of globalization. On this point, globalization theory requires a dialogical ethic that privileges the position of the most disadvantaged, weakly organized social groups and communities, notably non-Western women (Hutchings 2003).

To counteract the hardening of global divides, social scientists have advocated various political reforms. Scholte (1998) advocates 'humane global futures' through the redistribution of power and resources across the North–South, gender and ethnic divides; creation of more democratic frameworks for supra-state governance; and political and cultural empowerment of civil society. DeMartino (2000: 237–8) makes the case for a global social charter, a 'social index tariff' that rewards nations for making internationalist, egalitarian improvements, a global code of conduct for corporations, a global tax on TNCs, a global convention on migration, and greater global solidarity and co-operation.

In anticipation of a global community, Habermas (1999: 58) has argued that if it is possible to produce an 'artificial form of solidarity amongst strangers' at national level, 'then why should it be impossible to extend this [democratic] learning process beyond national borders?' Drawing heavily upon Habermasian theory, Held (1995) has argued for the foundation of a 'cosmopolitan democracy' at global level. This would extend democratic principles over the whole world, allowing all citizens to 'have a voice, input and political representation in international affairs' (1995: 13). Held advocates *inter alia* the creation of a democratically elected assembly within a reformed UN that is itself recognized by an international convention of governments, NGOs and social movements. We also require more 'cosmopolitan citizens' 'capable of mediating between national traditions, communities of fate and alternative styles of life' (Held 2000: 402).

Other political philosophers like Honig (2001) advocate 'democratic cosmopolitanism' that prioritizes practical democratic empowerment at local level (Rengger 2003). However, a practical democratic ethic still requires institutional support if its abuse by elite groups is to be curtailed. After all, sports governing bodies preach humanist definitions of 'fair play' and respect for all opponents, but institutional weaknesses allow these ethics to be inverted by the corrupt, Machiavellian, unexposed practices of leading sports administrators.

If reformed global governance is to function economically, then a new system of exchange must be introduced, and Hart (2000, 2001) has offered a particularly radical rethink. Bringing classical political theory into the information age, Hart proposes that we humanely redefine 'money' as not 'state-made' but as a form of personal credit within a potentially global web of exchange circuits (2000: 322–3). In this way, money marks and mediates social interaction; 'credits' are accumulated and stored in 'memory banks'. The 'loyalty card' principle is thus extended across the community, its units logged and transferred through digital technology. To adapt Hart's thesis to the ideas of Held and DeMartino, the memory bank should credit internationalist egalitarian actions. The reformed cosmopolitan democracy would have substantial credit reserves, and would institutionally guarantee the ethical currency of this new exchange system.

Held and Hart might be accused of 'hopeless utopianism'; they are certainly weak in formulating a praxis for delivering these reforms (Goldblatt 1997). I disagree also with Hart's belief that the contemporary bourgeoisie will one day 'revitalize' their revolutionary historical project. Moreover, I recognize that a cosmopolitan democracy needs to be protected by democratically cosmopolitan ethics of dialogue and interaction, enabling the world to become 'for-itself'. One way to explore how such reforms might be realized is through their application within specific cultural laboratories. Sporting disciplines provide one such testing ground, due to their ethical and institutional content.

First, the discourse ethics of humanist universalism already exist within sport, albeit in rather unrefined form. Governing bodies constantly proclaim sport's universalist virtues. For some academics, sport's organizing ethics already anticipate aspects of democratic global practice. For Van Bottenburg (2001: 206), sport enables a 'renewed realization of collectivity', supplying our supranational interdependence with a set of global symbols. Guttmann (1994: 188) implores sport to afford 'the expression of *communitas*' for humanity *per se* alongside idioms of tribal identification. Morgan (2000) indicates that the use of numbers discloses sport's universalist dimensions: dominated nations are numbered literally alongside dominant nations, as the 'conversational partners' of Western representatives.

Second, modern sport's governing bodies mirror the UN in terms of infrastructure and procedure, and are ripe for reform. An elected governing assembly would need to represent the interests of all relevant sections: not only nations and continents, but also amateur and professional athletes and event officials, spectator movements, the retired, and those in sports-related employment. While paralleling Morgan's (1993) vision of a democratized 'practice-community', the reformed model would include more than athletes (see Walsh and Giulianotti 2001). The small executive cabals controlling each sports organization need to be abolished. The new body must have political superiority over national associations, NGOs, TNCs and social movements within each sport. New economic systems and circuits of exchange can evolve within each sport. For example, social actors can accumulate sporting credits through their time and expertise in contributing to sports development, notably coaching and health education in the developing world, rather than through their monetary contribution to that sport.

Thus, I favour a vision of supranational political and economic reform that takes a 'realist' position regarding globalization. Against a parasitic cosmopolitanism, I favour a democratic cosmopolitan ethic enabling cross-cultural dialogue, as guaranteed institutionally through new democratic frameworks, and through a radically reformed economy built on new definitions of money. As I have noted, globalization does not abolish the nation-state or procure a blanket cultural homogenization. Nevertheless, powerful nations and their associated TNCs in the Northern hemisphere, abetted by economic neo-liberalism and political influence within global institutions, can direct and control the global flows in capital, people, images and commodities. In such circumstances, and without buying into the deterministic Americanization thesis, I would argue that glocalization projects are always likely to be skewed in favour of some cultures over others. Hence, these political reforms would serve to promote human development and life-chances across all societies. They would provide comparatively weak cultures with material and dialogical resources to act fully and more critically within global cultural exchanges. In the glocal interplay of contemporary sports, all global players deserve a fair go.

Epilogue: The Critical Sociology of Sport: Some Recommendations

I conclude this sociology of sport by drawing together my various arguments to provide some recommendations for our sub-discipline, towards the pursuit of emancipation, justice and democratic participation within sport. It is clear by now that I prefer to dissociate investigation of sport from particular perspectives. Specifically, I resist explanations that presuppose the overweening, deterministic might of social structures or the pure agency of individualistic voluntarism. Anthropological and historical strains within sociology ensure that I am hostile to the evolutionism of structural-functionalists like Parsons and (less nakedly) the cross-cultural assumptions of Elias. I am opposed analytically to the cultural conservatism of functionalism (including the functionalist assumptions in some Marxism), and empirically to arguments regarding global homogeneity as opposed to the anthropological complexity and diversity of human societies. Of course, it is easier to state in categorical terms what I disagree with rather than support. To clarify the latter, I have parcelled the discussion into seven parts, to set out key research domains and approaches for the sociology of sport.

Sport, sociology and the academy. There are empirical, disciplinary and trans-disciplinary dimensions to reforming sport sociology. First, sport's societal importance continues to expand rapidly. As a core element of postmodern popular culture, sports dominate greater and greater volumes of media content and are bloated by hyper-commodification. Physical exercise is central to consumerism's regimens of bodily discipline and cultural government. In an age of heightened globalization, the fullest manifestations of transnational connectivity and community often occur at global sports events.

Second, as sociologists, we should sustain Bourdieu's and Elias's location of sport at the heart of sociological analysis. Sport assists specific domains of sociological research. On 'hegemonic masculinity', as I have suggested, sport and leisure may constitute a fifth defining feature in Connell's analytical structures concerning gender relations. Similarly, we should note sport's crucial historical and contemporary roles in constructing and reproducing international systems of subjugation and control with regard to race, imperialism and ethnic intolerance. The ethical overhaul of sport's governing bodies can provide a controlled demonstration of the potentialities for more fundamental global political reform.

Third, with Bourdieu, any sociologist (of sport, or otherwise) needs to undergo rigorous sociological training. Despite the popularity of interdisciplinary degrees (including 'sport studies'), broad and deep grasps of sociology as an academic discipline must be acquired before shifting into diverse substantive domains. However, I cannot subscribe to Bourdieu's ideal scenario wherein only qualified sociologists may pronounce on social phenomena. Disciplinary training should provide sociologists with a springboard for entering into markedly greater levels of interdisciplinary dialogue and research. The research object of sociologists – human societies – can be better explained through working relationships with other disciplines rather than by insisting upon the hypocritical, asocial conceit of splendid isolation. Specifically, the investigation of sport can become, alongside globalization studies, an essentially *trans-disciplinary* research domain. Elias provided an early argument for, if not demonstration of, the trans-disciplinary investigation of the emotions and the body. Our faith in sociology's explanatory merits should inspire the conviction that trans-disciplinary dialogue strengthens rather than weakens sociology's position within the academy and the public sphere. For example, the research fields of gender and ethnicity within sport indicate that interdisciplinary dialogue can force other disciplines to account for sociological evidence and argument.

Methodology, theory and sport sociology. I favour a *structured polyphonic* research perspective. Such a standpoint is highly cognizant of the structural context of social actors, their life-chances and resources; its polyphonic dimension refers to their critical reflexivity, to the open-endedness of social actions that do not silently follow a predetermined narrative. Sport's theorization must be qualitatively informed and contain a comparatively action-focused understanding of social hegemony, as envisioned in Marx and adumbrated through early Cultural Studies research.

Obviously, sport sociology is most effective when blending empirical research (particularly fieldwork) with theoretical analysis. Fieldwork revitalizes the Cultural Studies mission to connect interpretivist insights concerning the complexity of social roles, identities, meanings and practices to critical readings of the structural location of specific research groups. I favour genuinely 'grass roots' research that examines informal, everyday social practices, rather than 'landscaped' research that considers how institutions relate to social actors.

Fieldwork must be a dialogical process wherein research objectives, hypotheses and tentative conclusions are constantly reformulated through communication with research subjects. The researcher must engage in self-critical reflexivity, seeking to negate the kind of research biases identified by Bourdieu. The researcher must also produce critical (or 'para-doxal', in Bourdieu's terms) analyses that challenge dominant assumptions and ideologies, and deconstruct the dominant discourses of sport rooted in the structural inequalities of gender, ethnicity, class and age.

Social theorists need to be selectively and imaginatively deployed – for example, in combining interpretivism with postmodern thinking to explain fan identities, or in mixing Elias with Foucault to disclose body discipline in sport. I favour a softened Durkheimian position that keeps the significance of societal totality in our purview while undertaking fieldwork and analysis. Globalization theory lends that macroscopic inclination greater coherence while simultaneously expanding our sociological imagination. However, I favour Merton's cautious, middle-range epistemology. We cannot forcibly simplify the complexity or ignore the *sui generis* elements of specific research groups; nor should we assume that functional relations exist between various social groups before we enter the field.

History, culture and comparative studies. I advocate a strongly comparative approach across time (historically) and space (cross-culturally). Historical approaches illuminate the continuities and changes within the social structures and practices of specific sports, thereby revealing the social conflicts and transgressions within modern play. Our discussions of gender, race and space (baseball stadiums) have been indicative. We need to identify the sociogenesis of the salient features of postmodernity while recognizing that longer-standing, modern social inequalities remain within the contemporary epoch.

I favour critical histories of sport that synthesize the nuanced Marxism of Gramsci and Williams with the strongly cultural thinking of Eichberg (alongside a smattering of Foucault). Williams's 'dominant-emergent-residual' model is a useful, generalizing tool for registering shifting power relations. It focuses the eye of Marx (in *The Eighteenth Brumaire*) through a Gramscian lens to visualize the complex patterns of modern systems of domination. As the chapters on the body and space have demonstrated, I am drawn to Eichberg's 'trialectic' model, which differentiates between folk, modern and late/postmodern cultures within sport. Eichberg, with a twist of Foucault, reveals how folk practices diverge from, yet survive amidst, the disciplinary regimes of modern sports.

Cross-cultural studies must be intensified. Anthropologists and globalization analysts can assist in expanding discussion of 'race' within sport to include far more developing nations, particularly in Africa. Glocalization processes confirm that all cultures are increasingly cross-cultural in identity construction. Cross-cultural research reveals interconnections, continuities and differences between the sporting genealogies of specific societies. Such research illuminates the empirical and theoretical weaknesses of rather narrow associations of hegemonic masculinity with instrumental violence; a similar point holds regarding reductive arguments, on femininity, social class, ethnicity and the major differences in how societies experience postmodern culture.

Sport, political economy and hegemony. I favour a political economic perspective that is neither deterministic nor purely individualistic. Sports constitute relatively autonomous elements of cultural superstructures, which are themselves not simply determined by the material base.

A political economic framework critically augments the insights of Durkheim and Weber. We may consider how social institutions are rationally organized, and functionally interconnected, to sustain elite interests. Critical political economy arguments give teeth to Elias's mapping of manners, to Beck's writings on risk, and to postmodernist premonitions about sport. Bourdieu's analyses of struggles for distinction within sport are congruent with critical political economic perspectives, but I would argue against his practice of interpreting culture (including sport) as a mere trace of more fundamental structural battles between class fractions and strata.

Critical political economy arguments assist in examining the hypercommodification of professional and mediated sports, the *de facto* economic exclusion of many from full sports participation, the corporeal subjugation of athletes, the nexus of consumer culture and the governing of bodily pleasures, and the transformation of sporting landscapes to suit the *flâneur*'s gaze.

I advocate the application of a *political economy of glocalization* to explore how structural inequalities impact upon the cultural practices and interpretations of specific societies within the context of intensifying globalization. We must examine interrelations between different forms of social exclusion and subjugation, such as class, gender and ethnicity, as expressed, for example, through the practices of lower-class African-Americans within sport. Such a variant of hegemony theory registers the limitations of relatively deterministic readings of gender inequalities, as evidenced by Connell and Pronger. I consider the approach adopted here to be highly attuned to work by other major social thinkers on the institutionalized reproduction of social identities. Bourdieu puts forward some brilliant insights into the symbolic violence of major institutions: notably in education, but also in the mass media and sport. Foucault's genealogies of corporeal discipline and government, and the micro-political struggles generated therein, invite elucidation. On globalization, structured polyphonic research can explore how the politics of cosmopolitanism engenders particular forms of social exclusion within sport. Meanwhile, theorizations of power relations should identify social 'resistance' where it is a deliberative strategy of social actors. Exploration of sport's carnivalesque enables the sociologist to register 'transgressions' by social actors.

Sport, community and cultural aesthetics. Sport's role in constructing community and collective identity requires close sociological inspection. Durkheimian sociology opens understanding of sport's ritual construction of community. The Cultural Studies work of Raymond Williams promotes a critical focus on the structural inequalities and collective cultural identifications that underlie a community's 'structure of feeling' and its representative sporting institutions. Sport's cultural politics emanate from social struggles in cementing community identity, notably among ethnic minorities and within social classes. The body in sport is a venue of strengthened community influence and identification, as specific social groups found and embellish collective identity through pleasurable sporting practices. Strong affective community bonds are symbolized within 'topophilic' sporting spaces that acquire distinctive 'patinas'. Cultural relativization induced by intensified globalization can stimulate greater senses of particularistic identity that are increasingly deterritorialized. On community postmodernization, we need to recognize how the reproduction of core subcultures facilitates more temporary, expressive and neo-tribal modes of association. In ethically reformulating sport communities, I favour stretching Morgan's idea of 'practice-community' to include all interested parties, especially long-term custodians of a specific sport.

Despite their compelling significance to players and spectators, sport's aesthetic dimensions have been largely ignored by sport sociology. Historical and cross-cultural variations in sport's aesthetics are particularly fascinating. Sport entails social-psychological pleasures that are connected to forms of somatic transcendence and sports-specific eroticism. Regarding globalization and cultural postmodernity, sport facilitates the interplay of different corporeal techniques and tactical systems, reflecting broader relativization of cultural identities. Critical research questions surround the potentially disenchanting consequences of the rationalization, professionalization and hyper-commodification of sport's aesthetics. Sport's cultural politics include inter-group struggles to establish dominant aesthetic traditions and codes within sporting cultures, excluding alternative forms of corporeal and collective pleasure.

The political reinvention of sport. I advocate critical understandings of sport that challenge instrumental reason, social inequality and exclusion that collectively preclude human enjoyment and development within sport. There are three strands to this argument.

First, sport's communicative and social ethics must be reformulated along *dialogical* lines. Critical sociologies of education within sport should focus on how coaching may shift from pedagogy to *andragogy*. Regarding athlete identity, sports practice should avoid the deadening of the self as entailed by specialization and routinization, and promote diverse sporting roles and disciplinary interests among individuals. Sports events provide carnivalesque occasions that should stimulate, rather than stifle, dialogue between diverse bodies, cultural identities, folk customs, and tiers of authority. Such a dialogical principle must be democratically founded, necessitating the major reform of some cultural traditions and practices to safeguard the participatory rights of all citizens. Dialogue facilitates common strategies and practices among different social groups, and thus accords with Jennifer Hargreaves's 'co-operation' strategy on gender relations in sport.

Second, sport's institutional reform should work towards an inclusive, democratically defined 'practice-community' that minimizes the money principle and maximizes distributive justice within the reformed governing bodies. While sport's globalization registers the pleasing interplay of relativized identities and glocalized practices, hyper-commodification functions to exclude or transform the participation of particular communities. Governing bodies should ensure that global sport is not dominated by the signs, practices and identities of a cosmopolitan elite.

Third, sociologists can adopt more pro-active roles in sport's political transformation. As Bourdieu suggests, we may certainly engage with labour unions, new social movements and humanitarian NGOs to promote the interests of subordinate groups within sport. We should undertake and publicize research that exposes the empirical falsities and divisive interests that underlie the conservative discourses and unjust practices of major sports institutions and corporations. We should work with progressive elements within sports governing bodies that employ play and games, for example, to assist in the rehabilitation of traumatized children or to promote positive communication across divided societies.

Sport, sociology and humankind. We noted earlier Robertson's (1992) argument that contemporary globalization is shaped by the interplay of four elemental reference points: the individual, the nation, the international society and humankind. A more significant move towards human emancipation is likely only when the issue of humankind gains greater influence over individual practices, the domestic policies of nation-states, and the activities of transnational institutions within international society.

Sport is a vehicle for, and an index of, the growing juridico-cultural importance of human rights and the greater relevance of humankind. Sporting disciplines and institutions, notably football and Olympism, are in theory committed to universal participation, and certainly reach deeply into most societies' popular cultures. Major sports events occasion global fascination, and thereby represent cultural media through which their followers can more vividly imagine the community of humankind. Sports participation enables the dissemination of humanitarian messages and the implementation of contemporary policy initiatives. Major international organizations like the United Nations and ICRC view sport and play generally as essential human rights, particularly for children (Giulianotti, with Armstrong and Hognestad 2003). Some nations, notably Finland, have legislated on the right of all individuals to participate in sport and physical recreation (Kidd and Donnelly 2000: 145).

Sport's internationalism can be manipulated to the detriment of justice, equality and democracy. Since the late 1970s, centrist and

right-wing governments have dominated the developed world, imposing neo-liberal domestic and international policies. Sport's popularity
is exploited by political leaders to introduce, and add symbolic lustre
to, inadequate domestic policies that are avowedly intended to tackle
major problems like youth unemployment, urban crime, institutionalized racism and educational failure. Charitable sports-related aid
programmes have had a positive material impact on specific locations
in the developing world. But, in neither economic volume nor political value, should they be considered as viable substitutes for the true
'Weapons of Mass Salvation' that the largest Western governments still
fail to release, such as capital, food and anti-AIDS drugs, to protect
the existence of millions of people (Sachs 2002).

On this concluding point I request some crucial perspective on sport.
This book has sought to demonstrate that a critical sociology of sport
is valuable if only because its subject matter is of increasing economic,
political, cultural and social significance within a global context. But
sport, like all cultural domains, needs to be put in its place. As Terry
Eagleton (2000: 130–1) has argued, since the late 1960s the idea of
'culture' has gained greater theoretical prominence for many intellectuals, to the point that it is sometimes, and erroneously, depicted as
the dominant societal force.

> The primary problems which we confront in the new millennium –
> war, famine, poverty, disease, debt, drugs, environmental pollution, the
> displacement of peoples are not especially 'cultural' at all. They are not
> primarily questions of value, symbolism, language, tradition, belonging
> or identity, least of all the arts. Cultural theorists *qua* cultural theorists
> have precious little to contribute to their resolution ... they are cultural
> problems only in a sense which risks expanding the term to the point
> of meaninglessness.

Substitute the word 'sport' for 'culture', and you have my point. Sport
is characterized by complex cultural processes relating to social solidarity, rationalization, community and identity, political authority,
the environment, the body and aesthetic codes. Sports, and other institutionalized cultural practices, have certainly contributed markedly
to the political struggles involving the lower classes, women and colonized populations. But ultimately, sport sociologists should always
appreciate that games do not feed, house or inoculate people; they do
not reclaim polluted lands or terminate ethnic conflicts. Resolution of
the world's fundamental problems is not simply a matter for play.

Notes

1 These football codes include soccer, American football (or gridiron), Australian Rules football, rugby union and rugby league, and Gaelic football. Unless otherwise indicated, from here on 'football' designates the sport of soccer only.

CHAPTER 1   DURKHEIMIAN ELEMENTS: RELIGION, INTEGRATION AND SOCIAL ORDER IN SPORT

1 An early analysis developed Durkheim to explain how American baseball enhanced social solidarity (Cohen 1946: 334–6). This kind of study reflects the breadth of interpretation that is possible for examining the social functions of religion (Robertson 1970: 17–18).
2 Interestingly, in the early post-war period, the American government assigned a 'function' to every region of the poor Southern hemisphere. Each function was intended to support US interests in rebuilding Europe, rather than to assist these poor regions to develop for their own benefit (Chomsky 1998: 5).
3 A similar complaint can be targeted at another neo-functionalist, Niklas Luhmann, whose work I do not have room to discuss.

CHAPTER 2   WEBERIAN TRENDS: MEANING AND RATIONALIZATION IN SPORT

1 Of course, this discussion is necessarily selective. I do not have space to elaborate Weber's other arguments relating to the scientific procedures of sociology.

CHAPTER 3   MARX AND NEO-MARXISTS: SPORT, WORK, ALIENATION
AND IDEOLOGY

1   See http://www.worldbank.org/data/databytopic/GNI.pdf.
2   As Marx (1965/1845: 35) put it, 'The class which has the means of material production at its disposal, has control at the same time over the means of mental production, so that in consequence the ideas of those who lack the means of mental production are, in general, subject to it.' It should be added that Marx's conception of ideology went through several stages.
3   The commodification of the athlete's body may take extreme forms. In Australian Rules football, the Geelong captain Gary Hocking changed his name by deed poll to Whiskas for one week in the summer of 1999, as part of a deal with the eponymous cat food company to reduce his club's AUS$7 million debt.
4   As further examples, we may cite the actions of political demagogues like Franco in Spain and Mugabe in Zimbabwe in scheduling major matches on key national holidays, either to distract workers from taking to the streets in protest or to present full stadiums as evidence of mass support for the ruling party.
5   Marcuse (1964: 5) adds: 'Most of the prevailing needs to relax, to have fun, to behave and consume in accordance with the advertisements, to love and hate what others love and hate, belong to this category of false needs.'
6   The Frankfurt School's broad contempt for mass culture has had notable political and cultural allies. In the UK, Keir Hardie, a founding father of the Labour Party, described sport as 'degrading' and football as an 'abomination' (Smith and Williams 1980: 121). In the early post-war era, popular working-class pastimes like wrestling or greyhound racing were excluded from BBC coverage, since they did not fit the corporation's bourgeois ethics and cultural 'responsibility' towards its preferred audience. The post-war Labour government, with its own version of 'puritan socialism', adopted a similarly discriminatory stance towards greyhound racing, prompting a significant public backlash (N. Barker 1996).
7   Rowe (1995: 20) aptly describes Adorno and colleagues as 'Left Leavisites'.
8   Adorno (2001: 163) is critical of how modern mass culture is fixed to 'the almost unchanged ideology of early middle-class society', and so is out of date with the ideas of consumers. He illustrates this comment with reference to the anachronistic puritanism of mass culture in post-war England.
9   Some sporting bodies invoked the amateurism rule in extreme ways to exclude working-class competitors. The Amateur Rowing Association in England banned the 1920 Olympic champion from competing at the

upper-class Henley Regatta on the grounds that the American had once been employed as a bricklayer (Allison 1980: 19).

10 At one match in the early 1950s, Sussex's David Sheppard, the future bishop of Liverpool, had batted superbly against Gloucestershire. At close of play, a Gloucestershire professional congratulated Sheppard with the words, 'Well played David!' only to be strongly censured by his captain for over-familiarity and causing serious offence to the amateur (Ryder 1995: 182).

CHAPTER 4   CULTURAL STUDIES: HEGEMONY THEORY BEYOND RESISTANCE

1 McCree (2000) employs Williams's historical model to examine struggles over football's professionalization in the Caribbean.

2 There are ambiguities. In one passage, Gramsci (1971: 208) argues that the state (as the 'political society') and civil society are in balance; elsewhere, he suggests that the two are 'one and the same'.

3 In 1999, Kansas City Royals fans staged a 'Share the Wealth' protest at their home stadium when the champion New York Yankees were visiting. Home fans booed leading Yankees player Bernie Williams, whose $10 million annual salary was higher than the salary costs of the entire Royals first team. Early in the fourth inning, many fans in the left-field 'bleachers' vacated their seats in protest.

4 The 'Rabbitohs', based in the declining working-class district of Redfern, are one of Australian rugby league's oldest teams. They had been pressurized to merge with other clubs to survive, as part of a deal signed between the NRL and television companies, to reduce the number of clubs in the tournament while creating new teams outside Sydney, such as in Melbourne and Auckland.

5 Rojek complains that Cultural Studies can produce highly facile and banal conclusions regarding, for example, how cultural relations are neither 'wholly free nor totally determined activity'. This is fair criticism, but it fits many other sociological perspectives, notably Elias's 'figurational' approach and Giddens's 'structurations' theory.

6 In contrast to the restrained civility of English cricket crowds, the Barmy Army are known for very informal dress, heavy drinking, chanting and singing throughout play. Their leadership has been openly critical of the English cricket authorities.

7 See Stallybrass and White (1986), Eco (1984), and Fiske (1989).

8 Paintings and sketches by Bruegel, Hogarth and Beckmann deal with scenes of carnival and excessive folk culture.

9 The key writer on this subject, Mikhail Bakhtin (1984: 5), differentiated three interrelated forms of 'folk culture': ritual spectacles (including carnival pageants), comic verbal compositions, and various genres of Billingsgate (such as cursing).

10 Vrcan (2002) has demonstrated how the 'colonization of the lifeworld' can arise within sport: for example, through the process by which leaders within the new Croatian state sought to rename and culturally reinvent the football club, Dynamo Zagreb, as an institutional symbol of official Croatian nationalism, against the wishes of the club's supporters.

CHAPTER 5 'RACE', ETHNICITY AND INTOLERANCE IN SPORT

1 In 1941, one white sports coach argued of the black athlete, 'It is not long ago that his ability to sprint and jump was a life-and-death matter to him in the jungle. His muscles are pliable, and his easy-going disposition is a valuable aid to the mental and physical relaxation that a runner and jumper must have' (quoted in Miller 1998: 129–30).
2 In Africa and India, local chiefs and high-caste Brahmins wanted their boys to gain practical instruction in English to improve business skills and employment prospects. New cultural habits, like knowledge of British games, were not priorities, but tolerable diversions (Mangan 1998a: 188).
3 Specific Hindu beliefs and customs further reduced the boys' sporting propensity: swimming was a distinctly low-caste activity; rowing built muscular arms associated with lower castes; leather balls were unholy; the boys' favoured garments of long gowns and clogs were ill-fitting apparel for outdoor games like football; the long rings in noses and ears caused injuries, infections and lacerations during boxing bouts or games of leap-frog (Mangan 1998a: 182–6).
4 Stacking theory may be extended to other body cultures relative to aesthetics. For example, while the 'rhythms' of jazz and modern popular music are said to be attuned to African-American dance patterns, ballet has been presented by some as too academic, European and technical for the black temperament and physiology (Miller 1998: 119).
5 I discuss this kind of argument more fully in chapter 12 with regard to 'Orientalism'.
6 The great Italian-American baseball star Joe DiMaggio adopted a strategy of media avoidance, rather than become caught in a celebrity identity that would include ethnic stereotyping (Altimore 1999).

CHAPTER 6 GENDER IDENTITIES AND SEXUALITY IN SPORT

1 Mangan (1998a: 182–3) describes this as a 'complacent and confident ethnocentricity', driven partly by the 'transformation of the famous concept of "fair play" from a utilitarian instrument of private control into a moralistic public virtue largely "peculiar" to the upper- and middle-class English schoolboy'.
2 Exercises involving strength, endurance or opening the legs were prohibited!

3   The increasingly militarist regime in pre-1945 Japan founded women's sports organizations and promoted female participation at national and international tournaments. One brilliant athlete, Hitomi Kinue, produced world-class performances in the 100 and 400 metres and the long jump, although not in Olympic competition (Guttmann and Thompson 2001: 120–1).

4   As Guttmann puts it, 'an athletic body in an evening gown can cause the same kind of cognitive dissonance as obesity in a track suit' (1991: 261).

5   Lenskyj (1995: 55) rejects the 'reverse discrimination' or 'heterophobia' arguments that criticize the alleged majority presence of gays or lesbians in some sports. If such scenarios ever do arise, then these can help heterosexuals, who suddenly find themselves in a minority, to get a taste of the marginalization routinely experienced by gays and lesbians.

6   Cox and Thompson (2001) advance similar arguments with respect to New Zealand football.

7   The entry of a female *torero* (bullfighter) in Spain in the mid-1990s provoked strong protests, notably among other bullfighters, forcing her to retire within three years (*The Australian*, 20 May 1999).

8   J. Williams (2001: 105) captures this well when explaining how working-class Liverpool football fans during the 1960s were particularly appreciative of the aesthetic 'grace, style and pace' found in the best players.

CHAPTER 7   THE BODY: DISCIPLINE, CONDUCT AND THE
PLEASURES OF SPORT

1   In the next chapter, I discuss the transfer of techniques of surveillance within prisons or militarized zones to city centres, suburban malls and sports stadiums.

2   Participation levels and public interest have grown steadily: the Sydney Paralympics saw over 10,000 athletes from 125 nations competing before more than 1.2 million live spectators. The Special Olympics now organizes sport programmes for over 1 million people across more than 150 nations.

3   African-American boxers tie the slave metaphor partly to their ancestors' racial subjugation; indeed some slaves fought brutal, often lethal contests at their owners' behest.

4   Boxing may enable fighters to escape the unpredictable violence of their lower-class peers and social milieu, and offset the poor job prospects of young black men by placing a 'career' and social glamour within reach (Wacquant 1995a).

5   Theodore Roosevelt declared, 'I would a hundred fold rather keep the game as it is now with the brutality, than give it up.' A true leader, Roosevelt opined, 'can't be efficient unless he is manly'; and American football's

violence cultivated masculinity (quoted in McQuilkin and Smith 1993: 59).

6   Elite gymnastic careers are concentrated in childhood and adolescence, lasting generally from around 12 to 18 years of age. Most girls abandon gymnastics after entering adulthood, not by choice but because their bodies 'expire' through unchecked regimens of work (Ryan 1996: 31).

7   Recent cases involving Minnesota Vikings' Korey Stringer (killed by heat-stroke in pre-season training) and the Jacksonville Jaguars' Jeff Novak (whose serious shin injury was not properly rested) have exposed further NFL deficiencies in standardizing care responsibilities of club coaches, medics and officials.

8   Most famously, Dick Butkus (a Hall of Fame linebacker) settled for $600,000 in 1974 following his case against the Chicago Bears' team physician. Fifteen years later, Charlie Krueger settled for $1.5 million in a similar case against the San Francisco 49ers and the team orthopaedist.

9   There are five main categories of banned substance, each with differ-ent competitive functions: anabolic steroids and peptide hormones (both improve training capabilities); stimulants (increase heart rate); analgesics (such as opiates); and diuretics (for weight control).

10   High-profile cases include Ben Johnson (Canadian sprinter), Petr Korda (Czech tennis player), Alain Baxter (Scottish skier), Richard Virenque (French cyclist), Diego Maradona (Argentinian football player) and Merlene Ottey (Jamaican sprinter).

CHAPTER 8   SPORTING SPACES: VALUING TOPOPHILIA

1   See e.g., Bale (1982, 1989, 1992, 1994; Bale and Vertinsky 2003).

2   The disaster occurred through crowd crushing inside one ground 'pen'; fearing a violent invasion of supporters, police initially refused to allow fans to escape on to the field of play.

3   At the 1985 European Cup final at the Heysel Stadium in Brussels, 39 fans of the Italian team Juventus perished, and 400 were injured when they fled a charge by Liverpool supporters and were subsequently crushed after a stadium wall collapsed.

4   According to Roger Clarke, dataveillance involves 'the systematic use of personal data systems in the investigation or monitoring of the actions or communications of one or more persons' (see http://www.anu.edu.au/people/Roger.Clarke/DV/CACM88.html).

5   Deleuze (1997) notes that disciplinary techniques have been superseded by apparatuses of control. Whereas the former were overt and more ma-terial in their forms of spatial confinement, the latter are more hidden, less 'placed' and more multi-layered. For sport spectators, the disciplinary gaze of police officers and CCTV inside stadiums might be outmoded. A more efficient control strategy involves self-policing, imposed through membership of spectator associations, or through ticket sales by credit

card that render the purchasers legally responsible for their collective behaviour. In turn, top athletes have moved from the more disciplinary experience of powerful sports clubs to the subtle control functions that arise through diverse relationships with public image advisers, sponsors and media contacts.

CHAPTER 9   ELIAS ON SPORT: THE INTERPLAY OF FIGURATIONS

1 The civilizing process may promote some rules that are actually more harmful to individuals. For example, Sheard (1997) notes that boxing has in many ways become more dangerous for contestants following its 'sportization'. Bare-knuckle prize-fighting was viewed increasingly as barbaric by the Victorian aristocracy. The introduction of the Queensberry Rules in the 1860s brought padded gloves and the ten-second count for grounded fighters. While the blood and violence of earlier pugilism was greatly reduced, the new rules encouraged new blows (particularly 'knock-out' punches) that are far more harmful to the brain.

2 Johansson (2000) found that Swedish football matches were notably violent during the 1930s, primarily because of the way in which local coaches applied English playing systems through close man-to-man marking. In other circumstances, the civilizing process cannot be said to have determined the rise of instrumental, often brutal, football tactics in Italy during the 1960s, at a time of increasing prosperity and less violence involving organized crime.

3 See, e.g., Dunning's (1992: 254–7) attack on Jennifer Hargreaves's feminist perspective, and Hargreaves's (1994: 12–16) later demonstration of how her arguments had been seriously misrepresented. See also the absurd claim by Dunning, Murphy and Waddington (1991) that their critics (Armstrong and Harris 1991) had 'gone native' when undertaking a study of football hooligans.

CHAPTER 10   BOURDIEU ON SPORT: *DISTINCTION*, SYMBOLIC VIOLENCE AND STRUGGLE

1 The term 'genetic structuralism' has an earlier sociological usage: Williams (R. 1981: 144), e.g., locates it in the work of Goldmann (1970) that 'puts a decisive emphasis on the evolution of forms, analyzing their building and dissolution, by contrast with the idea of permanent forms which simply exhibit variations'.

2 As he argues elsewhere, 'the sociology of sociology is a fundamental dimension of sociological epistemology' (Bourdieu and Wacquant 1992: 68).

3 Witness those occasions when elite athletes seek to show their versatility in other sports, only to find their lack of technical skills being criticized by

media experts, while established professionals seek to 'teach the rookies a lesson' in the new game.

4 Bourdieu (2000: 170) notes how symbolic violence socializes black children into their subaltern position; even before recognizing 'difference', and the various conventions and boundaries imposed upon the dominated group, black children still construct their 'colour' identity out of their elders' voices, and the positions and dispositions that these adults adopt in social relations.

5 Obviously Bourdieu was not the first social analyst to explore how social classes are differentiated through cultural preference. In the United States prior to the First World War, Veblen (1970/1899) examined class dynamics via analyses of materialism and consumption patterns. For example, the upper-class penchant for the rustic and the natural, seen in their visiting parks and purchasing handicrafts, distinguishes this class's liberation from memories of thrift (1970/1899: 84). However, Bourdieu notes that Veblen connects the pursuit of distinction with distinguished behaviour. Conversely, Bourdieu (1990a: 11) argues that striving for distinction is actually discrediting, since it confirms that the individual is both aware that she lacks some distinguishing qualities and does not have the unthinking virtuosity of those who do have true distinction.

6 In early modern times in America, the different sporting preferences of the aristocracy and middle classes reflected the cultural values that imbued their respective *habituses*. The rich and super-rich favoured sport and country clubs for their 'inutility', whereas the middle classes viewed sport as enabling life's work to be done in a practicable and morally correct manner (Mrozek 1983).

7 Urry (1995: 225–8) describes a similar study of middle-class consumption patterns, by Savage et al. (1992), suggesting three categories rooted in socio-economic differences. First, public sector professionals adopt an 'ascetic' approach towards leisure, favouring a healthy, outdoor life-style and activities such as climbing, skating and tennis. Second, the professional middle classes engage in a 'postmodern' mode of consumption, adopting healthy life-styles and aspects of asceticism while 'living rich'. Third, the managerial middle classes show-case an 'indistinct' life-style that is more escapist, and results in higher engagement with country sports, squash and golf.

CHAPTER 11   THE POSTMODERN: PREMONITIONS OF VIRTUAL, POST-INDUSTRIAL SPORT

1 Postmodern thinking can empathize with pre-modern cultural forms or patterns of social organization. For example, Baudrillard's penchant for symbolic exchange relationships in non-industrial societies reflects a pre-modern ethos within his anti-modern theory.

2   For an application of a softer, 'middle-range' version of Lévi-Strauss's thinking to sport, see Giulianotti and Armstrong (2001).
3   The degree to which Foucault really broke with structuralism tends to be exaggerated. There are strong continuities between structuralism and his initial, archaeological method; and the latter has strong overlaps with his later, more celebrated, genealogical approach.
4   See *Otobiographies* in which Derrida (1984) develops a deconstructionist analysis of the American constitution.
5   See Cole (1998) for a Derridean analysis of the problems inherent in sport rules and regulations that relate to the body.
6   Kruger (1996) traces this back further, to at least the late nineteenth century. He argues that the founder of the modern Olympics, Pierre de Coubertin, was heavily influenced by John Ruskin, the English art critic and social analyst. In postmodern vein, Ruskin dismissed the notion of art as a 'high' modern phenomenon; he argued instead that 'all art is a low and common thing', and that one should respect only the 'instinct' or 'inspiration' behind artistry. Similarly, Ruskin argued that 'commodification' and 'beautification' went together, in line, according to Kruger (1996: 34–5), with the postmodernist Baudrillard, who insists that signs as well as products are central to contemporary consumption.
7   Virilio distances himself from postmodernism, particularly in architecture, though he recognizes the validity of post-structuralist theory. He accepts that his social theory addresses the problems of 'hypermodernism' (Armitage 2000: 25–6). Yet, given his concern with the radical cultural changes wrought by new technology, notably in relation to virtual reality, one does not need to reinvent the basic definition of the postmodern to include Virilio. Indicatively, Virilio and Baudrillard attract similar communities of scholars.
8   The scale of neo-tribal participation within the hooligan group varies according to several factors, such as the hooligan reputation of the opposing group, how well the favoured football team is currently playing, or the specific status of hooligan styles relative to other youth styles. Differentiating subcultural and neo-tribal hooliganism helps to explain why 30 young men following one specific football team may come together as part of a hooligan formation for a football match, then their numbers swell to 100 for another fixture the following week.
9   Pastiche arises in other cultural realms, such as music 'sampling' or avant-garde fashion. But eclecticism connotes a partial return to pre-modern artistic practices. Renaissance and Baroque artists were less concerned with modernist displays of authentic, individual creativity, and more willing to integrate other artists' ideas and work into fresh music, paintings or poems. A crucial difference between then and now concerns the wider 'aestheticization of everyday life' that marks the consumer culture of postmodernity.

10 There is an interesting difference between Baudrillard and Virilio on sim-
    ulation. Whereas for Baudrillard, reality seems to disappear or dissolve
    into hyperreality, for Virilio, reality is substituted by the more seductive
    force of simulation (Kellner 2000: 115). The difference may be illustrated
    by the case of video sports games. For Virilio, video games displace mod-
    ern, object-related social exercises by virtual play on consoles. For Bau-
    drillard, 'real' sport disappears as its simulated model comes to dominate
    how players experience and envision its practice, whether on television
    screens or in the excessively manicured landscapes of postmodernity.

CHAPTER 12   GLOBALIZATION: THE POLITICS OF 'GLOCAL' SPORT

1 Gramsci (1971: 318) considered that 'Americanism', in its Rotary Club
   form at least, represented an intensification of (rather than a radical
   departure from) European civilization. More conservative intellectuals
   like T. S. Eliot and F. R. Leavis connected Americanization with the
   dangerous advances of mass culture.
2 Thus French sports policy rejects American free-market thinking to
   favour non-profit-making, public sector investment, volunteer-based
   sports development, public sector sports infrastructure, and usually
   strong partnerships between local authorities and professional clubs.
3 This can mean that sports modernization takes highly distinctive
   local forms. In modern sumo wrestling, for example, the Japanese
   sought to re-emphasize distinctive cultural traditions by insisting that the
   yokozuna (grand champion) should be chosen on the grounds of his tournament performance *and* his symbolic value as a Japanese (Guttmann
   1994: 162–3).

References

Adams, R. L. A. (1995) Golf. In K. Raitz (ed.), *Theater of Sport*, Baltimore: Johns Hopkins University Press.

Adler, P. A. and P. Adler (1991) *Backboards and Blackboards*. New York: Columbia University Press.

Adorno, T. W. (1982) *Prisms*. Cambridge, Mass.: Harvard University Press.

Adorno, T. W. (2001) *The Culture Industry*. London: Routledge.

Adorno, T. W. and M. Horkheimer (1979, 1944) *Dialectic of Enlightenment*. London: Verso.

Alabarces, P. (1999) Post-modern times. In G. Armstrong and R. Giulianotti (eds), *Football Cultures and Identities*, Basingstoke: Macmillan.

Albert, E. (1999) Dealing with danger: the normalization of risk in cycling. *International Review for the Sociology of Sport*, 34 (2), 157–71.

Alexander, J. C. (1992) Citizen and enemy as symbolic classification: on the polarizing discourse of civil society. In M. Lamont and M. Fournier (eds), *Cultivating Differences*, Chicago: University of Chicago Press.

Allison, L. (1980) Batsman and bowler: the key relation of Victorian England. *Journal of Sport History*, 7 (2), 5–20.

Allison, L. (1998) Biology, ideology and sport. In L. Allison (ed.), *Taking Sport Seriously*, Aachen: Meyer & Meyer.

Alomes, S. (1994) Tales of a dreamtime. In I. Craven (ed.), *Australian Popular Culture*, Melbourne: Cambridge University Press.

Alt, J. (1983) Sport and cultural reification. *Theory, Culture and Society*, 1 (3), 93–107.

Althusser, L. (1971) *Lenin and Philosophy and Other Essays*. London: New Left Books.

Altimore, M. (1999) Gentleman athlete: Joe DiMaggio and the celebration and submergence of ethnicity. *International Review for the Sociology of Sport*, 34 (4), 359–67.

Anderson, P. M. (1997) Playing the stadium game. *Journal of Sport & Social Issues*, 21 (1), 103–11.

Andrews, D. L. (1997) The [trans]National Basketball Association. In A. Cvetovitch and D. Kellner (eds), *Articulating the Global and the Local*, Boulder, Colo.: Westview Press.

Andrews, D. L. (2001) The fact(s) of Michael Jordan's blackness. In D. L. Andrews (ed.), *Michael Jordan, Inc.*, New York: SUNY Press.

Andrews, D. L. (2002) Coming to terms with Cultural Studies. *Journal of Sport & Social Issues*, 26 (1), 110–17.

Andrews, D. L., R. Pitter, D. Zwick and D. Ambrose (1997) Soccer's racial frontier. In G. Armstrong and R. Giulianotti (eds), *Entering the Field*, Oxford: Berg.

Appadurai, A. (1990) Disjuncture and difference in the global cultural economy. In M. Featherstone (ed.), *Global Culture: Nationalism, Globalization and Modernity*, London: Sage.

Appadurai, A. (1995) Playing with modernity: the decolonization of Indian cricket. In C. A. Breckenridge (ed.), *Consuming Modernity*, Minneapolis: University of Minnesota Press.

Appadurai, A. (2000) Grassroots globalization and the research imagination. *Public Culture*, 12 (1), 1–20.

Apter, M. J. (1982) *The Experience of Motivation*. London: Academic Press.

Arbena, J. L. (1986) Sport and the study of Latin American history. *Journal of Sport History*, 13 (2), 87–96.

Archetti, E. (1998) *Masculinities*. Oxford: Berg.

Archetti, E. (1999) The spectacle of heroic masculinity. In A. M. Klausen (ed.), *Olympic Games as Performance and Public Event*, Oxford: Berg.

Aristotle (1981) *Politics*. Harmondsworth: Penguin.

Armitage, J. (2000) An interview with Paul Virilio. In J. Armitage (ed.), *Paul Virilio*, London: Sage.

Armstrong, G. (1998) *Football Hooligans: Knowing the Score*, Oxford: Berg.

Armstrong, G. and R. Giulianotti (1998) From another angle: police surveillance and football supporters. In C. Norris, G. Armstrong and J. Moran (eds), *Surveillance, CCTV and Social Control*, Aldershot: Gower.

Armstrong, G. and R. Giulianotti (eds) (2004) *Football in Africa*. Basingstoke: Palgrave.

Armstrong, G. and R. Harris (1991) Football hooligans: theory and evidence. *Sociological Review*, 39 (3), 427–58.

Aronowitz, S. (1973) *False Promises*. New York: McGraw-Hill.

Ascherson, N. (2002) *Stone Voices: The Search for Scotland*. London: Granta.

Bachelard, G. (1969) *The Poetics of Space*. Boston: Beacon Press.

Bairner, A. (2001) *Sport, Nationalism and Globalization*. Albany, NY: SUNY Press.

Baker, N. (1996) Going to the dogs. *Journal of Sport History*, 23 (2), 97–119.

Baker, W. J. (1992) Muscular Marxism and the Chicago Counter-Olympics of 1932. *International Journal of the History of Sport*, 9, 397–410.

Bakhtin, M. (1984) *Rabelais and his World*. Bloomington: Indiana University Press.

Bale, J. (1982) *Sport and Place*. London: Hurst.

Bale, J. (1989) *Sports Geography*. London: Spon.

Bale, J. (1990) In the shadow of the stadium. *Geography*, 75 (4), 324–34.

Bale, J. (1991) Playing at home. In J. Williams and S. Wagg (eds), *British Football and Social Change*, Leicester: Leicester University Press.

Bale, J. (1992) *Sport, Space and the City*. London: Routledge.

Bale, J. (1993) The spatial development of the modern stadium. *International Review for the Sociology of Sport*, 28 (2/3), 121–34.

Bale, J. (1994) *Landscapes of Modern Sport*. London: Leicester University Press.

Bale, J. (1995) Cricket. In K. Raitz (ed.), *Theater of Sport*, Baltimore: Johns Hopkins University Press.

Bale, J. (1998) Virtual fandoms. In A. Brown (ed.), *Fanatics!*, London: Routledge.

Bale, J. (2000) Sport as power. In J. P. Sharp, P. Routledge, C. Philo and R. Paddison (eds), *Entanglements of Power*, London: Routledge.

Bale, J. and J. Sang (1996) *Kenyan Running*. London: Frank Cass.

Bale, J. and P. Vertinsky (2003) *Sites of Sport: Space, Place, Experience*, London: Frank Cass.

Banton, M. (1988) *Racial Consciousness*. London: Longman.

Barnes, J. (1999) *John Barnes*. London: Headline.

Barrett, M. (1982) Feminism and the definition of cultural politics. In R. Brunt (ed.), *Feminism, Culture and Politics*, London: Lawrence & Wishart.

Barron, A. (1992) Lyotard and the problem of justice. In A. Benjamin (ed.), *Judging Lyotard*, London: Routledge.

Barthes, R. (1972) *Mythologies*. London: Paladin.

Baudrillard, J. (1983) *In the Shadow of the Silent Majorities*. New York: Semiotext(e).

Baudrillard, J. (1989) *America*, trans. Chris Turner. London: Verso.

Baudrillard, J. (1990) *Seduction*. Cambridge: Polity.

Baudrillard, J. (1993) *The Transparency of Evil*, trans. James Benedict. London: Verso.

Baudrillard, J. (1994a) *The Gulf War Did Not Take Place*. Sydney: Power Institute.

Baudrillard, J. (1994b) *The Illusion of the End*, trans. Chris Turner. Cambridge: Polity.

Baudrillard, J. (1995) The virtual illusion. *Theory, Culture and Society*, 12, 97–107.

Baudrillard, J. (1996a) *Cool Memories*, vol. 2, trans. Chris Turner. Cambridge: Polity.

Baudrillard, J. (1996b) Disneyworld Company. *Liberation*, 4 March.

Baudrillard, J. (1996c) *The Perfect Crime*, trans. Chris Turner. London: Verso.

Baudrillard, J. (1998) *Paroxysm*. London: Verso.

Baudrillard, J. (2002) *Screened Out*. London: Verso.

Bauman, Z. (1992) *Intimations of Postmodernity*. London: Routledge.

Beamish, R. (1993) Labor relations in sport. In A. G. Ingham and J. W. Loy (eds), *Sport in Social Development*, Champaign, Ill.: Human Kinetics.

Beck, U. (1992) *Risk Society*. London: Sage.

Beck, U. (2000) *What is Globalization?* Cambridge: Polity.

Becker, H. S. (1953) Becoming a marihuana user. *American Journal of Sociology*, 59 (Nov.), 235–43.

Beckles, H. (1998) *The Development of West Indies Cricket*, vol. 1. London: Pluto.

Bellah, R. (1975) *The Broken Covenant*. New York: Seabury.

Ben-Ari, E. (1998) Golf, organization, and body projects: Japanese business executives in Singapore. In S. Linhart and S. Frühstück (eds), *The Culture of Japan as Seen Through its Leisure*, Albany, NY: SUNY Press.

Benedict, J. (1998) *Public Heroes, Private Felons*. Boston: Northeastern University Press.

Benjamin, W. (1999) *The Arcades Project*. London: Belknap.

Bennett, T. (1998) *Culture: A Reformer's Science*. London: Sage.

Bentham, J. (1791) *Panopticon, or....* London: T. Payne.

Birrell, S. (1978) Sporting Encounters. Unpublished doctoral dissertation, University of Massachusetts, Amherst.

Birrell, S. (1981) Sport as ritual. *Social Forces*, 60, 354–76.

Blake, A. (1995) *The Body Language*. London: Lawrence & Wishart.

Bogard, W. (1996) *The Simulation of Surveillance: Hypercontrol in Telematic Societies*. Cambridge: Cambridge University Press.

Booth, D. (1998) *The Race Game: Sport and Politics in South Africa*. Landon: Frank Cass.

Booth, D. (2001) *Australian Beach Cultures*. London: Frank Cass.

Booth, D. and C. Tatz (2000) *One-Eyed: A View of Australian Sport*. St Leonards, NSW: Allen & Unwin.

Bottenburg, M. Van (2001) *Global Games*. Urbana: University of Illinois Press.

Bottomore, T. and M. Rubel (1963) *Karl Marx: Selected Writings*. Harmondsworth: Penguin.

Bourdieu, P. (1978) Sport and social class. *Social Science Information*, 17 (6), 819–40.

Bourdieu, P. (1984) *Distinction*. London: Routledge.

Bourdieu, P. (1990a) *In Other Words*. Stanford, Calif.: Stanford University Press.

Bourdieu, P. (1990b) *The Logic of Practice*. Cambridge: Polity.

Bourdieu, P. (1992) Deux impérialismes de l'universel. In C. Fauré and T. Bishop (eds), *L'Amérique des Français*, Paris: Seuil.

Bourdieu, P. (1993) *Sociology in Question*. London: Sage.

Bourdieu, P. (1998a) *Acts of Resistance*. New York: New Press.

Bourdieu, P. (1998b) The State, economics and sport. *Culture Sport Society*, 1 (2), 15–21.

Bourdieu, P. (2000) *Pascalian Meditations*. Cambridge: Polity.

Bourdieu, P. and G. Balazs (1993) Such a fragile equilibrium. In P. Bourdieu et al., *The Weight of the World*, Stanford, Calif.: Stanford University Press.

Bourdieu, P. and J.-C. Passeron (1977) *Reproduction in Education, Society and Culture*. London: Sage.

Bourdieu, P. and L. J. D. Wacquant (1992) *An Invitation to Reflexive Sociology*. Cambridge: Polity.

Bourdieu, P. et al. (1999) *The Weight of the World*. Stanford, Calif.: Stanford University Press.

Boyd, T. (1997) The day the niggaz took over. In A. Baker and T. Boyd (eds), *Out of Bounds*, Bloomington: Indiana University Press.

Boyne, R. (2000) Post-panopticism. *Economy & Society*, 29 (2), 285–307.

Brackenridge, C. (2001) *Spoilsports*. London: Routledge.

Brailsford, D. (1985) Morals and maulers. *Journal of Sport History*, 2, 126–42.

Brohm, J.-M. (1978) *Sport: A Prison of Measured Time*. London: Pluto.

Bromberger, C. (1995) Football as world-view and as ritual. *French Cultural Studies*, 6, 293–311.

Brophy, J. (1997) Carnival in Cologne. *History Today*, July.

Bruce, S. (2000) Comparing Scotland and Northern Ireland. In T. M. Devine (ed.), *Scotland's Shame?* Edinburgh: Mainstream.

Bruce, T. (1998) Postmodernism and the possibilities for writing 'vital' sports texts. In G. Rail (ed.), *Sport and Postmodern Times*, Albany, NY: SUNY Press.

Bryman, A. (1998) *Disney and his Worlds*. London: Routledge.

Buch, E. (2003) *Beethoven's Ninth*. Chicago: University of Chicago Press.

Burns, T. (1992) *Erving Goffman*. London: Routledge.

Canclini, N. G. (1995) *Hybrid Cultures*. Minneapolis: University of Minnesota Press.

Carleheden, M. and R. Gabriels (1997) An interview with Michael Walzer. *Theory, Culture & Society*, 14 (1), 113–30.

Carr, K. G. (1993) Making way: war, philosophy and sport in Japanese *judo*. *Journal of Sport History*, 20 (2), 167–88.

Carrington, B. (2001) Postmodern blackness and the celebrity sports star'. In D. L. Andrews and S. J. Jackson (eds.), *Sport Stars*, London: Routledge.

Carrington, B. and I. McDonald (2001) Introduction. In B. Carrington and I. McDonald (eds), *'Race', Sport and British Society*, London: Routledge.

Carroll, J. (1985) Sport: virtue and grace. *Theory, Culture & Society*, 3 (1), 91–8.

Cashman, R. (1988) Cricket and colonialism. In J. A. Mangan (ed.), *Pleasure, Profit, Proselytism*, London: Frank Cass.

Cashman, R. (1995) *Paradise of Sport*. Oxford: Oxford University Press.

Cashman, R. and A. Hughes (eds) (1998) *The Green Games*. Sydney: Centre for Olympic Studies.

Cashmore, E. (1982) *Black Sportsmen*. London: Routledge & Kegan Paul.

Cashmore, E. (2002) *Beckham*. Cambridge: Polity.

Castells, M. (1997) *The Power of Identity*. Oxford: Blackwell.

Castells, M. (1998) *End of Millennium*. Oxford: Blackwell.

Chomsky, N. (1998) Power in the global arena. *New Left Review*, 230, 3–27.

Clarke, A. (1992) Figuring a brighter future. In E. Dunning and C. Rojek (eds), *Sport and Leisure in the Civilizing Process*, Toronto: University of Toronto Press.

Clarke, G. (2002) Difference matters. In D. Penney (ed.), *Gender and Physical Education*, London: Routledge.

Clarke, J. (1976) Style. In S. Hall and T. Jefferson (eds), *Resistance through Rituals*, London: Hutchinson.

Clarke, J. and C. Critcher (1985) *The Devil Makes Work*. Basingstoke: Macmillan.

Clément, J.-P. (1981) La force, la souplesse et l'harmonie: étude comparée de trois sports de combat (lutte, judo, aikido). In C. Pociello (ed.), *Sports et société*, Paris: Vigot.

Clément, J.-P. (1985) Etude comparative de trois sports de combat et de leurs usages sociaux. Unpublished Ph.D. thesis, Université Paris III, Paris, France.

Clément, J.-P. (1995) Contributions of the sociology of Pierre Bourdieu to the sociology of sport. *Sociology of Sport Journal*, 12, 147–57.

Coates, D. and B. R. Humphreys (2000) The stadium gambit and local economic development. *Regulation*, 23 (2), 15–20.

Cohen, M. B. (1946) *The Faith of a Liberal*. New York: Transaction.

Cohen, S. and L. Taylor (1976) *Escape Attempts*. London: Routledge.

Cole, C. L. (1998) Addiction, exercise and cyborgs. In G. Rail (ed.), *Sport and Postmodern Times*, Albany, NY: SUNY Press.

Connell, R. W. (1987) *Gender and Power*. Stanford, Calif.: Stanford University Press.

Connell, R. W. (1990) An iron man. In M. Messner and D. Sabo (eds), *Sport, Men and the Gender Order*, Champaign, Ill.: Human Kinetics.

Connell, R. W. (1995) *Masculinities*. Cambridge: Polity.

Connell, R. W. (2000) *The Men and the Boys*. Cambridge: Polity.

Coser, L. (1964) Durkheim's conservatism and its implications for sociological theory. In K. H. Wolff (ed.), *Emile Durkheim et al.: Essays on Sociology and Philosophy*, New York: Harper & Row.

Cox, B. and S. Thompson (2001) Facing the bogey: women, football and sexuality. *Football Studies*, 4 (2), 7–24.

Critcher, C. (1979) Football since the war. In J. Clarke, C. Critcher and R. Johnson (eds), *Working Class Culture*, London: Hutchinson.

Crossett, T. (1995) *Outsiders in the Clubhouse*. Albany, NY: SUNY Press.

Csikszentmihalyi, M. (1975) *Beyond Boredom and Anxiety*. San Francisco: Jossey-Bass.

Csikszentmihalyi, M. and I. S. Csikszentmihalyi (1988) *Optimal Experience*. Cambridge: Cambridge University Press.

Da Matta, R. (1982) Esporte na Sociedade. In R. Da Matta (ed.), *Universo do Futebol*, Rio de Janeiro: Pinakotheke.

Da Matta, R. (1991) *Carnivals, Rogues and Heroes*. Notre Dame, Ind.: University of Notre Dame Press.

Dauncey, H. (1998) Building the finals. *Culture, Sport, Society*, 1 (2), 98–120.

Davis, L. R. (1997) *The Swimsuit Issue and Sport*. Albany, NY: SUNY Press.

Dean, P. (2002) 'Dear Sisters' and 'Hated Rivals'. In P. B. Miller (ed.), *The Sporting World of the Modern South*, Urbana: University of Illinois Press.

De Certeau, M. (1984) *The Practice of Everyday Life*. Berkeley: University of California Press.

Defrance, J. (1976) Esquisse d'une histoire sociale de la gymnastique. *Actes de la Recherche en Sciences Sociales*, 6, 22–46.

Defrance, J. (1987) *L'Excellence corporelle*. Rennes: Presses Universitaires de Rennes.

Defrance, J. (1995) The anthropological sociology of Pierre Bourdieu. *Sociology of Sport Journal*, 12, 121–31.

Deleuze, G. (1997) Postscript on the societies of control. In N. Leach (ed.), *Rethinking Architecture*, London: Routledge.

DeMartino, G. F. (2000) *Global Economy, Global Justice*. London: Routledge.

Denzin, N. K. (1995) *The Cinematic Society*. London: Sage.

Derrida, J. (1978) *Writing and Difference*. Chicago: University of Chicago Press.

Derrida, J. (1984) *Otobiographies*. Paris: Galilée.

Donnelly, P. (1993) Subcultures in sport. In A. G. Ingham and J. W. Loy (eds), *Sport in Social Development*, Champaign, Ill.: Human Kinetics.

Dreyfus, H. L. and P. Rabinow (1983) *Michel Foucault*. Chicago: University of Chicago Press.

Dunning, E. (1977) Power and authority in the public schools (1700–1850). In P. R. Gleichmann, J. Goudsblom and H. Korte (eds), *Human Figurations*, Amsterdam: Amsterdam Sociologisch Tijdschrift.

Dunning, E. (1992) Figurational sociology and the sociology of sport. In E. Dunning and C. Rojek (eds), *Sport and Leisure in the Civilizing Process*, Toronto: University of Toronto Press.

Dunning, E. (1994) The social roots of football hooliganism. In R. Giulianotti, N. Bonney and M. Hepworth (eds), *Football, Violence and Social Identity*, London: Routledge.

Dunning, E. and K. Sheard (1979) *Barbarians, Gentlemen and Players*. Oxford: Blackwell.

Dunning, E., P. Murphy and I. Waddington (1991) Anthropological versus sociological approaches to the study of soccer hooliganism. *Sociological Review*, 39 (3), 459–78.

Dunning, E., P. Murphy and J. Williams (1988) *The Roots of Football Hooliganism*. London: Routledge.

Durkheim, E. (1938/1895) *The Rules of Sociological Method*. New York: Free Press.

Durkheim, E. (1961/1915) *The Elementary Forms of the Religious Life*. New York: Collier Books.

Durkheim, E. (1964/1893) *The Division of Labour in Society*. London: Routledge & Kegan Paul.

Durkheim, E. (1970/1897) *Suicide: A Study in Sociology*. London: Routledge & Kegan Paul.

Dworkin, S. L. and F. L. Wachs (2000) The morality/manhood paradox. In J. McKay, M. A. Messner and D. Sabo (eds), *Masculinities, Gender Relations and Sport*, London: Sage.

Dyck, N. (2000) Games, bodies, celebrations and boundaries: anthropological perspectives on sport. In N. Dyck (ed.), *Games, Sports and Cultures*, Oxford: Berg.

Eagleton, T. (2000) *The Idea of Culture*. Oxford: Blackwell.

Eco, U. (1984) The frames of comic freedom. In T. A. Sebeok (ed.), *Carnival!*, New York: Mouton.

Edelman, R. (1993) *Serious Fun*. New York: Oxford University Press.

Eichberg, H. (1986) The enclosure of the body. *Journal of Contemporary History*, 21, 99–121.

Eichberg, H. (1995) Stadium, pyramid, labyrinth. In J. Bale and O. Moen (eds), *The Stadium and the City*, Keele: Keele University Press.

Eichberg, H. (1998) *Body Cultures*, ed. J. Bale and C. Philo. London: Routledge.

Eitzen, D. S. (1999) *Fair and Foul*. Lanham, Md.: Rowman & Littlefield.

Elias, N. (1978, 1939) *The Civilizing Process: The History of Manners*. Oxford: Blackwell.

Elias, N. (1978) *What is Sociology?* London: Hutchinson.

Elias, N. (1982/1939) *The Civilizing Process: State Formation and Civilization*. Oxford: Blackwell.

Elias, N. (1987) *Involvement and Detachment*. Oxford: Blackwell.

Elias, N. (1991) *The Society of Individuals*. Oxford: Blackwell.

Elias, N. (1996) *The Germans*. Cambridge: Polity.

Elias, N. and E. Dunning (1986) *Quest for Excitement*. Oxford: Blackwell.

Entine, J. (2000) *Taboo*. New York: Public Affairs.

Euchner, C. C. (1993) *Playing the Field*. Baltimore: Johns Hopkins University Press.

Evans, C. H. (2002) Baseball as civil religion. In C. H. Evans and W. R. Herzog II (eds), *The Faith of 50 Million*, Louisville, Ky.: Westminster John Knox Press.

Evanson, P. (1982) Understanding the people. *South Atlantic Quarterly*, 81 (4), 399–412.

Featherstone, M. (1991a) The body in consumer culture. In M. Featherstone, M. Hepworth and B. S. Turner (eds), *The Body*, London: Sage.

236   *References*

Featherstone, M. (1991b) *Consumer Culture and Postmodernism*. London: Sage.
Featherstone, M. (1995) *Undoing Culture*. London: Sage.
Feifer, M. (1985) *Going Places*. London: Macmillan.
Feuer, L. S. (1969) *Marx and the Intellectuals*. New York: Anchor Books.
Fine, G. (1987) *With the Boys*. Chicago: University of Chicago Press.
Finn, G. P. T. (1990) Prejudice in the history of Irish Catholics in Scotland. Paper read to the 24th History Workshop Conference, Glasgow Polytechnic, November.
Finn, G. P. T. (1994a) Football violence. In R. Giulianotti, N. Bonney and M. Hepworth (eds), *Football, Violence and Social Identity*, London: Routledge.
Finn, G. P. T. (1994b) Sporting symbols, sporting identities. In I. S. Wood (ed.), *Scotland and Ulster*, Edinburgh: Mercat Press.
Finn, G. P. T. (1999) Scottish myopia and global prejudices. *Culture Sport Society*, 2 (3), 54–99.
Finn, G. P. T. (2000) A culture of prejudice. In T. M. Devine (ed.), *Scotland's Shame?*, Edinburgh: Mainstream.
Fiske, J. (1987) *Television Culture*. London: Methuen.
Fiske, J. (1989) *Reading the Popular*. London: Unwin Hyman.
Fiske, J. (1993) *Power Plays, Power Works*. London: Verso.
Foley, D. (1990) The great American football ritual. *Sociology of Sport Journal*, 7 (2), 111–35.
Foucault, M. (1977) *Discipline and Punish*. London: Peregrine.
Foucault, M. (1979) *The History of Sexuality*, vol. 1. London: Penguin.
Foucault, M. (1980) *Power/Knowledge*. Brighton: Harvester.
Foucault, M. (1983) The subject and power. In H. L. Dreyfus and P. Rabinow, *Michel Foucault*, Chicago: University of Chicago Press.
Fowler, B. (1997) *Bourdieu and Cultural Theory*. London: Sage.
France, A. and M. Roche (1998) Sport mega-events, urban policy and youth identity. In M. Roche (ed.), *Sport, Popular Culture and Identity*, Aachen: Meyer & Meyer Verlag.
Freeman, P. (1998) *Ian Roberts*. Sydney: Random House.
Freyre, G. (1963) *The Mansions and the Shanties*. London: Weidenfeld & Nicolson.
Freyre, G. (1964) O negro no futebol brasileiro. In M. Filho (ed.), *O Negro no Futebol Brasileiro*, Rio de Janeiro: Civilização Brasileira.
Freyre, G. (1967) *Sociologia*. Rio de Janeiro: José Olympio.
Frisby, W. (1982) Weber's theory of bureaucracy and the study of voluntary sports organizations. In A. O. Dunleavy, A. W. Miracle and C. R. Rees (eds), *Studies in the Sociology of Sport*, Fort Worth: Texas Christian University Press.
Gane, M. (1993) *Baudrillard Live*. London: Routledge.
Gane, M. (2000) Paul Virilio's bunker theorizing. In J. Armitage (ed.), *Paul Virilio*, London: Sage.

Gannon, M. J. (2000) *Understanding Global Cultures*, 2nd edn. London: Sage.

Gans, H. J. (1999) *Popular Culture and High Culture*. New York: Basic Books.

García, D. L. (2002) The architecture of global networking technologies. In S. Sassen (ed.), *Global Networks, Linked Cities*, London: Routledge.

Gartman, D. (1991) Culture as class symbolization or mass reification? A critique of Bourdieu's *Distinction*. *American Journal of Sociology*, 97 (2), 421–47.

Gavora, J. (2002) *Tilting the Playing Field*. New York: Encounter Books.

Geertz, C. (1973) *The Interpretation of Cultures*. New York: Basic Books.

Gems, G. R. (1995) Blocked shot. *Journal of Sport History*, 22 (2), 135–48.

Giddens, A. (1971) *Capitalism and Modern Social Theory*. Cambridge: Cambridge University Press.

Giddens, A. (1991) *Modernity and Self-Identity*. Cambridge: Polity.

Giulianotti, R. (1991) Scotland's tartan army in Italy. *Sociological Review*, 39 (3), 503–27.

Giulianotti, R. (1993) Soccer casuals as cultural intermediaries. In S. Redhead (ed.), *The Passion and the Fashion*, Aldershot: Avebury.

Giulianotti, R. (1995) Football and the politics of carnival. *International Review for the Sociology of Sport*, 30 (2), 191–224.

Giulianotti, R. (1996) 'All the Olympians: A Thing Never Known Again'? *Irish Journal of Sociology*, 6, 101–26.

Giulianotti, R. (1997) Enlightening the North. In G. Armstrong and R. Giulianotti (eds), *Entering the Field*, Oxford: Berg.

Giulianotti, R. (1999) *Football*. Cambridge: Polity.

Giulianotti, R. (2001) Conducting play. *Youth & Policy*, 73, 45–65.

Giulianotti, R. (2002) Supporters, followers, fans and *flâneurs'*. *Journal of Sport and Social Issues*, 26 (1), 25–46.

Giulianotti, R. and G. Armstrong (2001) Constructing social identities. In G. Armstrong and R. Giulianotti (eds), *Fear and Loathing in World Football*, Oxford: Berg.

Giulianotti, R. and G. Armstrong (2002) Avenues of contestation. *Social Anthropology*, 10 (2), 211–38.

Giulianotti, R. and M. Gerrard (2001) Evil genie or pure genius? In D. L. Andrews and S. Jackson (eds), *Sportstars*, London: Routledge.

Giulianotti, R. and R. Robertson (2001) Die globalisierung des fußballs: 'Glokalisierung', transnationale konzerne und demokratische regulierung. In P. Lösche, U. Ruge and K. Stolz (eds), *Fussballwelten: Zum Verhältnis von Sport, Politik, Ökonomie und Gesellschaft*, Jahrbuch Europa und Nordamerika-Studien 5, Opladen: Leske & Budrich.

Giulianotti, R., with G. Armstrong and H. Hognestad (2003) Sport and peace. Paper read to the international conference *Sport and Development*, Swiss Academy for Development, Magglingen, 16–18 February.

Gmelch, G. (1972) Magic in professional baseball. In G. P. Stone (ed.), *Games, Sports and Power*, New Brunswick, NJ: Dutton.

Gmelch, G. and P. M. San Antonio (1998) Groupies and American baseball. *Journal of Sport & Social Issues*, 22 (1), 32–45.

Goffman, E. (1959) *The Presentation of Self in Everyday Life*. Harmondsworth: Penguin.

Goffman, E. (1967) *Interaction Ritual*. Harmondsworth: Penguin.

Goffman, E. (1971) *Relations in Public*. London: Allen Lane.

Goldblatt, D. (1997) The limits of political possibility. *New Left Review*, 225, 140–50.

Goldmann, L. (1970) *Marxism et Sciences Humaine*. Paris: Minuit.

Goody, J. (2002) Elias and the anthropological tradition. *Anthropological Theory*, 2 (4), 401–12.

Gorn, E. J. and W. Goldstein (1993) *A Brief History of American Sports*. New York: Hill & Wang.

Gottdiener, M. (1995) *Postmodern Semiotics*, Oxford: Blackwell.

Goudsblom, J. (1995) The theory of the civilizing process. *Amsterdams Sociologisch Tijdschrift*, 22 (2).

Gould, S. J. (1997) *Life's Grandeur*. London: Jonathan Cape.

Goulstone, J. (1974) *Modern Sport*. Bexleyheath: author.

Goulstone, J. (2000) The working-class origins of modern football. *International Journal of the History of Sport*, 17, 135–43.

Gramsci, A. (1971) *Selections from the Prison Notebooks*. London: Lawrence & Wishart.

Griffin, P. (1998) *Strong Women, Deep Closets*. Champaign, Ill.: Human Kinetics.

Grint, K. (1991) *The Sociology of Work*. Cambridge: Polity.

Grossberg, L. (1988) *It's a Sin*. Sydney: Power Publications.

Grosz, E. (1995) Women, *chora*, dwelling. In S. Watson and K. Gibson (eds), *Postmodern Cities and Spaces*, Oxford: Blackwell.

Grundlingh, A. (1994) Playing for power? In J. Nauright and T. J. L. Chandler (eds), *Making Men*, London: Frank Cass.

Gruneau, R. (1999) *Class, Sports and Social Development*. Champaign, Ill.: Human Kinetics.

Gruneau, R. and D. Whitson (1993) *Hockey Night in Canada*. Toronto: Garamond.

Guelke, A. (1993) Sport and the end of *Apartheid*. In L. Allison (ed.), *The Changing Politics of Sport*, Manchester: Manchester University Press.

Guttmann, A. (1978) *From Ritual to Record*. New York: Columbia University Press.

Guttmann, A. (1988) *A Whole New Ball Game*. Chapel Hill: University of North Carolina Press.

Guttmann, A. (1991) *Women's Sports*. New York: Columbia University Press.

Guttmann, A. (1992) Chariot races, tournaments and the civilizing process. In E. Dunning and C. Rojek (eds), *Sport and Leisure in the Civilizing Process*, Toronto: University of Toronto Press.

Guttmann, A. (1994) *Games & Empires*. New York: Columbia University Press.

Guttmann, A. (1996) *The Erotic in Sports*. New York: Columbia University Press.

Guttmann, A. and L. Thompson (2001) *Japanese Sports*. Hawaii: University of Hawaii Press.

Habermas, J. (1999) The European nation-state and the pressures of globalization. *New Left Review*, 235, 46–59.

Hall, M. A. (2002) *The Girl and the Game*. Toronto: Broadview.

Hall, S. (1977) Re-thinking the 'base and superstructure' metaphor. In J. Bloomfield (ed.), *Class, Hegemony and Party*, London: Lawrence & Wishart.

Hall, S. (1978) The treatment of football hooliganism in the press. In R. Ingham (ed.), *Football Hooliganism*, London: Inter-Action.

Hall, S. and T. Jefferson (eds) (1976) *Resistance through Rituals*. London: Hutchinson.

Hall, S., C. Critcher, T. Jefferson, J. Clarke and B. Roberts (1978) *Policing the Crisis*. Basingstoke: Macmillan.

Hall, S., S. Szymanski and A. S. Zimbalist (2002) Testing causality between team performance and payroll. *Journal of Sports Economics*, 3 (2), 149–68.

Hallinan, C. (1991) Aborigines and positional segregation in the Australian Rugby League. *International Review for the Sociology of Sport*, 12 (1), 69–82.

Hallinan, C. (1999) Aboriginal involvement in elite football. Paper read to The First International Conference on Sports and Human Rights, Sydney, Australia, 1–3 September.

Hannigan, J. A. (1998) *Fantasy City*. London: Routledge.

Hardy, S. (1986) Entrepreneurs, organizations and the sports marketplace. *Journal of Sport History*, 13, 14–33.

Hargreaves, Jennifer (1993) Gender on the sports agenda. In A. G. Ingham and J. W. Loy (eds), *Sport in Social Development*, Champaign, Ill.: Human Kinetics.

Hargreaves, Jennifer (1994) *Sporting Females*. London: Routledge.

Hargreaves, Jennifer (2002) The Victorian cult of the family and the early years of female sport. In S. Scraton and A. Flintoff (eds), *Gender and Sport: A Reader*, London: Routledge.

Hargreaves, John (1986) *Sport, Power and Culture*. Cambridge: Polity.

Harpalani, A. (1998) The athletic dominance of African-Americans. In G. Sailes (ed.), *African-Americans in Sport*, New Brunswick, NJ: Transaction Publishers.

Harris, O. (1998) The role of sport in the Black community. In G. Sailes (ed.), *African-Americans in Sport*, New Brunswick, NJ: Transaction Publishers.

Harriss, I. (1986) Cricket and rational economic man. *Sporting Traditions*, 3, 51–68.

Harriss, I. (1988–9) Cricket and capitalism. *Melbourne Historical Journal*, 19.

Harriss, I. (1990) Packer, cricket and postmodernism. In D. Rowe and G. Lawrence (eds), *Sport and Leisure*, Sydney: Harcourt Brace Jovanovich.

Hart, K. (2000) *The Memory Bank*. London: Profile.

Hart, K. (2001) Money in an unequal world. *Anthropological Theory*, 1 (3), 307–30.

Harvey, A. (1999) Football's missing link. In J. A. Mangan (ed.), *Sport in Europe*, London: Frank Cass.

Harvey, D. (1989) *The Condition of Postmodernity*. Oxford: Blackwell.

Harvey, J. and F. Houle (1994) Sport, world economy, global culture, and new social movements. *Sociology of Sport Journal*, 11, 337–55.

Haynes, R. (1992) *The Football Imagination*. Aldershot: Arena.

Hebdige, D. (1979) *Subculture*. London: Methuen.

Hebdige, D. (1988) *Hiding in the Light*. London: Routledge.

Heinilä, K. (1998) *Sport in Social Context*. Jyväskylä: University of Jyväskylä Press.

Heino, R. (2000) New sports. *Journal of Sport & Social Issues*, 24 (1), 176–91.

Held, D. (1995) *Democracy and the Global Order*. Cambridge: Polity.

Held, D. (2000) Regulating globalization? The reinvention of politics. *International Sociology*, 15 (2), 394–408.

Henderson, R. (1995) Is it in the blood? *Wisden Cricket Monthly*, July.

Henderson, R. W. (2001) *Ball, Bat and Bishop*. Champaign, Ill.: University of Illinois Press.

Herrnstein, R. J. and C. Murray (1994) *The Bell Curve*. Glencoe, Ill.: Free Press.

Hess, R. (1998) The Victorian football league takes over, 1897–1914. In R. Hess and B. Stewart (eds), *More than a Game*, Melbourne: Melbourne University Press.

Hirst, P. and G. Thompson (1999) *Globalization in Question*. Cambridge: Polity.

Hoberman, J. (1984) *Sport and Political Ideology*. Austin: University of Texas Press.

Hoberman, J. (1995) Toward a theory of Olympic internationalism. *Journal of Sport History*, 22 (1), 1–37.

Hoberman, J. (1997a) *Darwin's Athletes*. Boston: Houghton Mifflin.

Hoberman, J. (1997b) How Not to Misread *Darwin's Athletes*. *Journal of Sport History*, 24 (3), 389–96.

Hobsbawm, E. and T. Ranger (eds) (1983) *The Invention of Tradition*. Cambridge: Cambridge University Press.

Hoch, P. (1972) *Rip Off the Big Game*. Garden City, NY: Doubleday.

Hoggart, R. (1958) *The Uses of Literacy*. London: Pelican.

Holmes, M. (1994) Symbols of national identity and sport: the case of the Irish football team. *Irish Political Studies*, 9, 81–98.

Holt, R. (1991) Women, men and sport in France, c.1870–1914. *Journal of Sport History*, 18 (1), 121–34.

Hong, F. (1997) *Footbinding, Feminism and Freedom*. London: Frank Cass.

Honig, B. (2001) *Democracy and the Foreigner*. Princeton: Princeton University Press.

Hope, W. (2002) Whose All Blacks? *Media, Culture & Society*, 24, 235–53.

Houlihan, B. (1997) *Sport, Policy and Politics*. London: Routledge.

Howe, D. (2001) An ethnography of pain and injury in professional Rugby Union. *International Review for the Sociology of Sport*, 36 (3), 289–304.

Hughson, J. (1999) A tale of two tribes. In G. P. T. Finn and R. Giulianotti (eds), *Football Culture*, London: Frank Cass.

Humphreys, D. (1996) Snowboarders. *Sporting Traditions*, 13 (1), 3–23.

Hunter, D. W. (1998) Race and athletic performance. In G. Sailes (ed.), *African-Americans in Sport*, New Brunswick, NJ: Transaction Publishers.

Hutchings, K. (2003) Feminist international ethics and the civil society argument. Paper read to the conference *Global Ethics in the Context of Global Democracy and Globalization*, University of Aberdeen, 7–10 March 2003.

Ingham, A. G. (1975) Occupational subcultures in the work world of sport. In D. Ball and J. Loy (eds), *Sport and Social Order*, Reading, Mass.: Addison-Wesley.

Ingham, A. G. and S. Hardy (1993) Sport studies through the lens of Raymond Williams. In A. G. Ingham and J. W. Loy (eds), *Sport in Social Development*, Champaign, Ill.: Human Kinetics.

Ingham, A. G. (and friends) (1997) Toward a Department of Physical Cultural Studies and an end to tribal warfare. In J.-M. Fernández-Balboa (ed.), *Critical Postmodernism in Human Movement, Physical Education and Sport*, Albany, NY: SUNY Press.

Jackson, S. J. (2001) Gretzky nation. In D. L. Andrews and S. J. Jackson (ed.), *Sport Stars*, London: Routledge.

Jaireth, S. (1995) Tracing Orientalism in cricket. *Sporting Traditions*, 12 (1), 103–20.

James, C. L. R. (1963) *Beyond a Boundary*. London: Paul.

Jameson, F. (1979) Reification and utopia in mass culture. *Social Text*, 1, 130–48.

Jameson, F. (1981) *The Political Unconscious*, Ithaca, NY: Cornell University Press.

Jameson, F. (1991) *Postmodernism or, the Cultural Logic of Late Capitalism*. London: Verso.

Jamison, B. (1996) The Sandgate handicap riot. *Sporting Traditions*, 12 (2), 17–48.

Jenkins, R. (1992) *Pierre Bourdieu*. London: Routledge.

Jhally, S. and J. Lewis (1992) *Enlightened Racism*. Boulder, Colo.: Westview Press.

Johansson, S. (2000) Våldet på de Svenska Fotbollsplanerna 1936–1939. Unpublished paper, Department of History, University of Gothenburg, Sweden.

Johns, D. P. and J. S. Johns (2000) Surveillance, subjectivism and technologies of power. *International Review for the Sociology of Sport*, 35 (2), 219–34.

Katz, D. R. (1994) *Just Do It*. New York: Random House.

Kay, J. and S. Laberge (2002) The 'New' corporate habitus in adventure racing. *International Review for the Sociology of Sport*, 37 (1), 17–36.

Kellner, D. (1989) *Jean Baudrillard*. Cambridge: Polity.

Kellner, D. (2000) Virilio, war and technology. In J. Armitage (ed.), *Paul Virilio*, London: Sage.

Kerry, D. S. and K. M. Armour (2000) Sport sciences and the promise of phenomenology. *Quest*, 52, 1–17.

Kidd, B. (1996) *The Struggle for Canadian Sport*. Toronto: University of Toronto Press.

Kidd, B. and P. Donnelly (2000) Human rights in sport. *International Review for the Sociology of Sport*, 35 (2), 131–48.

Kildea, G. and J. Leach (1979) *Trobriand Cricket*. Video documentary.

Kimmel, M. S. (1990) Baseball and the reconstitution of American masculinity 1880–1920. In M. A. Messner and D. F. Sabo (eds), *Sport, Men and the Gender Order*, Champaign, Ill.: Human Kinetics.

Klein, A. (1989) Baseball as underdevelopment. *Sociology of Sport Journal*, 6, 95–112.

Klein, A. (1991) *Sugarball*. New Haven: Yale University Press.

Klein, A. (1993) *Little Big Men*. Albany, NY: SUNY Press.

Klein, A. (1994) Transnational labour and Latin American baseball. In J. Bale and J. Maguire (eds), *The Global Sports Arena*, London: Frank Cass.

Klein, A. (1997) *Baseball on the Border: A Tale of Two Laredos*. Princeton: Princeton University Press.

Klein, A. (2000a) Dueling machos: masculinity and sport in Mexican baseball. In J. McKay, M. A. Messner and D. Sabo (eds), *Masculinities, Gender Relations and Sport*, London: Sage.

Klein, A. (2000b) Latinizing Fenway Park. *Sociology of Sport Journal*, 17, 403–22.

Klein, A. (2003) Progressive ethnocentrics. Unpublished paper.

Knowles, M. (1973) *The Adult Learner*. Houston, Tex.: Gulf Publishing.

Kobayashi, T. (2001) Developing countries. *Japan Journal of Sport Sociology*, 9.

Koppett, L. (1981) *Sports Illusion, Sports Reality*. Urbana: University of Illinois Press.

Kruger, A. (1996) The Masses are Much More Sensitive to the Perfection of the Whole than to any Separate Details. *Olympika*, 5, 25–44.

Laberge, S. and D. Sankoff (1988) Physical activities, body *habitus* and lifestyles. In J. Harvey and H. Cantelon (eds), *Not Just a Game*, Ottawa: University of Ottawa Press.

LaFeber, W. (2002) *Michael Jordan and the New Global Capitalism*. New York: W. W. Norton.

Lanfranchi, P. and M. Taylor (2001) *Moving with the Ball*. Oxford: Berg.

Lapchick, R. (1991) *Five Minutes to Midnight*. Lanham, Md.: Madison Books.

Lapchick, R. (2003) *2003 Racial and Gender Report Card*. Orlando: University of Central Florida Press.

Lasch, C. (1979) *The Culture of Narcissism*. London: Abacus.

Lash, S. (1990) *Sociology of Postmodernism*. London: Routledge.

Lash, S. and J. Urry (1987) *The End of Organized Capitalism*. Cambridge: Polity.

Lash, S. and J. Urry (1994a) *Economies of Signs and Space*. London: Sage.

Lash, S. and J. Urry (1994b) Expert-systems or situated interpretation? In U. Beck, A. Giddens and S. Lash, *Reflexive Modernization*, Cambridge: Polity.

Latour, B. (1993) *We Have Never Been Modern*. Cambridge, Mass.: Harvard University Press.

Le Breton, D. (2000) Playing symbolically with death in extreme sports. *Body & Society*, 6, 1–11.

Leavy, J. (2002) *Sandy Koufax*. London: HarperCollins.

Lenin, V. I. (1997/1916) *Imperialism*. New York: International Publishers.

Lenin, V. I. (1998/1902) *What is to be Done?* Harmondsworth: Penguin.

Lenskyj, H. (1986) *Out of Bounds*. Toronto: Women's Press.

Lenskyj, H. (1995) Sport and the threat to gender boundaries. *Sporting Traditions*, 12 (1), 47–60.

Lenskyj, H. (2000) *Inside the Olympic Industry*. Albany, NY: SUNY Press.

Lenskyj, H. (2002) *The Best Olympics Ever?* Albany, NY: SUNY Press.

Lenskyj, H. (2004) The Olympic industry and civil liberties. In R. Giulianotti and D. McArdle (eds), *Sport and Human Rights*, London: Taylor & Francis.

Levine, P. (1992) *Ellis Island to Ebbets Field*. Oxford: Oxford University Press.

Lewis, R. W. (1996) Football hooliganism in England before 1914. *International Journal of the History of Sport*, 13 (3), 310–39.

Lithman, Y. G. (2001) Reflections on the social and cultural dimensions of children's elite sport in Sweden. In N. Dyck (ed.), *Games, Sports and Cultures*, Oxford: Berg.

Llobera, J. (1994) *The God of Modernity*. Oxford: Berg.

Loland, S. (2000) Justice and game advantage in sporting games. In T. Tännsjö and C. Tamburrini (eds), *Values in Sport*, London: E & FN Spon.

Loland, S. (2002) *Fair Play in Sport*. London: Routledge.

Loy, J. W. and J. F. McElvogue (1970) Racial segregation in American sport. *International Review for the Sociology of Sport*, 5, 5–24.

Lucas, S. (2000) Nike's commercial solution. *International Review for the Sociology of Sport*, 35 (2), 149–64.

Lukács, G. (1967/1923) *History and Class Consciousness*. London: Merlin.

Lüschen, G. (1967) The interdependence of sport and culture. *International Review of Sport Sociology*, 2 (1), 27–41.

Lynch, R. (1992) A symbolic patch of grass. *ASSH Studies in Sports History*, 7, 44–68.

Lyng, S. (1990) Edgework. *American Journal of Sociology*, 95 (4), 851–86.

Lyotard, J.-F. (1984) *The Postmodern Condition*. Manchester: Manchester University Press.

Lyotard, J.-F. (1993) *The Postmodern Explained*. Minneapolis: University of Minnesota Press.

MacClancy, J. (1993) Female bullfighting, gender stereotyping and the state. In J. MacClancy (ed.), *Sport, Identity and Ethnicity*, Oxford: Berg.

Maffesoli, M. (1996) *The Time of the Tribes*. London: Sage.

Maguire, J. (1991) Sport, racism and British society. In G. Jarvie (ed.), *Sport, Racism and Ethnicity*, London: Falmer.

Maguire, J. (1994) Sport, identity politics, and globalization. *Sociology of Sport Journal*, 11, 398–427.

Maguire, J. (1999) *Global Sport*. Cambridge: Polity.

Majors, R. (1990) Cool Pose. In M. Messner and D. Sabo (eds), *Sport, Men and Gender Order*, Champaign, Ill.: Human Kinetics.

Mangan, J. A. (1981) *Athleticism in the Victorian and Edwardian Public School*. Cambridge: Cambridge University Press.

Mangan, J. A. (1986) *The Games Ethic and Imperialism*. London: Viking.

Mangan, J. A. (1987) Ethics and ethnocentricity. In W. J. Baker and J. A. Mangan (eds), *Sport in Africa*, London: Holmes & Meier.

Mangan, J. A. (1998a) *The Games Ethic and Imperialism: Aspects of the Diffusion of an Ideal*. London: Frank Cass.

Mangan, J. A. (1998b) Sport in society: the Nordic world and other worlds. In H. Meinander and J. A. Mangan (eds), *The Nordic World*, London: Frank Cass.

Mangan, J. A. (1999) Prologue: global Fascism and the male body: ambitions, similarities and dissimilarities. *International Journal for the History of Sport*, 16 (4), 1–26.

Marcano, A. J. and D. P. Fidler (1999) The globalization of baseball. *Global Legal Studies Journal*, 6, 511–77.

Marcuse, H. (1964) *One-Dimensional Man*. London: Ark.

Markula, P. (1995) Firm but shapely, fit but sexy, strong but thin. *Sociology of Sport Journal*, 12, 424–53.

Marqusee, M. (1994) *Anyone but England*. London: Verso.

Marqusee, M. (1996) *War Minus the Shooting*. London: Mandarin.

Martin, C. R. and J. L. Reeves (2001) The whole world isn't watching (but we thought they were). *Culture, Sport, Society*, 4 (2), 213–36.

Martin, P. (1995) *Leisure and Society in Colonial Brazzaville*. Cambridge: Cambridge University Press.

Marvin, G. (1994) *Bullfight*. Urbana: University of Illinois Press.

Marx, K. (1937/1869) *The Eighteenth Brumaire of Louis Bonaparte*. Moscow: Progress.

Marx, K. (1965/1845) *The German Ideology*, London: Lawrence & Wishart.

Marx, K. (1973/1844) *Economic and Philosophical Manuscripts of 1844*. London: Victor Kamkin.

Marx, K. (1999/1867) *Capital*. Oxford: Oxford University Press.

Marx, K. and F. Engels (1998/1848) *The Communist Manifesto*. Oxford: Oxford University Press.

Mason, A. (1980) *Association Football and English Society 1863–1915*. Brighton: Harvester.

Mason, C. and R. Roberts (1991) The spatial externality fields of football stadiums. *Applied Geography*, 11, 251–66.

McChesney, R. W. (2002) Whatever happened to Cultural Studies? In C. A. Warren and M. D. Vavrus (eds), *American Cultural Studies*, Urbana: University of Illinois Press.

McCree, R. (2000) Professional soccer in the Caribbean. *International Review for the Sociology of Sport*, 35 (2), 199–218.

McCrone, K. (1988) *Sport and the Physical Emancipation of Women, 1870–1914*. London: Routledge.

McInman, A. D. and J. R. Grove (1991) Peak moments in sport. *Quest*, 43, 333–51.

McKay, J. (1995) Just Do It. *Discourse*, 16 (2), 191–205.

McKay, J. (1997) *Managing Gender*. Albany, NY: SUNY Press.

McKay, J. and T. Miller (1991) From old boys to men and women of the corporation. *Sociology of Sport Journal*, 8, 86–94.

McPherson, B. D., J. E. Curtis and J. W. Loy (1989) *The Social Significance of Sport*. Champaign, Ill.: Human Kinetics.

McQuilkin, S. A. and R. A. Smith (1993) The rise and fall of the flying wedge. *Journal of Sport History*, 20 (1), 57–64.

Mead, G. H. (1934) *Mind, Self and Society*. Chicago: University of Chicago Press.

Mennesson, C. (2002) 'Hard' women and 'soft' women: the social construction of identities among female boxers. *Intermational Review for the Sociology of Sport*, 35 (1), 21–33.

Merrett, C. (1994) Sport, racism and urban policy in South Africa. *Sporting Traditions*, 11 (2), 97–122.

Merton, R. K. (1938) Social structure and anomie. *American Sociological Review*, 3 (6), 672–82.

Merton, R. K. (1968) *Social Theory and Social Structure*. New York: Free Press.

Messner, M. (1992) *Power at Play*. Boston: Beacon Press.

Messner, M. A. (1994) AIDS, homophobia and sport. In M. A. Messner and D. F. Sabo (eds), *Sex, Violence and Power in Sports*, Freedom, Calif.: Crossing Press.

Messner, M. A., M. Dunbar and D. Hunt (2000) The televised sports manhood formula. *Journal of Sport & Social Issues*, 24 (4), 380–94.

Messner, M. A., M. C. Duncan and C. Cooky (2003) Silence, sports bras, and wrestling porn. *Journal of Sport & Social Issues*, 27 (1), 38–51.

Metcalfe, A. (1974) Some background influences on nineteenth-century Canadian sport and physical education. *Canadian Journal of Sport & Physical Education*, 6 (May), 62–73.

Miliband, R. (1977) *Marxism and Politics*. Oxford: Oxford University Press.

Miller, P. (1998) The anatomy of scientific racism. *Journal of Sport History*, 24 (1), 119–51.

Miller, T., D. Rowe, J. McKay and G. Lawrence (2003) The over-production of US sports and the new international division of cultural labor. *International Review for the Sociology of Sport*, 38 (4), 427–40.

Mills, C. W. (1959) *The Sociological Imagination*. Harmondsworth: Penguin.

Min-Seok, A. (2002) The political economy of the World Cup in South Korea. In J. Horne and W. Manzenreiter (eds), *Japan, Korea and the 2002 World Cup*, London: Routledge.

Morgan, W. J. (1988) Adorno on sport. *Theory and Society*, 17, 813–38.

Morgan, W. J. (1993) *Leftist Theories of Sport*. Urbana: University of Illinois Press.

Morgan, W. J. (1998) Hassiba Boulmerka and Islamic green. In G. Rail (ed.), *Sport and Postmodern Times*, Albany, NY: SUNY Press.

Morgan, W. J. (2000) Sports as the moral discourse of nations. In T. Tännsjö and C. Tamburrini (eds), *Values in Sport*, London: E & FN Spon.

Morgan, W. J. (2002) Social criticism as moral criticism. *Journal of Sport and Social Issues*, 26 (3), 281–99.

Morgan, W. J. (2004) Habermas on sports. In R. Giulianotti (ed.), *Sport and Modern Social Theorists*, Basingstoke: Palgrave.

Morson, G. S. with C. Emerson (1997) Extracts from a *Heteroglossary*. In M. Macovski (ed.), *Dialogue and Critical Discourse*, Oxford: Oxford University Press.

Mrozek, D. (1983) *Sport and American Mentality 1880–1910*. Knoxville: University of Tennessee Press.

Muchembled, R. (1985) *Popular Culture and Elite Culture in France 1400–1750*. Baton Rouge: Louisiana State University Press.

Müller, A. F. (2002) Sociology as a combat sport: Pierre Bourdieu (1930–2002) – admired and reviled in France. *Anthropology Today*, 18 (2), 5–9.

Murphy, P., E. Dunning and J. Williams (1990) *Football on Trial*. London: Routledge.

Murray, B. (1996) *The World's Game*. Urbana and Chicago: University of Illinois Press.

Nadel, D. (1998) The League goes national 1986–1997. In R. Hess and B. Stewart (eds), *More than a Game*, Melbourne: Melbourne University Press.

Nairn, T. (1994) *The Enchanted Glass*. New York: Vintage.

Noll, R. G. and A. S. Zimbalist (1997) *Sports, Jobs and Taxes*. Washington, DC: Brookings Institute.

Novak, M. (1994) *The Joy of Sports*. Lanham, Md.: Madison.

O'Donnell, H. (1994) Mapping the mythical. *Discourse & Society*, 5 (3), 345–80.

O'Neill, M. (2003) The Policing of Football Spectators. Unpublished Ph.D. thesis, University of Aberdeen.

Oriard, M. (1993) *Reading Football*. Chapel Hill: University of North Carolina Press.

Oriard, M. (1995) Muhammad Ali. In E. Gorn (ed.), *Muhammad Ali*, Urbana: University of Illinois Press.

Oriard, M. (2001) *King Football*. Chapel Hill: University of North Carolina Press.

Overman, S. J. (1997) *The Influence of the Protestant Ethic on Sport and Recreation*. Aldershot: Avebury.

Park, J. K. (1999) Sports industry and the Korean economy. *Japan Journal of Sport Sociology*, 7.

Park, R. J. (1978) Embodied Selves. *Journal of Sport History*, 5 (2), 5–41.

Parsons, T. (1951) *The Social System*. New York: Free Press.

Parsons, T. (1966) *Societies*. Englewood Cliffs, NJ: Prentice-Hall.

Pfister, G. (2002) Sport for women. In R. Naul and K. Hardman (eds), *Sport and Physical Education in Germany*, London: Routledge.

Phillips, J. (1994) The hard man. In J. Nauright and T. J. L. Chandler (eds), *Making Men*, London: Frank Cass.

Pitt-Rivers, J. A. (1984) El sacrificio del toro. *Revista de Occidente*, 36, 27–47.

Popper, K. (1963) *Conjectures and Refutations*. London: Routledge & Kegan Paul.

Poster, M. (1988) *Jean Baudrillard*. Cambridge: Polity.

Poster, M. (1990) *The Mode of Information*. Cambridge: Polity.

Prasad, D. (1999) Environment. In R. Cashman and A. Hughes (eds), *Staging the Olympics*, Sydney: University of New South Wales Press.

Pronger, B. (1990) *The Arena of Masculinity*. New York: St Martin's Press.

Pronger, B. (1999) Outta my endzone. *Journal of Sport & Social Issues*, 23 (4), 373–89.

Pronger B. (2000) Homosexuality and sport: who's winning? In J. McKay, M. A. Messner and D. Sabo (eds), *Masculinities, Gender Relations and Sport*, London: Sage.

Pye, G. (1986) The ideology of Cuban sport. *Journal of Sport History*, 13 (2), 119–27.

Rail, G. (1998) Seismography of the postmodern condition. In G. Rail (ed.), *Sport and Postmodern Times*, Albany, NY: SUNY Press.

Raitz, K. (1995) The theater of sport: a landscape perspective. In K. Raitz (ed.), *The Theater of Sport*, Baltimore: Johns Hopkins University Press.

Ranger, T. (1987) Pugilism and pathology. In W. J. Baker and J. A. Mangan (eds), *Sport in Africa*, London: Holmes & Meier.

Real, M. (1999) Aerobics and feminism. In R. Martin and T. Miller (eds), *SportCult*, Minneapolis: University of Minnesota Press.

Redhead, S. (1991) Some reflections on discourses on football hooliganism. *Sociological Review*, 39 (3), 479–88.

Redhead, S. (1998) Baudrillard, Amérique and hyperreal World Cup. In G. Rail (ed.), *Sport and Postmodern Times*, Albany, NY: SUNY Press.

Reiss, S. (1991) *City Games*. Urbana: University of Illinois Press.

Rengger, N. (2003) The moral constitution of international society in the twenty-first century. Paper read to the conference *Global Ethics in the Context of Global Democracy and Globalization*, University of Aberdeen, 7–10 March 2003.

Ribeiro, D. (2000) *The Brazilian People*. Gainesville: University of Florida Press.

Rigauer, B. (1981) *Sport and Work*. New York: Columbia University Press.

Rigauer, B. (2001) Marxist theories. In J. Coakley and E. Dunning (eds), *Handbook of Sports Studies*, London: Sage.

Rinehart, R. E. (1996) Fists Flew and Blood Flowed. *Journal of Sport History*, 23 (2), 120–39.

Riordan, J. (1976) Marx, Lenin and physical culture. *Journal of Sport History*, 2, 152–61.

Riordan, J. (1991) The rise, fall and rebirth of sporting women in Russia and the USSR. *Journal of Sport History*, 18 (1), 183–99.

Ritzer, G. (1993) *The McDonaldization of Society*. Thousand Oaks, Calif.: Pine Forge.

Ritzer, G. (1996) *Modern Sociological Theory*, 4th edn. New York: McGraw-Hill.

Ritzer, G. and T. Stillman (2001) The postmodern ballpark as leisure setting. *Leisure Sciences*, 23, 99–113.

Roberts, R. and J. Olsen (1989) *Winning is the Only Thing*. Baltimore: Johns Hopkins University Press.

Robertson, R. (1970) *The Sociological Interpretation of Religion*. Oxford: Blackwell.

Robertson, R. (1990a) After nostalgia? Wilful nostalgia and the phases of globalization. In B. S. Turner (ed.), *Theories of Modernity and Post-modernity*, London: Sage.

Robertson, R. (1990b) Mapping the global condition. *Theory, Culture & Society*, 7, 15–30.

Robertson, R. (1992) *Globalization*. London: Sage.

Robertson, R. (1995) Glocalization. In M. Featherstone, S. Lash and R. Robertson (eds), *Global Modernities*, London: Sage.

Robertson, R. and K. White (2003) Globalization: an overview. In R. Robertson and K. White (eds), *Globalization: Critical Concepts in Sociology*, London: Routledge.

Robson, G. (2000) *No One Likes Us, We Don't Care*. Oxford: Berg.

Rojek, C. (1993) Disney culture. *Leisure Studies*, 12, 121–35.

Rojek, C. (1995) *Decentring Leisure*. London: Sage.

Rorty, R. (1991) *Objectivity, Relativism and Truth*. Cambridge: Cambridge University Press.

Rose, N. (1996) Governing advanced liberal democracies. In A. Barry, T. Osborne and N. Rose (eds), *Foucault and Political Reason*, London: UCL Press.

Rose, N. (1999) *Powers of Freedom*. Cambridge: Cambridge University Press.

Rosemblatt, K. A. (2000) Domesticating men. In E. Dore and M. Molyneux (eds), *Hidden Histories of Gender and State in Latin America*, Durham, NC: Duke University Press.

Rowe, D. (1995) *Popular Cultures*. London: Sage.

Rowe, D. (1999) *Sport, Culture and the Media*. Buckingham: Open University Press.

Rowe, D. and P. McGuirk (1999) Drunk for three weeks. *International Review for the Sociology of Sport*, 34 (2), 125–41.

Russell, D. (1999) Associating with football. In G. Armstrong and R. Giulianotti (eds), *Football Cultures and Identities*, Basingstoke: Macmillan.

Ryan, J. (1996) *Little Girls in Pretty Boxes*. London: Women's Press.

Ryder, R. (1995) *Cricket Calling*. London: Faber & Faber.

Sabo, D. F. (1994) Doing time doing masculinity. In M. Messner and D. F. Sabo (eds), *Sex, Violence and Power in Sports*, Freedom, Calif.: Crossing Press.

Sachs, J. (2002) Weapons of mass salvation. *The Economist*, 24 October.

Said, E. (1994) *Culture and Imperialism*. London: Chatto & Windus.

Said, E. (1995) *Orientalism*. Harmondsworth: Penguin.

Sailes, G. A. (1998) The African-American athlete. In G. Sailes (ed.), *African-Americans in Sport*, New Brunswick, NJ: Transaction Publishers.

Sammons, J. (1997) A proportionate and measured response to the provocation that is *Darwin's Athletes*. *Journal of Sport History*, 24 (3), 378–88.

Sandiford, K. and B. Stoddart (1995) The elite schools and cricket in Barbados. In H. McD. Beckles and B. Stoddart (eds), *Liberation Cricket*, Manchester: Manchester University Press.

Sassen, S. (2000) Spatialities and temporalities of the global: elements for a theorization. *Public Culture*, 12 (1), 215–32.

Savage, M. et al. (1992) *Property, Bureaucracy and Culture*. London: Routledge.

Schimmel, K. S. (2001) Take Me Out to the Ball Game. In C. L. Harrington and D. B. Bielby (eds), *Popular Culture*, Oxford: Blackwell.

Schimmel, K., A. G. Ingham and J. W. Howell (1993) Professional team sport and the American city: urban politics and franchise relocations. In A. G. Ingham and J. W. Loy (eds), *Sport in Social Development*, Champaign, Ill.: Human Kinetics.

Scholte, J. A. (1998) *Globalization*. Basingstoke: Macmillan.

Segel, H. G. (1999) *Body Ascendant*. Baltimore: Johns Hopkins University Press.

Seidman, S. (1994) *Contested Knowledge*. Oxford: Blackwell.

Sennett, R. (1977) *The Fall of Public Man*. London: Faber & Faber.

Sheard, K. (1997) Aspects of boxing in the civilizing process. *International Review for the Sociology of Sport*, 32 (1), 31–58.

Shmanske, S. (2000) Gender, skill, and earnings in professional golf. *Journal of Sports Economics*, 1 (4), 385–400.

Sklair, L. (1995) *Sociology of the Global System*. Baltimore: Johns Hopkins University Press.

Smith, A. D. (1999) *Myths and Memories of the Nation*. Oxford: Oxford University Press.

Smith, C. (1997) Control of the female body. *Sporting Traditions*, 14 (2), 59–71.

Smith, D. (2001) *Norbert Elias and Modern Social Theory*. London: Sage.

Smith, D. and G. Williams (1980) *Fields of Praise*. Cardiff: University of Wales Press.

Smith, P. (1997) *Millennial Dreams*. London: Verso.

Snow, C. P. (1959) *The Two Cultures*. Cambridge: Cambridge University Press.

Sperber, M. (2003) *Beer and Circuses*. Bloomington: University of Indiana Press.

Spivey, D. (1985) Black consciousness and the Olympic protest movement, 1964–1980. In D. Spivey (ed.), *Sport in America*, Westport, Conn.: Greenwood Press.

St Pierre, M. (1995) West Indian cricket as cultural resistance. In M. A. Malec (ed.), *The Social Roles of Sport in Caribbean Societies*, Luxembourg: Gordon & Breach.

Stallybrass, P. and A. White (1986) *The Politics and Poetics of Transgression*. London: Methuen.

Stewart, B. (1993) A theoretical framework for analysing the commercial development of Australian first-class cricket. Paper read to the ASSH Annual Conference, Launceston, Australia.

Stoddart, B. (1989) Gary Sobers and cultural identity in the Caribbean. *Sporting Traditions*, 5 (1), 131–46.

Strange, S. (1994) *The Retreat of the State*. Cambridge: Cambridge University Press.

Stuart, O. (1989) Good Boys, Footballers and Strikers. Unpublished Ph.D. thesis, SOAS, University of London.

Sugden, J. (1987) The exploitation of disadvantage. In J. Horne, D. Jary and A. Tomlinson (eds), *Sport, Leisure and Social Relations*, London: Routledge & Kegan Paul.

Suttles, G. (1968) *The Social Order of the Slum*. Chicago: University of Chicago Press.

Suttles, G. (1972) *The Social Construction of Communities*. Chicago: University of Chicago Press.

Tännsjö, T. (2000) Is it fascistoid to admire sports heroes? In T. Tännsjö and C. Tamburrini (eds), *Values in Sport*, London: E & FN Spon.

Tatz, C. (1984) Race, politics and sport. *Sporting Traditions*, 1 (1), 2–36.

Tatz, C. (1999) Winning isn't Black and White. *Sunday Herald*, 5 September.

Taylor, I. (1969) Hooligans: soccer's resistance movement. *New Society*, 7 August.

Taylor, I. (1970) Football mad: a speculative sociology of soccer hooliganism. In E. Dunning (ed.), *The Sociology of Sport*, London: Frank Cass.

Taylor, I. (1971) Soccer consciousness and soccer hooliganism. In S. Cohen (ed.), *Images of Deviance*, Harmondsworth: Penguin.

Taylor, I. (1987) Putting the boot into a working-class sport: British soccer after Bradford and Brussels. *Sociology of Sport Journal*, 4, 171–91.

Taylor, I. (1991) English football in the 1990s. In J. Williams and S. Wagg (eds), *English Football and Social Change*, London: Leicester University Press.

Taylor, P., Lord Justice (Chairman) (1990) *Inquiry into the Hillsborough Stadium Disaster: Final Report*. London: HMSO.

Theberge, N. (2000) *Higher Goals*. Albany, NY: SUNY Press.

Thompson, E. P. (1963) *The Making of the English Working Class*. London: Pelican.

Thompson, J. B. (1995) *The Media and Modernity*. Cambridge: Polity.

Thompson, S. M. (1999) The game begins at home. In J. Coakley and P. Donnelly (eds), *Inside Sports*, London: Routledge.

Thornton, S. (1995) *Club Cultures*. Cambridge: Polity.

Thrane, C. (2001) Sport spectatorship in Scandinavia. *International Review for the Sociology of Sport*, 36 (2), 149–63.

Tomlinson, A. (2004) Pierre Bourdieu and the sociological study of sport. In R. Giulianotti (ed.), *Sport and Modern Social Theorists*, Basingstoke: Palgrave.

Tönnies, F. (1955) *Community and Association*. London: Routledge & Kegan Paul.

Tranter, N. L. (1998) *Sport, Economy and Society in Britain 1750–1914*. Cambridge: Cambridge University Press.

Tuan, Y.-F. (1974) *Topophilia*. Englewood Cliffs, NJ: Prentice-Hall.

Turner, B. S. (1999) The possibility of primitiveness. *Body & Society*, 5(2–3), 39–50.

Urry, J. (1990) *The Tourist Gaze*. London: Sage.

Urry, J. (1995) *Consuming Places*. London: Routledge.

Vahed, G. (2001) What do they know of cricket who only cricket know? *International Review for the Sociology of Sport*, 36 (3), 319–36.

Vamplew, W. (1994) Australians and sport. In W. Vamplew and B. Stoddart (eds), *Sport in Australia*, Melbourne: Cambridge University Press.

Vasili, P. (1998) *The First Black Footballer: Arthur Wharton 1865–1930, An Absence of Memory*. London: Frank Cass.

Veblen, T. (1970/1899) *The Theory of the Leisure Class*. London: Allen & Unwin.

Vertinsky, P. and G. Captain (1998) More myth than history. *Journal of Sport History*, 25 (3), 532–61.

Vigarello, G. (1995) The sociology of sport in France. *Sociology of Sport Journal*, 12, 224–32.

Vinnai, G. (1973) *Football Mania*. London: Ocean.

Virilio, P. (1986) *Speed and Politics*. New York: Semiotext(e).

Vrcan, S. (2002) The curious drama of the president of a republic versus a football fan tribe. *International Review for the Sociology of Sport*, 37 (1), 59–77.

Wacquant, L. J. D. (1995a) The pugilistic point of view. *Theory & Society*, 24, 489–535.

Wacquant, L. J. D. (1995b) Pugs at work. *Body & Society*, 1, 65–93.

Wacquant, L. J. D. (2001) Whores, slaves and stallions. *Body & Society*, 7(2–3), 181–94.

Wacquant, L. J. D. (2002a) From slavery to mass incarceration. *New Left Review*, 13, 41–60.

Wacquant, L. J. D. (2002b) The sociological life of Pierre Bourdieu. *International Sociology*, 17 (4), 549–56.

Walby, S. (1997) *Gender Transformations*. London: Routledge.

Wallerstein, I. (1974) *The Modern World System*, vol. 1, London: Academic Press.

Walsh, A. and R. Giulianotti (2001) This sporting mammon. *Journal of the Philosophy of Sport*, 28, 53–77.

Wearing, B. (1998) *Leisure and Feminist Theory*. London: Sage.

Weber, M. (1958/1905) *The Protestant Ethic and the Spirit of Capitalism*. New York: Charles Scribner's Sons.

Weber, M. (1968/1922) *Economy and Society*. New York: Bedminster Press.

Weber, M. (1978) *Max Weber: Selections in Translation*, ed. W. G. Runciman. Cambridge: Cambridge University Press.

Weiss, L. (1998) Globalization and the myth of the powerless state. *New Left Review*, 225, 3–27.

Weiss, O. (2001) Identity reinforcement in sport. *International Review for the Sociology of Sport*, 36 (4), 393–405.

White, P. and B. Wilson (1999) Distinctions in the stands. *International Review for the Sociology of Sport*, 34 (3), 245–64.

Wiggins, D. K. (1989) Great speed but little stamina. *Journal of Sport History*, 16 (2), 158–85.

Williams, J. (1991) Having an away day. In J. Williams and S. Wagg (eds), *British Football and Social Change*, Leicester: Leicester University Press.

Williams, J. (2001) *Cricket and Race*. Oxford: Berg.

Williams, R. (1958) *Culture and Society*. New York: Columbia University Press.

Williams, R. (1961) *The Long Revolution*. New York: Columbia University Press.

Williams, R. (1975) *The Country and the City*. St Albans: Paladin.

Williams, R. (1977) *Marxism and Literature*. Oxford: Oxford University Press.

Williams, R. (1981) *The Sociology of Culture*. Chicago: University of Chicago Press.

Willis. P. (1982) Women in sport in ideology. In J. A. Hargreaves (ed.), *Sport, Culture and Ideology*, London: Routledge & Kegan Paul.

Willis, P. (1990) *Common Culture*. Buckingham: Open University Press.

Wilson, E. (1995) The invisible *flâneur*. In S. Watson and K. Gibson (eds), *Postmodern Cities and Spaces*, Oxford: Blackwell.

Wilson, J. Z. (2002) Invisible racism: the language and ontology of 'white trash'. *Critique of Anthropology*, 22 (4), 387–401.

Wilson, T. C. (2002) The paradox of social class and sports involvement. *International Review for the Sociology of Sport*, 37 (1), 5–16.

Wouters, C. (1977) Informalisation and the civilising process. In P. R. Gleichman, J. Goudsblom and H. Korte (eds), *Human Figurations*, Amsterdam: Amsterdams Sociologisch Tijdschrift.

Wouters, C. (1986) Formalization and informalization. *Theory, Culture & Society*, 3, 1–18.

Wouters, C. (1990) Social stratification and informalization in global perspective. *Theory, Culture & Society*, 7, 69–90.

Wren-Lewis, J. and J. Clarke (1983) The World Cup: a political football. *Theory, Culture & Society*, 1, 123–32.

Yelvington, K. A. (1995) Cricket, colonialism, and the culture of Caribbean politics. In M. A. Malec (ed.), *The Social Roles of Sport in Caribbean Societies*, Luxembourg: Gordon & Breach.

Zaman, H. (1997) Islam, well-being and physical activity. In G. Clarke and B. Humberstone (eds), *Researching Women and Sport*, Basingstoke: Macmillan.

Index

Aborigines, Australian: racist treatment of, 69–70, 73, 74
Adler, P. A. and P.: college basketball study, 17
Adorno, Theodor, 34, 35, 42, 219 nn.7 & 8; Foucault and, 104
aerobics, 88, 95, 106
Africa, 68–9; introduction of European sports, 68
African-Americans: athleticism of, 63–5, 73; and dance, 221 n.4; and sporting segregration, 66, 74; see also under baseball; basketball
Afro-Caribbeans: in British sport, 70, 71
aikido, 7, 165
alpine sports, xv; see also skiing
Althusser, Louis, 43, 50
Amateur Rowing Association, 219 n.9
amateurism, 22, 33; v. professionalism, 37, 219 n.9, 220 n.10
American football (gridiron), xiv, 36; African-Americans in, 66, 67; commodified, 47; and

cultural values, 10; ethos of, 81; injuries in, 109–10, 222 ch.7 n.5; and masculinity, 97, 222 ch.7 n.5; multi-ethnic players in, 77–8; stars of, 99; women in, 86
Americanization, 199–200, 227 n.1
anthropology: and sport, xi, 3, 14; and masculinity, 97
apartheid: and sport, 68
Appadurai, A, 202–3: 'globalization from below', 207
archery: suitable for women, 83
Archetti, E., 98
arenas, sporting, see space: stadiums
Argentina: football, 53, 98–9, 132, 204; masculinity in, 98; polo, 98, 204
arm-wrestling: by prisoners, 96
Arnold, Matthew: elitist cultural theory, 34
Aronowitz, S., 32–3
Asians: in English cricket, 70–1
athletes: and alcoholism, 112; black/African-American,

63–4, 66, 221 ch.5 n.1; as celebrities, 12, 36; in college basketball team, 17; commodified, 219 n.3; disciplining of, 104–5, 223 n.5; and drug abuse, 112–13; exploitation of, 32–3, 35, 88–9; financial opportunities/ rewards, 39; gay, 91–3, 100; greatness in, 12; industrial action by, 36

athletics, track and field, xi; developed in Britain, xiv;

Australia, xiv, 69–70; Aborigines in sport, 69–70, 73; commercialization of sport, 39; economics of sport, 200–1; legal battle over rugby league, 53; masculine sporting subcultures, 81; resists Americanization, 200

Australian Rules football, xiv; commodified, 219 n.3; ethos of, 81; and racism, 73; as 'secular religion', 6; television deal, 200; women and, 83

authorities, sports, *see* governing bodies

Bale, J., 121, 122
Bali, 18, 27
ballparks, *see* baseball: grounds
Barmy Army, 56, 220 n.6
Barnes, John, 70, 79; quoted, 76
Barthes, Roland, 43
baseball, xiv, xv, 118; African-Americans in, 66, 73, 75; batting consistency, 22–3; capitalist distortion of, 41; ethos of, 81–2; girls in, 86; grounds (ballparks), 123–4, 126–8; Latino, study of, 17; myth of origin, 6; players' strike, 36; resists

commercialization, 54; and rounders, 204; rituals, 5; as 'secular religion', 6; and social solidarity, 218 ch.1 n.1

basketball, xi, xiv; African-Americans in, 66–7, 75, 75–6; 'feminine' rules for, 83; invention of, 20; and media deals, 29, 39–40

Baudrillard, Jean, 121, 172, 177, 184, 187, 188–9, 225 n.1, 226 nn.6 & 7, 227 n.10

Baxter, Jim, 112

Beck, Ulrich: 'risk society' theory, 110–11, 115, 118–19, 213

Beckham, David, 36, 46, 199

Behr, Sammy, 78

Bergman-Osterberg, Martina, 83–4

Best, George, 112

betting scandals, *see under* corruption

Bias, Len, 113

blood sports, xiii

body, the: and consumerism, 117, 118, 219 n.3; disabled, 107; non-white, 107; and self-identity, 117; sociology of, xvi, 102–4, 117, 155

body-building: and 'femiphobia', 94; steroids used in, 113; study of, 17; women in, 87

Boston, David, 113

Bourdieu, Pierre, xvi, xvii, 102, 104, 117, 168–70, 200, 212, 213, 214, 224 ch.9 n.2, 225 n.5; *Acts of Resistance*, 166; on 'colour' identity, 225 n.4; *Distinction*, 153, 161, 170; followers of, 164–5; on social stratification, 159–60, 161–2; on sport, 153–4, 160, 161–4, 165–6, 167–8, 211; on Western liberal culture, 166–7

bowling, xiii
boxing, xiv, 108–9, 118, 162, 222 ch.7 n.4, 224 ch.9 n.1; in Africa, 68; and African-Americans, 66, 222 ch.7 n.3; corruption in, 40; Queensberry Rules, 143, 224 ch.9 n.1; southern African, xiv; studies on, 164
Bradman, Don, 37–8
Brazil, 27, 75, 193; Orientalist view of, 201–2; as 'seductive culture', 184
Britain, *see* United Kingdom
Brohm, J.-M., 32, 33, 34
Brooklyn Dodgers, 121, 137
bullfighting: and masculinity, 97; woman *torero*, 222 n.7
bureaucracy: Weber's theory of, 19–20; and sport, 21, 23
Butkus, Dick, 223 n.8

'Californian' sports, 118, 164
calisthenics, 84
Calvinism, 4
Canada: amateurist principles, 33; ice hockey, 67, 125; native Americans and sport, 67; sport 'equity', 89; sporting ethos, 81; and US, 200; women and sport, 90, 165
'capital' (Bourdieu), 157
capitalism: and discipline, 104; 'disorganized', 182–3; and sport, xvi, 29–31, 32–3, 34, 39, 41, 42, 183–4; *see also* globalization
Carey, Wayne, 199
Carlos, Jon, 67, 79
Carroll, J.: on women in sport, 82
Castells, M., 55
CCTV, 129, 135, 136, 223 n.5

Celtic (Glasgow), 7, 77; globalization of, 203
'character': in sport, 12
Chicago Bulls, 198
children: and sport, 17, 117, 118, 175; and injuries, 111
Chile; boycott of national stadium, 54; masculine subculture and sport in, 98
China: Red Sport Movement, 84–5
chora, concept of, 132, 133
Clarke, Ron, 114
class divisions: and UK sport, 52–3
Cleveland Browns, 125
clubs, social, 19
coaching: and discipline, 104; McDonaldization of, 25–6
cockfighting, Balinese, 17, 18, 27, 28
colonialism: and 'muscular Christianity, 71, 81; and sport, 62, 68, 69, 71–2, 107, 194, 205
Colts, Indianapolis, 5; relocated from Baltimore, 125
Commonwealth Games (2002): disabled competitions, 107
'community': critiques of, 47–8
Connell, R. W., 94, 95–6, 214
Constantine, Learie, 79
consumerism, 39, 41, *see also* sport: commodified
corruption, 61; betting scandals, 40; results fixing, 40
cosmopolitanism, 206, 209
Coubertin, Baron Pierre de, xiv, 81, 82, 226 n.6
Counter-Olympics (Chicago 1932), 32
'creolization', 204

cricket: amateur–professional divide, 37, 220 n.10; commodified, 37–8; and corruption, 40; developed in Britain, xiv; and elitism, 34, 37, 163, 176; English supporters (Barmy Army), 56; grounds, 122, 130; and hegemony theory, 51; in Indian subcontinent, xiv; in North America, xiv; one-day, 38–9; Pakistani, 201; racial politics in, 70–2; television coverage of, 179; Trobriand, 27, 204; West Indian, 51, 53, 107; Zimbabwean, 196

croquet, 83

cross-cultural studies, 213

crowd control, 128, 131, 223 n.5; *see also* panopticism

Cuba: sport and 'new man' in, 97–8

cultural imperialism, 199–202

Cultural Studies, 43–61, 212, 220 n.5; Centre for Contemporary (CCCS); 43, 44, 45, 60; and sport, xvi, 18, 42, 44–61

cycling, xv

darts, xiii

Darwin, Charles: natural selection, 63

'dataveillance, 130, 223 n.4

Daum, Christoph, 113

De Certeau, Michel, 54

De La Hoya, Oscar, 36

Defrance, J., 164

Derrida, Jacques, 173–4, 188; *Otobiographies*, 226 nn.4 & 5

Didrikson, Babe, 84

dietrologia, 59, 96

DiMaggio, Joe, 221 n.6

discipline: forms of, in sport, 104–5; and football hooliganism, 106

D'Oliveira, Basil, 70, 79

Donoghue, Steve, 96

Doubleday, Abner, General: and baseball myth, 6

drinking culture, 112

drugs, 111–15, 119; abusers, 223 n.10; illicit, 112–13; medical, 112; performance-enhancing, 113–14, 223 n.9

Durkheim, Emile: critique of, 13; Foucault and; 104; on religion, 3; and social order, 1–2, 2–3, 4, 11; and sociology of sport, xv, 7, 12, 13–14

Dynamo Zagreb, 221 n.10

Eagleton, Terry: on cultural theorists, 217

economics of sport, xii

educational priorities: and sport, 24

Eichberg, H., 105, 107, 118, 119, 129, 131, 135, 213

Elias, Norbert, xvi–xvii, 102, 104, 120, 138–43, 147–52, 210, 211, 212, 220 n.5; *The Civilizing Process*, 138, 141–2; Eurocentrism, 148; evolutionism, 148–9; on figurations, 138–9; followers of, 138, 148, 150–1; and informalization theory, 151–2; on leisure, 140–1; *Quest for Excitement*, 138

Eliot, T. S.: elitist cultural theory, 34, 227 n.1

Entine, J.: sports genetics theories, 65

equestrianism: as elite sport, 161

Erving, Julius, 76
ethnic minorities, xvi
ethnicity, 62, 76–8; and
    stereotyping, 76–7, 221 n.6
Exley, Fred: *A Fan's Notes*, 106
extreme sports, 24, 116–17

'fair competition', ideal of, *see*
    meritocracy
'fair play', concept of, 81, 174,
    175, 221 ch.6 n.1
fans: defined, 48
'Fantasy City', 133–4
fanzines, 54, 181
FARE, 73
fascism, 85, 108, 118
Fashanu, Justin, 92
Favre, Brett, 112
Featherstone, M., 102
femininity, 87–8
feminism: and sport, 84, 89–90
'field' (Bourdieu), 157; as 'game',
    157–8, 161
FIFA, xv, 193
Finland, 216; class and sport in,
    169
Fiske, J., 53, 58
fixing results, *see under*
    corruption
Flamengo (Brazil), 5
flâneurs, 180, 181; concept of,
    132
Florida Marlins, 41
'flow experiences', 115–16, 119
folk culture, 56–7, 131, 220 n.9
football: aestheics, 222 n.8;
    African, xiv, 68; antiquity of,
    xiii; Argentinian, 98–9, 132;
    Brazilian, 27, 75, 169, 201–2;
    British, xiv, 144, 167, 176;
    capitalist distortion of, 41,
    167; Caribbean, 220 n.1;
    coaching methods, 23; codes,

218 prologue n.1;
    commodified, 39, 42, 47; and
    corruption, 40; disasters, 122,
    128; economics of, 29;
    European, xv; historic phases
    of, 193–4; Japanese, xv; Latin
    American, xv; players'
    boycott, 36; popularity of, xi,
    199; pre-modern, 20, 144,
    193; racism in, 70, 73; and
    ritual, 3–4; spectator profile,
    145; stadiums, 122, 129; stars
    of, 99, 179; supporters, 19,
    57, 178; and television, 200;
    violence in, 109, 224 ch.9 n.2;
    women and, 86, 145, 150; *see
    also* American football;
    Australian Rules football;
    Gaelic football, hooliganism,
    football
Fordism: and post-Fordism,
    182–3, 184
Formula One, 39, 186–7
Foucault, Michel, 18, 59, 121,
    173, 174, 226 n.3; on 'the
    body' xvi, 102–3, 118, 149;
    and 'panopticism', 128–30; on
    power, 102–3, 103–4; and
    sociology of sport, 104, 107–8,
    119, 212; and struggle, 188
fox-hunting, 143
France, xiv, xv; Stade de, 125;
    Tour de, xv; sports policy, 227
    n.2; world view of, 200
Franco, General Francisco:
    manipulates sporting events,
    219 n.4
Frankfurt School, 34–6, 41–2;
    on mass culture/sport, 34, 35,
    108, 219 n.6; *see also under
    individual members*
Freeman, Cathy, 79; as role
    model, 74

Freyre, Gilberto, 201–2
Friedman, Benny, 78
Fromm, Erich, 34
functionalist approaches, 1; and
  conflict, 6; critique of, 12–13;
  see also Durkheim, E.;
  Goffman, E.; Merton, R. K.;
  Parsons, T.

G-14 club (football), 41
Gaelic football, xv, 204
gambling: on sport, 40, 184
Gandhi, Mahatma: quoted, 148
Gardner, Gayle, 86
Gascoigne, Paul, 112, 179
Gay Games, 53, 93, 100
gays: pressures on, 91–2, 100,
  222 ch.6 n.5; *see also* lesbians
Geertz, Clifford, 17–18, 28
gender, xvi; discrimination
  within US sports prohibited
  (Title IX), 86; and
  participation in sport, 52,
  73–4, 80–93; and physical
  differentials, 87; and prize
  money discrimination, 87;
  roles in within sport, 99–101;
  see also gays; masculinity;
  women and girls
'genetic structuralism'
  (Bourdieu), 154, 224 ch.10 n.1
genetics: and sport, 65, 78; *see
  also* race
Germany: handball, xiv;
  Turnverein, xiv; women's
  sport and Nazism, 85, 142
Giddens, Anthony, 117, 154,
  168, 187, 220 n.5
Gilbert, Eddie, 69, 79
girls, *see* women and girls
globalization, 183–4, 190–209,
  212; 'from below', 207;
  complexities within, 202–3;

and the local, 204–6; phases
  of, 192–3; and politics, 206–9;
  and sport, xvii, 28, 176–7,
  184, 190–1, 208–9; sociology
  of, 190
'glocalization', 203, 205, 206,
  213, 214
Gobineau, Arthur de, 63
Goffman, Erving, xv, 8, 10–12,
  14, 18, 117; critique of, 13
golf, 73, 163; PGA European
  Tour, 205; Ryder Cup, 205;
  social value of, 162, 169;
  uniqueness of courses, 128;
  women and, 83, 86, 87, *see
  also* LPGA
Gould, Stephen J., 22–3
governing bodies (of sport), 8–9,
  215–16; and drugs, 113–14;
  see also FIFA; IOC; NBA;
  NCAA; NFL; NHL; NRL
Gramsci, Antonio, xvi, 43, 44,
  213, 220 n.2, 227 n.1;
  'hegemony theory', 49, 51, 59
Greaves, Jimmy, 112
greyhound racing, 176, 219 n.6
gridiron, *see* American football
Griffin, P., 93
Griffith-Joyner, Florence, 74
Grossberg, L.: quoted, 45
Guthrie, Janet, 86
Guttmann, A., xv, 15, 22, 23,
  26–7, 32, 89, 222 ch.6 n.4
gymnastics, xi, xv, 163, 223 n.6;
  and drugs, 113; injuries in,
  111

Habermas, Jürgen, 60–1, 175,
  207
'habitus' (Bourdieu), 156;
  postmodern, 179, 181
Hall, Stuart, 43, 49–50, 51
handball, xiv

Hannigan, J.A., 121
Hardie, Keir: on sport, 219 n.6
Hargreaves, Jennifer, 89–90,
　　215, 224 ch.9 n.3
Hargreaves, John, 52–3
Hart, K., 208
Harvey, D., 183
'hegemony theory', 49–50; and
　　sport, 50–3, 56, 58
Held, David, 207–8
Henderson, E. B., 63
Hepworth, Mike, 102
Heysel disaster, 128, 223 n.2
Hicks, Thomas, 113
Hillsborough disaster, 122, 128,
　　223 n.2
Hitomi Kinue, 222 ch.6 n.3
Hinduism: and sport, 71, 221
　　ch. 5 nn.2 & 3
history: and sport, xi, 212–13
HIV-AIDS, 92, 112
Hobbs, J., 38
Hoch, J., 32, 33
hockey, field, xiv; women and,
　　83
Hocking, Gary, 219 n.3
Hoggart, Richard, 43, 46
hooliganism, football, 144–7,
　　226 n.8; and boredom, 116;
　　control of, attempted, 106,
　　130–1; history of, 145,
　　149–50; studies of, 17, 51, 55,
　　144–5, 149–50, 151, 152, 224
　　ch.9 n.3; subculture of, 178–9
Horkheimer, Max, 34, 35
Hornby, N.: *Fever Pitch*, 106,
　　176
horse-racing, 23; courses for,
　　123; virtual, 185; women in,
　　86
Huizenga, Wayne, 41
Hungary, 53
hurling, xv

Husserl, Edmund, 116
Hutton, Len, 37
'hybridization', 204
'hyperreality' (Baudrillard), 185,
　　186, 187–8, 227 n.10

ice hockey, 67, 125;
　　Scandinavian, 169; stardom
　　in, 99; women's, 92
identity: spectator, 179–80, 181;
　　types of, 55
Indian subcontinent: cricket in,
　　71
individualism, cult of, 2
injuries, sporting, 109–10, 112;
　　and 'risk society', 110–11,
　　114–15
interactionism, 18, 28
'invented traditions', 48
IOC (International Olympic
　　Committee), 159, 191, 198
Ireland, xv, 203–4
Islam: and women's sports, 74

Jahn, Friedrich, xiv
James, C. L. R., 51, 71, 107
Jameson, F., 34, 183
Japan: baseball, xv, 27, 118;
　　football, xv; golf, 163;
　　gymnastics, xv, rugby, 118;
　　surfing, 118; traditional
　　martial arts, xv; women's
　　sports, 222 ch.6 n.3
Jeffries, Jim, 66
Jews: in US sport, 78
Jockey Club (UK), 23
Johnson, Jack, 66, 79
Johnson, Magic, 92, 112
Jordan, Michael, 39, 67, 76,
　　79, 175; as role model, 74,
　　75
judo, xv; modernization of,
　　21–2

kabbadi, xiv
Kansas City Royals: in protest, 220 n.3
karate, xv
Kenya, 68, 107, 192
King, Billie Jean, 86, 92
Korea, 197
Koufax, Sandy, 78
Kournikova, Anna, 88
Kratochvilova, Jarmila: and femininity, 88
Krone, Julie, 86
Krueger, Charlie, 223 n.8

lacrosse, 67
Lara, Brian, 79, 199
Lash, S., 183, 184
Latin America, xv; baseball, 194–5
Latour, B.: and 'oligopticon', 131
lawn tennis, xiv, *see also* tennis
Le Saux, Graeme, 92
Leavis, F. R.: elitist cultural theory, 34, 227 n.1
leisure, 25; and gender, 95; in modern UK, 51–2; *see also* spare-time spectrum
Lenin, V. I., 30; and sport, 31
lesbians, 100; demonized, 51
Lévi-Strauss, Claude, 173, 226 n.2
Lewis, Carl, 23, 114
Lewis, Leland T.: *The Tao of Golf*, 173
Liben, Meyer, 78
Louganis, Greg, 92
Louis, Joe, 66
Louisiana Superdome, 124
LPGA, 87; and lesbianism, 89, 91–2
Luhmann, N., 218 ch.1 n.3
Lyotard, Jean-François, 172, 173, 174, 188

McChesney, R. W., 58
McRobbie, Angela, 58
McTiernan, Kerri Ann, 86
Manchester United, 198; and consumerism, 40
Maradona, Diego, 99, 113
Marcuse, Herbert: on 'false needs', 34, 219 n.5
martial arts, xv, 173
Martin, Ashley, 86
Marx, K.: on capitalism, 29–30, 41; on mental production, 219 n.2; on religion, 30; and sociology of sport, xv, xvi, 29–31
Marxism-Leninism, 30; and sport, 31–2
masculinity, 94–100; anthropological perspectives on, 97; formation of, 95–6; historical perspectives on, 97; and nationality, 98; and sporting stardom, 99
mass culture, 34, 36–7, 219 n.6
Mauresmo, Amélie, 92
Mead, G. H., 16–17
media: and globalization, 176, 184; and hyperreality, 185; reinforce patriarchal norms, 88; and sports finance, 29, 175–6; and sports stars, 179; and sports voyeurism, 106
meritocracy, 20, 23
Merleau-Ponty, Maurice, 117
Merson, Paul, 113
Merton, Robert K., 1, 9–10, 12, 13, 14, 212
Mexico: baseball players' strike, 36; machismo in, 98
Miliband, Ralph, 35
Miller, Davis: *The Zen of Muhammad Ali*, 173
Mills, C. W., 13

Millwall football club, 46
Morgan, W. J., 61
Morrison, Tommy, 92
motor-racing, xiii; women in, 86
Mugabe, Robert: manipulates
    sporting events, 219 n.4
Muhammad Ali, 75, 76, 79
Murdoch, Rupert, 184: Foxtel,
    200

Naismith, J., 20
'nation', concept of, 178
nationalism: and sport, 5–6,
    108, 197–8, 221 n.10
native Americans; and sport, 67
Navratilova, Martina, 92
Nazism, 108, 142; and women's
    sport, 85
NBA, 39, 199; blacks and, 73;
    and cocaine use, 112–13;
    neo-colonialism of, 195; and
    Nike, 39
NCAA: and corruption, 40;
    media deals, 29, 39–40; and
    women, 86
'Negro Leagues', 66, 75
neo-liberalism, 196–7, 198, 206
neo-Marxists: 'containment
    model' of sport, 36; and
    sociology of sport, xvi, 29,
    32–3, 35–42, 41–2
New Left Review, 43
New York Yankees, 198; and
    consumerism, 40; in protest,
    220 n.3
New Zealand: rugby in, 39, 74,
    97
NFL, 39, 125, 199; and cocaine
    use, 113; and injured players,
    112, 223 n.7; media deal, 29;
    Super Bowl, xi
NHL, 39, 125
North America: development of
    sports in, xiv

Northern Ireland: Catholics in,
    77
Novak, Jeff, 223 n.7
NRL: excludes club, 54, 220 n.4

objectivism, 154
Olympics: 1936 (Berlin), 66,
    129; 1968 (Mexico), 67; 1972
    (Munich, 'Green'), 126; 1998
    (Seoul, South Korea), 198;
    2000 (Sydney), xi, 126;
    amateurism of, 22; ancient,
    xiii; and black civil rights, 67;
    and Cold War, 85; and
    globalization, 190–1; impact
    of, on local environment, 126;
    modern, culture of, 47, 159;
    and nationalism, 108;
    neo-Marxist critique of, 33;
    popularity of, xi; postmodern,
    186; professionalization of,
    159; protest commodified, 56;
    rationalization of, 22;
    refounded, xiv; sociological
    analysis of, 158–9, 167;
    women competitors in, 84, 85
Oriard, M., 36–7
Orientalism, 201–2
Overman, S. J., 4
Owens, Jesse, 66

'panopticism', 128–31; and
    resistance, 130
Paralympic Games, 107, 222 n.2
Parsons, Talcott, 1, 7–8, 10, 12,
    14, 154, 210; critique of, 13;
    AGIL model, 8
pastiche, 179, 226 n.9
People's Olympics, 32
Perkins, Charles, 69, 79
perruque, la (De Certeau), 54
Piazza, Mike, 92
Pitt-Rivers, J. A., 97
play, *see* sport: and play

polo: antiquity of, xiii; Argentinian, 98, 204; North American, xiv
'polyphony, structured', 60
pool, xiii
Porter, Darrell, 113
postmodern, the, 59, 133–5, 171–89; and capitalism, 183; and identity, 177–80; and knowledge, 172–3; and nostalgia, 205; and relativism, 174–5; sociology of, 180–4; and sport, xvii, 134–5, 171–4, 175–7, 178–82, 187–9
postmodernism/postmodernity: terms defined, 171
post-structuralism, 59, 173; and sport, 18; *see also* Foucault
'practice-community', of sport, 61, 215
Pronger, B., 93, 214
Protestantism: and sport, 2, 4; *see also* Puritans; Quakers
psychology, social: and sport, 115–17
pugilism, *see* boxing
Puritans: and sport, 6–7

Quakers: and sport, 6–7

race, xvi; 62–3; and colour, 63; and exclusion, 63; and physiological theories, 62, 63–5, 221 ch.5 n.1; *see also* racism
racism, 63, 65, 72–6, 78–9, 189; in Briitsh sport, 70–1; in US sport, 66–7; and ethnicity, 76–8
Rangers (Glasgow), 7, 77
Ranjitsinhji, Prince Kumasr Shri ('Ranji'), 70
Real Madrid: property deal, 125
record-setting/breaking, 21, 23

religion: Durkheim on, 3; social function of, 3, 218 ch.1 n.1; and sport, 2, 3, 4–5, 7, 20, 23
research, 60, 155–6, 170, 211–12; trans-disciplinary, 211
'resistance', xvi, 44, 53–6, 58, 79
Rhodesia: black footballers' strike, 36; *see also* Zimbabwe
Richards, V., 71
Rigauer, B., 32, 33, 34
Riggs, Bobby, 86
rituals: religious and sporting, 3
Ritzer, G., xv, 121, 128, 134, 135; McDonaldization thesis, 15, 24–6, 27, 126, 200
Rivaldo: as role model, 74
Roberts, Ian, 92
Robertson, R., 190, 191–2, 193,194, 203, 216
Robinson, Jackie, 66, 79
Robson, G., 46
Rockne, Knute, 77
Rodman, Dennis, 36
Roosevelt, Theodore: on American football, 222 ch.7 n.5
rugby league: legal battle over (Australia), 53; and media corporations, 40; resistance to commercialization of, 54; and television (Australia), 200; and working-class culture, 46, 176
rugby union: developed in Britain, xiv, 144; Japanese, 118; and masculinity, 97; New Zealand, 39, 74, 97; Samoan, 27; and social class, 162; South African, 81; stars of, 39, 99; and television (Australia), 200
Ruskin, John, 226 n.6

Sabo, D. F., 96–7
Sadler, Adam, 107
Said, Edward, 201
Samoa: rugby, 27
Samuels, Charlie, 69, 79
San Francisco 49ers, 198
Scandinavia: class and sport in, 169
Scotland: football and sectarianism in, 77
shooting, xv
Simpson, Tommy, 113
'simulacra' (Baudrillard), 195
skiing, xi, 45, 104, 163; stars stereotyped in, 98; unfair competition in, 23
Sklair, L., 195–6, 198
sky-diving, 117
Smith, Tommie, 67, 79
smoking: and sport, 9
snooker, xiii: televised, 40
Snow, C. P., 120
snowboarding: v. skiing, 45, 104
Snyder, J., 64
Sobers, Gary, 79, 107
soccer, *see* football
Social Darwinism, 63
socialism: and sport for women, 84–5; *see also* Marxism-Leninism
sociology: dichotomies in, 120; figurational, 138–40, 141, 144, 147, 150–1; interpretative, 15–18, 27; process, 138; recommendations for, 210–17; research/fieldwork, *see* research; of sport, xi, xii–xiii, xv–xvii, 16, 120, 138–41, 144–52, 154, 156, 160–6, 167–70; training in, 211
softball, 86
Sokol, xiv

Sorenstam, Annika, 86
South Africa, xiv, 68–9; rugby ethos, 81, 97
space (sports landscape), xvi, 121–37; economics of, 123, 124–5, 126, 132, 134; and folk culture, 131; McDonaldization of, 126, 127, 128; modernizing trends, 135–6; postmodern, 121, 127, 128, 133, 134; *potreros*, 132; and relocation of clubs, 121, 123–4, 125; stadiums, 121, 122–5, 126, 127–8; and 'topophilia', 122, 135; virtual, 134–5, 136
Spain: medieval ball games in, 4; sporting events and politics, 219 n.4
Spalding, A. G., 6
spare-time spectrum, 138, 140
Special Olympics, 107, 222 n.2
specialization (in sport), 20; and versatility, 23, 224 ch.10 n.3
sport: aesthetics of, 36, 215, 222 n.8; age-related, 163; antiquity of, xiii; appeal of, xi–xii; and carnival, 57, 119; commercialized, 29, 59; commodified, 39–40, 41, 118, 167, 177; and community, 12, 214–15; defined, xii–xiii; and the disadvantaged/disabled, 20, 107; and elites, xii, 20, 81, 100, 162, 225 n.6; globalization of, *see under* globalization; and human rights, 216–17; landscapes (space), *see* space; and local cultures, 26–7, 71, 72, 221 ch.5 nn.2 & 3; masculine subcultures in, 80–1; neo-Marxist critiques of,

32–3, 34–7; and play, 35–6, 115; pleasures of, 115–17, 119; political ethics of, xii; and political mobilization, 32, 207, 208–9, 219 n.4; and popular culture, 210–11; pre-modern, 4, 20, 105, 107–8, 143; productive v. seductive cultures in, 184–5; racism in, *see* racism; rationalization of, 15, 19–24, 25–6, 27–8, 61, 167; reinvention of, 215–16; 'romance' lost from, 15; as 'secular religion', 6; sexism in, 80, 189, *see also* gender; and social class, 162–3, 164–6, 169, 176, 181, 225 n.7; and social mobility, 73; sociology of, *see* sociology, of sport; as site of struggle, xvi, 72; and subordinated groups, xvi; and violence, *see* violence; and warfare, 177

'sportization' of games, 143, 144, *see also* sport: pre-modern

sports authorities/governing bodies, *see* governing bodies

sports clubs: membership of, 2; and consumerism, 40

squash, xiv

'stacking', 74, 221 n.4

Stade de France, 125

stadiums, sporting, *see under* space

Stalin, Joseph, 30; and sport, 31

statistics, sporting, 21, 23, 118

Stillman, T., 121, 126, 128, 134, 135

Strawberry, Darryl, 113

Stringer, Korey, 223 n.7

'structural adjustment programmes' (SAPs), 196

'stumbling', 105

subjectivism, 154

sumo wrestling, 20; and tradition, 227 n.3

surfing, 53, 118, 164

Sweet, Judith, 86

Sydney Cricket Ground, 130

tango, 98

tattoos, 178

Taylor, I., 55

Taylor, Lawrence, 113

Tebbit, N. (Lord); 'cricket test', 70

television: and sport, 36, 39, 40, 73, 106, 185–6; *see also* media

Tendulkar, Sachin, 74, 199

tennis, xiii; in North America, xiv; women and, 83

Thatcher, Margaret, 47, 51

Thompson, E. P., 43

Tomba, Alberto, 98, 199

Toronto Maple Leafs, 5

totemic objects: and club identity, 5

Tour de France, 113

tourism: postmodern, 181

'traditions, invented', *see* 'invented traditions'

'transgression', xvi, 44, 56–7, 58; and carnival, 56–7, 58, 220 n.8; and gender codes, 116

transnational capitalist class (TCC), 195–6

transnational corporations (TNCs), 195, 197

Trobriand Islands, 27, 204

Turner, B. S., 102

Turnverein, xiv; girls in, 83

Tyson, Mike, 67

Ueshiba Morihei, 7
Ulvang, Vegard, 98
UNICEF: Convention on the
Rights of the Child, 111
United Kingdom: equestrianism,
161–2; influential in
development of modern sport,
xxi, xiii–xiv; masculine
sporting subcultures, 81;
nineteenth-century sporting
ethos, 81; racist treatment of
black athletes, 70–1, 73;
sports, 52; women and sport,
83
United States: acculturation
through sport, 77–8; black
popular culture, 75; drug
abuse, 112–13; hyperreality
of, 186; masculine subcultures,
80–1; native Americans and
sport, 67; racial segregation of
sports, 66–7; social class and
sport, 225 n.6; and Southern
hemisphere countries, 218
ch.1 n.2; Title IX, 86, 100;
women and sport, 82–3;
world view of, 200
Urry, John, 183, 184

Veblen, Thorstein, 225 n.5
Versportlichung
('sportification'), 20
video sports games, 227 n.10
Vinnai, G., 32, 34
Virilio, P., 226 n.7, 227 n.10;
'dromology', 177;
'globalitarianism', 206
volleyball xi, xiv
violence; in contact sports,
108–10, 119; sports-related,
xvii, 13, 36, 61, 197, *see also*
hooliganism, football;
'symbolic', 160, 161

Wacquant, Loïc, 108, 164
WADA, 113
Wallerstein, I.: modern world
system, 195, 198
Walters, Mark, 70
Walzer, Michael, 206
water sports: black children
barred from, 104
Weber, Max: Foucault and; 104;
and interpretivism, 15; and
rationalization, 15, 17, 19;
and social stratification, 19;
on sociology, 15, 218 ch.2 n.1;
and sociology of sport, xv,
15–16; *verstehen*, 16
weight-lifting: and working
class, 162
West Ham United, 146, 148
West Indies: and cricket, 71, 72
Wharton, Arthur, 70, 79
When We Were Kings, 176
White Stockings, Chicago,
123–4
Williams, Bernie, 220
Williams, John, 150
Williams, Raymond, xvi, 43, 44,
45, 46–7, 58, 213, 214
Willis, P., 45–6, 58
Wills, Helen, 84
women and girls, xvi; barred
from contact sports, 104;
exclusion of, 24; gay, *see*
lesbians; non-participation of,
2; participation of, by social
class, 165; and reform of sport
institutions, 89–91; and
sexism, 82; sexist exploitation
of, 88–9; sports suitable for,
83, 221 ch.6 n.2; struggle for
equality, 82–91, 100–1
Woods, Tiger, 74
Workers' Rights Consortium:
and Nike, 206

working classes, xvi; and
  Cultural Studies, 43; exclusion
  of, 219 n.9; and UK sports,
  52
wrestling, 34, 165, 219 n.6

YMCA, 20
youth subcultures, 45–6, 56,
  181

YWCA: and sports for women,
  83

Zambia, 196–7
zapping, 135
Zimbabwe, 48; cricket, 196;
  sporting events and politics,
  219 n.4
see also Rhodesia